MW00610594

Margaret O'Brien

Margaret O'Brien

A Career Chronicle and Biography

by ALLAN R. ELLENBERGER

with forewords by
ROBERT YOUNG
and MARGARET O'BRIEN

McFarland & Company, Inc., Publishers
Jefferson, North Carolina, and London

ALSO BY ALLAN R. ELLENBERGER

*Ramon Novarro: A Biography of
the Silent Film Idol, 1899–1968; With a Filmography*
(McFarland, 1999)

*The present work is a reprint of the illustrated case bound edition
of* Margaret O'Brien: A Career Chronicle and Biography, *first
published in 2000 by McFarland.*

LIBRARY OF CONGRESS CATALOGUING-IN-PUBLICATION DATA

Ellenberger, Allan R., 1956–
    Margaret O'Brien : a career chronicle and biography / by Allan R.
Ellenberger ; with foreword by Robert Young and Margaret O'Brien.
       p.   cm.
    Includes bibliographical references and index.

    ISBN 0-7864-2155-X (softcover : 50# alkaline paper) ∞

    1. O'Brien, Margaret, 1937–   2. Actors—United States—Biography.
I. Title.
PN2287.O2 E44   2004
791.43'028'092—dc21
[B]   00-56241

British Library cataloguing data are available

©2000 Allan R. Ellenberger. All rights reserved

*No part of this book may be reproduced or transmitted in any form
or by any means, electronic or mechanical, including photocopying
or recording, or by any information storage and retrieval system,
without permission in writing from the publisher.*

On the cover: Margaret O'Brien in an MGM publicity pose

Manufactured in the United States of America

*McFarland & Company, Inc., Publishers
  Box 611, Jefferson, North Carolina 28640
    www.mcfarlandpub.com*

To the memory of Gladys O'Brien (1906–1958)

Table of Contents

THE FILMS

Acknowledgments

I would like to thank Margaret O'Brien for allowing me to interview her for this book and for her cooperation and commitment to see it through. I would also like to thank her for allowing me to use photographs of her career from her own personal collection.

Many, many thanks to film star Randal Malone; actor, film historian and writer Jimmy Bangley and literary aficionada Margaret Burk for their help in getting much needed celebrity quotes and interviews; your work is very much appreciated.

A special thanks to Jeanne DeVivier Brown, Ed Colbert, Erik Madden, the late Frances H. Malone, Hisato Masuyama and Michael Schwibs.

I would also like to thank the staff at the Margaret Herrick Library of the Academy of Motion Picture Arts and Sciences (AMPAS) including Faye Thompson, Sue Guldin, Barbara Hall, Stacey Belhmer, David Marsh and Scott Miller. Also to the staffs of the following institutions: Beverly Hills Public Library; Doheny Library, USC; Frances Howard Goldwyn Library, Hollywood; Glendale Public Library; Los Angeles Central Library; Louis B. Mayer Library of the AFI and the UCLA Research Library.

My thanks to Margaret O'Brien's costars and coworkers who allowed themselves to be quoted and interviewed, including June Allyson, Robert Blake, Conrad Brooks, Elinor Donahue, Joan Fontaine, Betty Garrett, the late Sydney Guilaroff, Marsha Hunt, Janet Leigh, Anita Page, Mickey Rooney, Theresa Saldana, the late Red Skelton and the late Robert Young.

Many, many thanks to the following Hollywood greats: singer Patti Andrews; former child star, author and historian Diana Serra Carey; former child star Gloria Jean; former child star and actor the late Roddy McDowall; legendary tap dancer Ann Miller and television writer and former president of the Writers Guild of America Del Reisman.

Thanks to my mother and members of my family who are always proud of me.

And last, but not least, to my very dear friends who have had to endure hearing about this project and others for months: Larry Arthur, Robbie Baker, Bob Bigge, Art Carrington, Willetta Carrington, Scott Carter, Stacey Chernin, Laura Cramer, Michael Dougher, Scott Drury, Dennis Fowler, Deborah Fullam, Jere Guldin, Sung Han, Rick Hernandez, Kevin McCauley, Renee McFadden, Michelle Mitchell, Kit Nakpil, Freda Novello, Michael Roman, Donna Ross, Rod Rounke, Mary Schlander, Jim Shippee, Sean Swayze, Justin Lee Wilson and Carl Youngblood.

Foreword

by Robert Young

Margaret O'Brien is my old and dear friend. I say this even though Margaret was that most threatening species to the mature thespian, a consummate, professional child star. No, better yet—an actress. Such creatures are rare, natural wonders, like Yosemite or Niagara Falls. No one, save God, can explain or understand this gift. I was privileged to witness this miracle firsthand in two films: *Journey for Margaret* and *The Canterville Ghost*. The fact that she stole scenes from me cannot be disputed. This pain was eased only by my knowledge of her great talent, and the lovely surprise that she was such a very nice person. Plus, she had a thoughtful and delightful "stage" mother. This combination is so rare as to belong in the Smithsonian.

I cannot help remembering how I ran across a downcast Charles Laughton on the set after he had been bested by little Margaret in a scene from *The Canterville Ghost*. "What's the matter, Charles?" I asked. Charles sighed and looked at me forlornly. "I really must kill that child," he said. For all his talent, Charles could sometimes be a pain. But the object of his ire, Margaret O'Brien, was and is a pleasure.

If memory serves me, and I hope it does, I used to call Margaret "my little lambchop." Well, my little lamb, my sincerest best wishes.

Robert Young
January 1996

Foreword

by Margaret O'Brien

First of all, I've always been a bit apprehensive about someone writing a book about my films and career. Being fortunate enough to be a part of Hollywood's "Golden Age" at the greatest studio of all, Metro-Goldwyn-Mayer, is a bit overwhelming for any writer. I felt such a project needed to be done with the utmost accuracy. Such a book should be written well enough to be both entertaining and informative. I wasn't sure if I'd ever find the time to write it myself or how I'd ever go about finding someone to undertake a book of this type.

One Sunday afternoon I was having brunch at the wonderful Roosevelt Hotel in the heart of Hollywood with my dear friend, film star Randal Malone. That particular Sunday afternoon we were joined by author Allan Ellenberger.

Allan explained that he was working on a biography of the late silent film actor Ramon Novarro. I told him that I had worked with Novarro, which he, of course, already knew. Allan was so complimentary, saying he loved and appreciated my work in films. He told me he would like to write a book about my career since I was one of his all time favorites.

I wasn't sure how much time I could dedicate to the project or even what was expected from me, but Allan explained that he would do all the work. So, over the next year we met for lunch or dinner a few times and simply talked about my film career. I told him my stories while he took notes and recorded our discussions. Happily, not only did we get a lot of work done, but we became good friends.

During these times, I remembered things I had not thought of in years. My film career, especially my time at MGM, is very special to me; I not only met, but worked with some of the biggest legends in film history. Such immortals as Lionel Barrymore, Elizabeth Taylor and the fabulous Judy Garland were people that I saw on a daily basis. My memories, along with Allan's exhaustive research, have produced a book that I feel will be a source of information for film historians for years to come.

I hope that you enjoy reading about my career as much as I enjoyed living it.

Margaret O'Brien
Los Angeles, California

Introduction

Child stars have presented something of a paradox since those first shadows flickered across the silver screen more than 100 years ago. From little Mary Pickford to Macaulay Culkin, they have been celluloid images to adore and cherish. Unfortunately, in real life, they sometimes have been more like the Bad Seed.

Many actors have dreaded working with child stars—if not for their preciousness, then for the mere fact that most youngsters are scene stealers. W. C. Fields was infamous in his disdain for child actors, which was summed up by the celebrated line attributed to him, "Any man who hates small dogs and children can't be all bad."[1] However, another former child star, Gloria Jean, who costarred with Fields in *Never Give a Sucker an Even Break* (1941), later declared that the comedian treated her wonderfully.

Contempt for child actors does not lie only with other actors. Producer Nunnally Johnson once claimed he would like to charge $500 for just looking at a talented child. "For *talking* to the same," he added, "$50,000!"[2] (Ironically, John-son's grandson is a child actor and appeared as Will Robinson in the 1998 feature film *Lost in Space*.)

During the thirties, Shirley Temple was the most popular child star that filmdom ever saw. In the forties, a new crop of youngsters popped up on the screen to challenge the former moppet, including Virginia Weidler, Bonita Granville and Jackie "Butch" Jenkins. But the one who was arguably the most talented of all the child stars of her day—or since—was Margaret O'Brien.

O'Brien was voted one of the Top Ten Box Office Stars two years in a row. The National Board of Review twice named her Best Actress, and the Academy of Motion Picture Arts and Sciences bestowed upon her their Most Outstanding Child Actress award. These honors and countless others were given to Margaret O'Brien all before the age of ten.

What is it that makes one child star stand out from all the rest? Is it charisma or just plain talent? In Margaret's case, it is probably the latter. She did not have the preciousness of Shirley Temple, or the impishness of Jane Withers. What

Margaret possessed was something that many adult actors in the business desperately lacked—she had talent.

And it is that talent that has earned her the respect and admiration of her peers. What follows is a sampling of what members of the Hollywood community have felt about the talent of Margaret O'Brien.

Hers is a great talent, as distinctly outstanding as the greatest stars we have. The O'Brien appeal is based on her naturalness. She's all America's child, the type every person in an audience wants to take into his arms.
>   —W. R. Wilkerson, founder of the
>   Hollywood Reporter[3]

She wasn't bubbling over with laughter, as small Shirley Temple had been, nor a natural clown like Jane Withers. As a child, Margaret had a dark-eyed, touchingly innocent quality which always left the impression that the adults in her films all seem to her to be just tall dolls.
>   —Louella Parsons, Hollywood gos-
>   sip columnist[4]

Acting is strictly play to Margaret. From the time she could first walk and talk she amused herself by playing theater. She has always preferred the theater and motion pictures to any other form of entertainment.
>   —Gladys O'Brien, mother[5]

Growing up in Brooklyn and watching her films on television like *The Secret Garden*, *Meet Me in St. Louis* and of course, *Little Women*, had inspired my dreams of becoming an actress.
>   —Theresa Saldano, actress[6]

Margaret was one of the all time greats. What made her great was that she was an American original and there was nobody like her nor has there been anyone since.
>   —Patti Andrews, of the singing
>   Andrews Sisters[7]

This grave little girl, who can give the screen a morning glow by simply stumping into camera range ... is something out of the ordinary in performing children. She belongs more with the Menuhins and Mozarts than with the Shirley Temples.
>   —C. A. Lejeune, film critic and
>   historian[8]

Margaret was a truly great little actress; she was so uniquely talented. There was just no one else like her.
>   —Ann Miller, legendary dancer[9]

As a child, she instinctively followed the famous James Cagney dictum: "You plant your feet, you look the other fella in the eye and you tell the truth." Margaret O'Brien was incapable of playing a scene falsely. Everything—her tone of voice, the conviction in her eyes—rang true.
>   —Del Reisman, television writer
>   and former president of the
>   Writers Guild of America[10]

Margaret O'Brien's brilliant and singular career as a child actress in Hollywood is unique and unparalleled. This bona fide box office star of the 1940s did not rely on a sugary "Mary Pickford Like" image so closely identified with Shirley Temple, nor did she attain stardom by the vapid good fortune of beauty. What this diminutive Duse did was act, and film audiences around the globe responded with laughter and tears.
>   —Jimmy Bangley, actor, writer and
>   film historian[11]

I say this with the utmost sincerity, Margaret is without a doubt the greatest child actor of them all. Her personality had a very rare magnetism all its own. This and large amounts of talent established little Margaret as a screen giant with whom few can compare.

—Roddy McDowall, actor[12]

Margaret O'Brien—
Her Journey

Margaret O'Brien began life as Angela Maxine O'Brien at St. Vincent's Hospital in Los Angeles on January 15, 1937. Her mother was Gladys Flores O'Brien, a young dancer of Spanish descent. At the age of thirteen, young Gladys ran away from home and found work as a specialty dancer in a show called *Dawn of Roses*. After staying with the show for thirty-three weeks of one night stands, she worked on the Pantages circuit and did a stint during the summer with the Ringling Brothers circus. During this time, Gladys also worked with dancer Eduardo Cansino, whose daughter, Margarita, would one day become the lovely Rita Hayworth.

The circumstances surrounding Margaret's father have always been clouded in mystery and have had many incarnations over the years, mostly due to studio publicity. For some reason Gladys never told young Margaret much about her father, but the most accepted version is that she met Larry O'Brien while working with the circus. O'Brien was reportedly a trumpet player in the cir-

cus band (another story had him as a bareback rider). The young couple were married in 1934, but separated two years later, shortly before he died under mysterious circumstances in Mexico City. Rumors circulated that he was killed in either a gambling hall duel or in a car accident. In any event, several weeks after his death, little Angela Maxine O'Brien was born.

Alone, and with a small child, Gladys needed to find support for herself, so she returned to the stage, the one thing she knew best. Soon, she met and married Larry Sears, a sailor in San Diego, but sadly this union lasted only three days before being annulled.

To make ends meet, Gladys moved in with her younger sister Marissa, who was also a dancer, and took over managing Marissa's career. During the next two years, Marissa appeared in supper clubs from California to Cuba, and Gladys and little Angela would go along. Finally the trio arrived in New York City where Marissa performed at the Wedgewood Room of the Waldorf-

Young Angela Maxine O'Brien at the tender age of 22 months.

Astoria Hotel with Xavier Cugat's orchestra.

Because she was constantly exposed to her aunt's act, little Angela knew all of Marissa's routines. One day, as Angela watched Marissa's act from a third row seat, she suddenly began reciting the dialogue out loud along with her aunt. Later, Marissa was introduced to the Broadway star Julie Hayden who was appearing in the play *Shadow and Substance*. "When Miss Hayden came in with George Jean Nathan, her co-star," Marissa later recalled, "Margaret looked at her and said, 'I bet I'm a better actress than you are.' Of course we hurried her out of the room and put her to bed."[1] Ironically, Margaret O'Brien would appear on stage with Julie Hayden 12 years later in the play *The Intruder.*

When Angela was four, the trio moved back to Los Angeles. At the time, Gladys was mostly concerned about Marissa's career and felt no great urge to push Angela into show business. "Of course," Gladys later said, "I hoped Margaret would have a theatrical career when she grew up. But I wanted her to decide that for herself."[2] Which is exactly what happened.

Like most little girls her age, little Angela loved dressing up and play acting. By the time she was three, she could mimic Scarlett O'Hara and Belle Starr. Learning what she saw on the screen came easily for her, but still no one looked on this behavior as anything that would eventually lead to stardom.

Soon, Angela expressed an interest in becoming an actress. Although most people saw it as a passing fancy, Gladys had enough faith in her daughter to know she was serious. So when she saw an ad placed by photographer Paul Hesse looking for youthful models, Gladys knew this was Angela's chance. Gladys realized that she was not curly-haired cute, and could not twinkle prettily like Shirley Temple; nor could she sing and dance. But Angela was an observant and very obedient child, and had a way of playing "pretend" that might be useful in films. When they arrived at Hesse's studio, Gladys noticed all the beautiful and seemingly accomplished children already waiting.

"When I saw that room full of beautiful children, my first impulse was to run," Mrs. O'Brien recalled years later. "There sat Margaret—or Angela at the time—not a wisp of curl in her hair, tiny freckles across her nose, thin and small for her age. I suggested we leave, but Margaret would have none of it."[3]

So they waited for more than an hour. Finally, Hesse came out of his office and looked around the room. "There is my model," he said pointing to little Angela, who was giving him her "look," that crinkly-eyed side glance that was later to capture the hearts of tens of millions of moviegoers.[4] Her appealing and completely natural face had caught his eye and she became his new model.

Because of Hesse's photographs, Angela appeared on several magazine covers, which caught the attention of the powers-that-be at Metro-Goldwyn-Mayer Studios. An audition was set up through Marissa's theatrical agent for a bit part in a Mickey Rooney–Judy Garland picture called *Babes on Broadway* (1941).

At the time, Gladys' brother Marty was having some problems with the law, and in a ploy to influence the judge, Gladys coached Angela to say in her most sympathetic voice, "Please judge, don't send my uncle to the chair." Obviously the ruse worked because the uncle was let go with a warning.

The day of the audition, Gladys dressed her daughter in a kilt and a tam and off they went to MGM studios in Culver City. The agent took Angela directly to the office of producer Arthur Freed, who was meeting with Vincente Minnelli. Standing before the two men, the agent said, "All right Angela, do something for Mr. Freed."

With her speech for her uncle fresh

Margaret O'Brien in a Paul Hesse photograph on the cover of *Photoplay*.

in her mind, the four-year-old improvised a bit and walked up to Freed, grabbed his shirt sleeve and cried, "Don't send my brother to the chair! Don't let him fry!" The two men sat transfixed for several seconds with their mouths agape before Minnelli ran to the office of Fred Finklehoffe, who was writing the screenplay for *Babes on Broadway*. "I know you're writing an audition scene with a producer," Minnelli told him. "I've just seen this extraordinary little girl. You must use her—just the way she is—kilts and all."[5] For the rest of his life, Vincente Minnelli boasted that he discovered Margaret O'Brien.

After her one scene in *Babes on Broadway*, nothing happened for several months. Then one day, Mrs. O'Brien received a call from MGM asking her to bring Angela in to test for the part of a war orphan in a film they were preparing called *Journey for Margaret* (1942). One of the producers of the film, B. P. Fineman, had seen her brief appearance in *Babes on Broadway*, and wanted her to test for the role along with dozens of other little girls.

Soon the choices were narrowed down to four girls, including Angela, so Fineman and executive producer Harry Rapf brought each of them into the studio for a reading. Before Angela was finished, Rapf turned to Fineman and cried, "Stop her, she's killing me!"[6] When director W. S. Van Dyke told Angela that she had the part, she replied, "I knew I'd get it. I prayed for it."

During production, the part of Margaret had such an effect on little Angela that she insisted on changing her name to that of the character she played. "Please don't call me anything but Margaret anymore," she pleaded. "Not ever!"[7] So adamant was she that her mother and the studio agreed. In court, the judge asked her what would happen if she made a picture called "Tea for Suzie."

"Nothing at all," she told the judge. "I just know my name should be Margaret."[8] And so little Angela Maxine became Margaret O'Brien and a star was born.

Journey for Margaret was a sensation, and so was the real Margaret. *Collier's* magazine said that she "tears at your heart-strings like a miniature Duse."[9]

All the acclaim and fanfare attributed to young Margaret during her career did not surprise her. She was always secure in the belief of her own talent. Unfortunately, this self-confidence sometimes appeared as brashness or impudence to the casual onlooker, but nothing could have been further from the truth.

Once while being photographed at Paul Hesse's studio, Margaret had the opportunity to meet the silent-screen legend Gloria Swanson. After being introduced, Swanson looked at Margaret and said, "You know, I used to be quite a movie star myself." With wide open eyes Margaret asked, "Did you? What happened?"[10] This may have seemed like a rude question, but to Margaret it was a statement of incredulity. She was truly concerned since she had known fame her entire short life and could not imagine it ever ending.

After *Journey for Margaret* premiered, MGM was unprepared for the public outpouring of love that their new star received. Studio chief Louis B. Mayer sent out an order to find a proper vehicle to star her in; however, it took a year before the right script was finished. In the meantime, they kept her before the public eye in cameo appearances in

Margaret O'Brien at school on the MGM lot (author's collection).

other films. In *Dr. Gillespie's Criminal Case* (1943) she played a young girl with a deadly disease. In the multi-starred *Thousands Cheer* (1943), her character requested an ice cream sundae from comedian Red Skelton. As the daughter of James Cagney, she recited the Gettysburg Address in an eight-minute short for the war effort titled *You, John Jones* (1943). A small role in the Academy Award– nominated *Madame Curie* (1943) was next before the studio loaned her out to 20th Century–Fox to play in the Victorian epic *Jane Eyre* (1944) with the multi-talented Orson Welles.

Finally after a year, *Lost Angel* (1944), the script written exclusively for her, was ready to begin filming. *Lost Angel*, which costarred James Craig and Marsha Hunt, was a smash. The critics were unanimous in their praise for Margaret. "It is little Miss O'Brien who steals the show," one reviewer wrote.[11] "This O'Brien kid is a natural-born actress," declared another.[12] The accolades were non-stop, and so was Margaret's work schedule. In 1943 alone she appeared in four films.

Margaret's schedule at the studio was much the same as any other actor, except she had to attend school on the MGM lot. She was fairly good at her lessons, except arithmetic, and was fond of drawing and literature. The welfare of child actors was provided for by the State Board of Education and the Producers Association, which agreed on the rules pertaining to their education. At Margaret's age, the regulations called for an eight-hour day, divided equally between school and acting. Mary MacDonald was the principal of the MGM school, and felt that child actors were not spoiled by their success, but were more likely improved by it. "Child actors

have a 17 percent higher I.Q. than ordinary children," MacDonald claimed.[13]

Since she was appointed by the Board of Education and was not hired by the studio, her only interest was in the children's welfare. She thought nothing of holding up production of a film costing thousands of dollars if one of her pupils was behind in their work, which gave her a reputation of being tough.

"I think everybody was scared to death of her," Margaret remembered. "She was very strict and none of the children liked her, and the studio didn't like her either because she obeyed the law and yanked us out of a scene when the time came, even if they only wanted to get that one last shot."[14]

Margaret's talent did not escape her costars, who always shook their heads in bewilderment. Lionel Barrymore, who appeared with her in *Three Wise Fools* (1946), probably paid her the highest compliment when he proclaimed that she was the "only actress, except for my sister Ethel, who has brought tears to my eyes in thirty years."[15]

After *Dr. Gillespie's Criminal Case*, Barrymore was quoted as saying that if Margaret had been unfortunate enough to be born in Salem, "They would have burned her as a witch." He later said that statement was taken somewhat out of context. "I meant it as the most envious of compliments," he insisted.[16] As a token of his affection, Barrymore gave Margaret his grandmother's pin of amethysts and seed pearls. "These are the crown jewels in a way," Margaret explained, "because they came from America's 'Royal Family.' And they're all the royalty we have in America."[17]

During the making of *Three Wise Fools* (1946), Barrymore first became aware of Margaret's scene-stealing

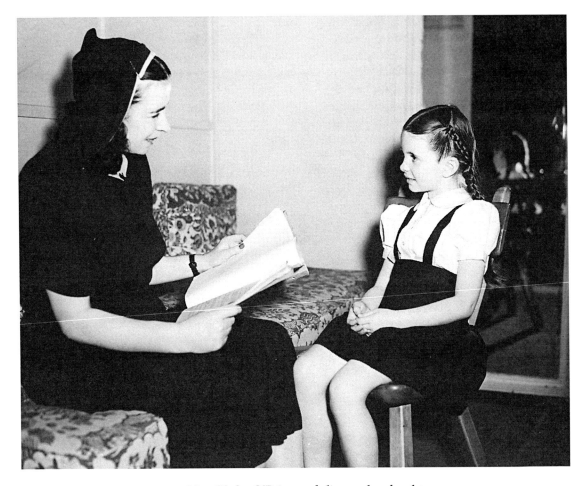

Mrs. Gladys O'Brien reads lines to her daughter.

ability, which was something that aggravated any good actor. "They should change the title to 'Three Fools.' Nobody will ever look at us on the screen," He said.[18]

This was also the case with Charles Laughton, one of the world's greatest actors, and an accomplished scenestealer himself. However, when he appeared in *The Canterville Ghost* (1944) with seven-year-old Margaret O'Brien, he had finally met his match. Laughton was very insecure about his work and according to costar Robert Young, he "couldn't play a scene with himself without competing." Exasperated, Laughton called Young into his dressing room complaining about "that child!" Young tried to convince him that there was nothing he could do.

"Charles, if you stand there and make faces or pick your nose, people will be looking at her anyway," Young told him. "You'll look like a fool if you try to compete with a seven-year-old child who wears an elfin hat and can make tears roll down her face at a look."

Young told Laughton that he had the best role because he wore outlandish costumes and walked through walls.

"You're bound to get attention," he assured the elder thespian.[19] Eventually, Laughton grew to love and respect Margaret, and the two became the best of friends. He did, however, later remark that he thought Margaret was a "changeling, somehow descended from royalty."[20]

Margaret's relationship with her mother was an endearing one, which made it appear as though they were more like sisters than mother and daughter. This gave credence to a studio rumor that Marissa was really Margaret's mother. All the gossip aside, Mrs. O'Brien tried to keep their home life separate from her work at the studio.

"Margaret plays with her stand-in on the set, and has other children in at home," Mrs. O'Brien said. "However, she sometimes becomes impatient with playing because she's likely to be rehearsing a movie scene with her dolls."[21]

When Margaret went outside to play, she preferred friends who didn't "tell"—or ones that did not boast that she was a movie star. On Saturdays, when she was not at the studio, she would play in the back yard, or go with friends to the beach for swims and barbecues. One such friend was child actress Elinor Donahue, who first met Margaret when they both appeared in *The Unfinished Dance* (1947). The two hit it off from the beginning and Mrs. O'Brien would send them off to the Del Mar Club in Santa Monica. "For some reason Margaret's mother approved of me," Donahue recalled. "She was a member of the Del Mar Club in Santa Monica and she paid a fee for us to join. That was so nice of her. She did this so I could play with Margaret on the weekends. I loved that club."[22]

Once, when she wanted a pony, she petitioned the neighbors at their Carthay Center apartment building, and asked their permission to keep a pony in her bedroom. After much persuasion, her mother—and the neighbors—convinced her it would be better to settle for a stuffed pink horse instead.

Regardless, Margaret was more of a dog lover anyway, and always had one with her through childhood. First, there was Maggie, a cocker spaniel; then a collie named Laddie, which was one of Lassie's pups. This was followed by Spotty, a miniature white fox terrier that was a gift from MGM mogul Louis B. Mayer, who adored Margaret. Many times, as a favor to her boss, Margaret would make appearances at the Home for the Aged, which was Mayer's sister's favorite charity. "You'd have to give a speech and listen to all the other speeches," she remembered. "For a child, it was hard to sit there and be on display for several hours." Another time, Mayer made the mistake of offering Margaret a gift for her birthday. "Anything you want," he told her.

"Well, what I really would like is Busher," she replied, undeterred by the fact that Busher, a member of Mayer's stable, happened to be one of the most valuable race horses in the world. "After all," she reasoned, "Mr. Mayer did ask me what I wanted, didn't he?"[23] He finally convinced her to settle for one of Lassie's puppies.

Her favorite movies were *National Velvet* (1944), which she saw eight times, and *Lassie Come Home* (1943). "I always wanted to do a Lassie movie but never got to do one," Margaret recalled. "I almost did *My Friend Flicka* (1943) with Roddy McDowall, but that was when *Meet Me in St Louis* came up. Only in later years did I get a chance to work

Margaret O'Brien with MGM mogul Louis B. Mayer.

with Lassie on the Lassie television show. But this was a descendant of Lassie and he didn't behave as well as his predecessor."[24]

Lassie Come Home was the first film to make Margaret cry, and even though she was renowned for her ability to cry on cue, Margaret usually did not show such emotion while watching a film. If her mother or aunt would happen to cry, she would taunt them by saying, "Why, it's only a picture."[25]

When she saw Elizabeth Taylor riding in the steeplechase sequence of *National Velvet*, she immediately decided to become the world's greatest female jockey. Later, after seeing *The Song of Bernadette* (1943), she switched her affections to Jennifer Jones, the star of the picture. "She was so beautiful in that," she told a reporter. "Almost holy, sort of." It was then that she decided she would become a nun when she grew up. "Nuns are the most beautiful people in the world," she said.[26]

But of all the movie stars in Hollywood, the one that made her heart flutter was Burt Lancaster, her soul mate, whose photograph Margaret kept in a place of honor at her home. Later, she was able to meet him when her dentist, who was also Lancaster's dentist, arranged a meeting between the two.

Clark Gable was another of her favorites. Once a reporter asked Gable how someone as young as Margaret could be such a good actress. "I wouldn't know," he replied. "It isn't years that count in show business. It's talent. There are plenty of actresses over 30 who aren't as mature, dramatically, as Margaret O'Brien."[27]

Regardless, their first meeting was somewhat unconventional. Gable, who had been flying missions over Germany in the war, had not seen any of her movies. "Tell me little girl," Gable said, "are you in pictures?" That evening, Margaret recounted the incident to her mother, saying philosophically, "I guess Mr. Gable just doesn't get around much."[28]

Even though Gable had not seen her films during the war, other servicemen did. Many times she entertained soldiers at the Hollywood Canteen, reciting the Gettysburg Address. During one particular visit to the Canteen, Margaret was virtually mobbed by servicemen who wanted her autograph. This rush of young men slightly frightened the young actress and years later made her wonder why such glamorous stars such as Hedy Lamarr and Lana Turner were being ignored. Many of the soldiers had Margaret's photograph tacked up on their lockers right next to Betty Grable and Rita Hayworth.

Margaret's popularity was reaching its zenith when she appeared in *Meet Me in St. Louis* (1944) with the legendary Judy Garland. She was the personal choice of director Vincente Minnelli for the role of Tootie, the youngest of the Smith girls. Of her performance in *Meet Me in St. Louis*, critic James Agee said that "Many of her possibilities and glints of her achievement hypnotize me as thoroughly as anything since Garbo."[29]

The making of *Meet Me in St Louis* was wracked with problems from the moment production began. Illnesses and accidents plagued the cast and crew, including Margaret, who was having problems with her teeth. When Louis B. Mayer refused to pay Margaret a higher salary, her mother yanked her out of the picture. Mrs. O'Brien had been on extremely friendly terms with the studio mogul, which enabled her to

Margaret O'Brien gazes at one of her idols, The King, Clark Gable.

march into his office and demand more money. "We'll come back when you pay our price," she told Mayer.[30] They were stuck with an unfinished picture, so Mayer relented and paid. "Mother was a smart business woman," Margaret admitted. "She put most of that money into bonds. But she also liked to spend, and so did I, so there was a lot we didn't save."[31]

Much of Margaret's money came from product endorsements. There were Margaret O'Brien hats, purses and dresses. Margaret O'Brien games, coloring books and dolls filled the toy stores, and in 1948, her published memoir called *My Diary* debuted during National Children's Book Week.

Margaret, who was now receiving more fan mail than anyone else at

Margaret O'Brien signs Elizabeth Taylor's cast as Jane Powell looks on.

MGM except Van Johnson and June Allyson, was collecting awards the way other children collected baseball cards. She was named one of the Top Ten Box Office Attractions of 1945 and 1946, and also received the *Film Daily* Critics Award, the *Look Magazine* Achievement Award, and *Parents* magazine Juvenile Award, to name just a few. She accumulated so many trophies and awards over her career that her mother built a special room in their home to contain them. Not since Shirley Temple had any child actress received so much acclaim.

On March 15, 1945, she received the industry's highest honor when she was given the Academy Award for Outstanding Child Actress of 1944. Because of the importance of that evening, Mrs. O'Brien helped Margaret prepare an acceptance speech. The ceremonies were held at Grauman's Chinese Theater in Hollywood, and the miniature statuette was presented to her by Mervyn LeRoy, who had directed her in the wartime short *You, John Jones* (1943) and the Academy Award nominated *Madame Curie* (1943).

"Thank you," she told LeRoy. "I really don't know what to say. Thank you very much."[32] Of course she had not forgotten her mother's speech, but instead decided to go with one of her own creation, which slightly displeased Mrs. O'Brien.

Bob Hope, who was the emcee that evening, called her award an "Oscar-ette." He then lifted her up to the microphone so she could be heard by the listening radio audience. "Will you hurry up and grow up, please?" Hope insisted as he struggled with the young winner.

"The Oscar didn't mean so much to me then," Margaret recalled. "It was more seeing Bob Hope. I was more interested in him than the Oscar that night. Of course I really appreciate it now, but as a child it was more seeing all the people."[33]

Grauman's Chinese Theater would also be the site of another honor given to Margaret O'Brien. The following year she was chosen to be the seventy-sixth star to place her hand and footprints in the famed forecourt outside the theater. Sid Grauman, the owner, allowed Margaret to pick the spot where she would like to sign.

On the evening of August 15, 1946, Margaret and her mother arrived at the theater for the ceremony. Given the choice, she decided to go barefoot because she didn't want to ruin her new shoes. Afterwards, she put her hand prints in the cement and signed it underneath. Her square, which is tinted green, reads, "Love to Mr. Grauman from Margaret O'Brien. Aug.15—1946."

"Mr. Grauman said that they will stay there for ever and ever," she said, "and anybody who has his name there can go to the movies free. That's nice."[34]

By now, the O'Briens had moved out of their Carthay Circle apartment and bought a house in Beverly Hills at 1502 South Beverly Boulevard. Margaret was making $2,500 a week under her new contract, which provided her payment for forty weeks a year whether she worked or not, and guaranteed her star or costar billing. The year before she had signed a $10,000 minimum, fourteen-month contract with Capitol Records for making narrative recordings of children's stories with musical backgrounds. Mrs. O'Brien also received 25 percent of the royalties for coaching.

During her years at MGM, Margaret O'Brien was the highest paid juvenile in

Director Mervyn LeRoy presents Margaret O'Brien with her Academy Award for *Meet Me in St. Louis* (1944, MGM).

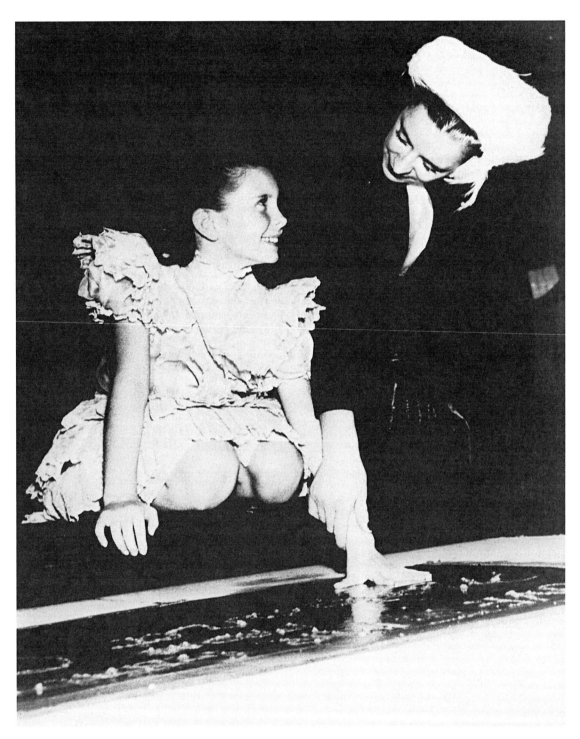

Margaret's mother helps her put her handprints in cement at the famed forecourt of Grauman's Chinese Theater.

motion pictures. At the height of her career she was making $5,000 a week which did not include the salary paid to Mrs. O'Brien, and the monies received for promotional tours, product endorsements, radio appearances and recording contracts. It was estimated that she had earned over $1,000,000 during her career.

Because of the so-called "Coogan Law," which was enacted to control the funds of juvenile actors after the astounding dissipation of $4,000,000 in film earnings of child actor Jackie Coogan, Margaret's money was protected for her, and invested properly, mostly in government bonds, until she turned twenty-one.

Because more and more of Mrs. O'Brien's time was spent looking over Margaret's affairs, she found it necessary to hire a nanny. A perfect one was found working at a Mexico City hotel. Margaret became entranced by the new nanny, who was named Guadalupe just like the shrine where the O'Briens made their devotions. Guadalupe taught Margaret how to speak Spanish and she in turn helped her with her English.

Margaret's financial independence allowed her family more leisure time. Mrs. O'Brien insisted that her daughter have more rest and planned recreation than other children. Between pictures they would take trips to Mexico, New York, or the seashore in order to give Margaret a change. "I try to get away after a picture," Mrs. O'Brien said. "It is more restful than staying in town where the studio can reach you."[35]

In 1947, Margaret took her mother and Uncle Marty on their first trip to Hawaii and got a chance to write about it for *Family Circle* magazine. When they arrived in Honolulu she was greeted by hundreds of fans who placed a total of fifty-six leis around her neck. "Of all the stars I have seen come and go here, she was the first one I ever saw literally smothered in orchids," wrote *Variety* correspondent Mabel Thomas to gossip columnist Hedda Hopper. While in Hawaii, Margaret hosted a cocktail party for more than 200 members of the press and theater representatives. The following day she made a personal appearance at a local store where 8,000 children waited for hours to see her. "Margaret has turned Honolulu upside down with her charm and graciousness," wrote Thomas. "It will be some time before Hawaii forgets the winsome, delightful, Margaret O'Brien."[36]

The following year the O'Briens traveled to Europe on vacation, but it turned out to be a lot of work. Margaret made numerous public appearances all through Europe, assisting in the work of European children's relief organizations. While in Ireland, Margaret interviewed the president of Ireland and the mayor of Dublin. "We saw O'Briens by the thousands in Ireland," Margaret told a reporter, "and they were all feuding like the Hatfields and McCoys."

In London, Prime Minister Atlee invited Margaret to dine at No. 10 Downing Street, and she also had the honor of introducing former First Lady Eleanor Roosevelt at the Empire Theater. A planned meeting with the king and queen fell through, but instead Margaret flew to Rome to meet the pope, who asked her if she went to school.

"No," Margaret replied. "I'm an actress."

"But you take lessons don't you?" the Pope inquired.

"Oh yes," she assured His Holiness,

Margaret O'Brien visits with President and Mrs. Truman.

"I take geography and history." Margaret later remarked that the pope was kind enough not to quiz her.[37]

During the voyage home on the *Queen Mary*, most everyone got seasick except Margaret and Eleanor Roosevelt. The two spent most of their time in the expansive dining room alone, talking. Upon her arrival in New York, Margaret was awarded the first Junior Humanitarian Medal by the Greenwich Village Humane League for her participation in charity affairs in Europe and America.

Before returning to California, Margaret stopped to visit with President Truman and continued raising money and food for the needy in Europe. When Truman asked her if she would like to be president someday, she replied, "I'd rather be Margaret O'Brien."[38]

When she returned to MGM after two months away, studio personnel noticed that their box office moppet had grown three inches. She was approaching the gangly period every young girl goes through and was no longer "cutesy." One day, an executive pointed at Margaret in the commissary and reportedly said to the man with him, "Don't look now, but the kid's growing awfully fast. We've got a headache on our hands."[39] Margaret was maturing and the studio was not sure what to do with her.

They made plans to star her in a film called *Violet*, which was based on a *Redbook* series. It was similar to the Andy Hardy films and was designed to bridge the gangling years between adolescence and young womanhood, but the project never materialized. Later, they tried to make a radio and television show from the same vehicle, but that too failed.

Part of the maturation process for any child is something called a birthday, and if you are Margaret O'Brien, the celebration is usually on a grand scale. Sometimes the parties would be held on the MGM lot, but once actress Mary Pickford hosted a celebration for Margaret at Pickfair. For her twelfth birthday, Mrs. O'Brien invited a few little girls for a party at Romanoff's, Margaret's favorite restaurant. Actress Elinor Donahue remembers that particular party vividly and has never shared this story before with anyone, until now.

"I have never told Margaret this, but I have a sad story," Donahue recalled. "Metro had just dropped me and at the time we didn't have as much money. My mother had neglected to buy Margaret a present and I was horrified. I had a beautiful porcelain ballerina mother had given me on my tenth birthday and I said I wanted Margaret to have this. And since we had done *The Unfinished Dance* together, I felt it was appropriate."

Elinor's mother was a little hurt that she wanted to give that particular doll and asked her daughter if something else would do, but there was nothing that looked new. Finally her mother relented and began to wrap the porcelain doll until suddenly they heard something break. The doll had accidentally broken while her mother was wrapping it.

"We were both horrified," Donahue said. "The limo was going to pick me up in less than an hour and I didn't have anything that looked new. Then, mother found a crappy fuzzy little dog, the kind you get at a carnival. It was one of those cheap giveaway toys, but it was the only thing that looked brand new. I was so ashamed; my heart was broken. I wanted to give Margaret something wonderful. When Margaret opened the present she was so gracious and cried, 'Oh how adorable,' but I was humiliated."[40]

What also should have been a celebration was Gladys O'Brien's announcement that she was going to marry orchestra leader Don Sylvio, who played at a club in Greenwich Village. Gladys had known Sylvio for five years and the couple planned to be married even though it was evident that Margaret did not approve. Some years earlier Gladys had asked Margaret what she thought of having a nice father. "No," Margaret responded, "I think I'll just stick to the same monotonous old family."[41]

Gladys knew the studio was finding less and less for Margaret to do, and held no delusions about her future. Although she believed her daughter was a talented actress, she also hoped that living an ordinary life away from Hollywood would help Margaret mature into a

well-rounded adult. Later, if she wanted, she could try for a stage career in New York.

She also saw this as a chance for a life of her own; a life that until now had centered around her daughter. For the better part of Margaret's life she had to wake up at dawn every morning, stand around all day in drafty movie stages then go home to fall into bed while other people were still planning their evenings. "First your feet get weary from a routine like that," she later said, "and then the ache spreads all over. For anyone who loves life, it's no life."[42]

After being postponed several times, the marriage ceremony was finally held on February 21, 1949, in a Palm Beach, Florida, hotel room with six people as witnesses. Mrs. O'Brien spent all day trying to get Margaret to say it would be all right to marry Sylvio. "She said she didn't think I realized what a big job I have been," Margaret later said. "I guess I didn't realize it but I am beginning to. She said she just doesn't feel she can do it alone, anymore." Mrs. O'Brien also reminded Margaret that when her Aunt Marissa got married she was also upset, yet she grew to love her Uncle Johnny.

Unfortunately, Mrs. O'Brien did not tell Margaret that she was getting married that day. Instead, she asked her to put on her prettiest white dress and go with her upstairs. Almost at the top of the stairs Mrs. O'Brien stopped and said, "I think you know what we are going upstairs for, darling."

"But I didn't know," Margaret recalled. "If she had had a wedding dress, I would have known what was going to happen. I didn't know until it really happened. I didn't know until we were in the room, and the judge was there, and

"America's Sweetheart," Mary Pickford, wishes a happy birthday to America's newest sweetheart, Margaret O'Brien.

Don was there, and Mummy and Don were married, and I was crying."[43]

Margaret wept through the entire ceremony and at one point sobbed, "Oh, Mother." Later, when she refused to kiss Sylvio for the photographers who had gathered, newspapers all over the country proclaimed, "Margaret O'Brien Shuns Stepfather."[44]

"It wasn't because I didn't like Don that I cried at Mummy's wedding," Margaret said. "I think Don is nice looking, and I like the way he plays the piano. It was just that I never have had anybody but my mother and never wanted anyone else."[45]

The following month, as a peace offering, Gladys took Margaret on a two-month trip to Europe, leaving Sylvio behind to fulfill his musical engagements. "I think it just as well I am not going," Sylvio said. "I don't want Margaret or Gladdy to feel there has been any change at all. I want it understood that it will be just the same between Margaret and her mother."[46] Mrs. O'Brien also failed to tell MGM they were going to Europe and the studio put Margaret on an unpaid suspension.

While in England, Margaret received a very special treat when she met her longtime idol, Vivien Leigh. Miss Leigh was appearing at the Old Vic Theater in *Anthony and Cleopatra* with her husband, Sir Laurence Olivier. After their performance, she went backstage for a special tea with them. Of all the actresses in Hollywood, Vivien Leigh was one she really wanted to meet. After a few pleasantries, Margaret turned to her and said, "Miss Leigh, you are my favorite actress."

"That is so sweet," Leigh told her. "Especially when you have so many to choose from."

Miss Leigh then moved closer to her and softly said, "Do you want to know a secret? You're my favorite too." Margaret was overjoyed to hear her say that. After the tea, Margaret shyly asked for an autograph, something she rarely did. Miss Leigh went to a drawer and took out several photographs and allowed her to pick the one she liked the best. After signing it, Olivier asked her if she would like to have his autograph also. "Oh, no thank you," she told him. "I only want Miss Leigh's." He seemed a little disappointed, but she hoped he understood how much Miss Leigh meant to her. Before leaving, Vivien Leigh sent her a dozen roses at her hotel.

When they returned home two months later, Gladys asked for an annulment of her marriage to Sylvio, and an immediate release of Margaret's $3,000 a week MGM contract, which still had six months to go. Margaret had been offered some independent film and stage work, which she couldn't accept if she were still at MGM. Also, the studio had no project for her at the time and had rejected several ideas her mother wanted to pursue. MGM released a statement saying that the parting was "mutually friendly."

Don Sylvio told the press he was going to fight the annulment, saying, "I still love Gladys. I never would have married her if I didn't love her. I'm hoping for a reconciliation."[47] Unfortunately the reconciliation never occurred and the fight turned nasty with Gladys claiming spousal abuse. The annulment was granted two years later. Gladys insisted that Margaret had nothing to do with her decision, but added, "She is happy about it."[48]

The day after Margaret left her MGM contract, Walt Disney announced

Margaret O'Brien has tea with her idol, Vivien Leigh, during a visit to London.

Two of the most popular child stars ever, Shirley Temple and Margaret O'Brien (courtesy of Ed Colbert).

that he would star her in his next film, *Alice in Wonderland*, which would be a combination of live-action and animation. The announcement, however, was a little premature, because Disney and Mrs. O'Brien could not agree on Margaret's salary, so she stormed out of his office. Vic Orsatti, Margaret's agent, later announced that the deal was off. "The contracts which had been ready for signatures over the weekend were withdrawn," Orsatti stated. "A mutual un-

derstanding to call off the engagement with the Disney studio was reached."[49]

That same week, Mrs. O'Brien received a phone call from New York offering Margaret the lead role in *Peter Pan* on Broadway. "But I think she is a little young to play *Peter Pan*," Gladys told a reporter. "I didn't turn the offer down. I said we'd think it over."[50]

The strain of Gladys' marital problems and Margaret's contractual difficulties with MGM and Disney had taken their toll; both mother and daughter needed a vacation. Margaret's aunt, Mrs. Jean Harris, released a statement saying that Gladys was "too upset at present to accompany Margaret to a studio. Furthermore, Margaret herself is too upset to do justice to the Disney film at this particular time. So we thought it would be the best thing for both of them to rest a while."[51]

For the first time in her career, Margaret had to deal with bad publicity, which was foreign to her. The press and the public blamed her for the breakup of her mother's marriage. A few months later, while in Chicago to appear on a television show, a woman came up to Margaret on the street and said, "You wretched girl. What a terrible thing to do to your poor mother."[52]

A year later Margaret was appearing in a play in Philadelphia and the audience hissed at her. In 1953, she played a stepchild scheming to shatter her parent's second marriage in the play *The Intruder*. Drama critics commented on the parallels of the play and her real life situation. Always the loving mother, Mrs. O'Brien defended her daughter.

"It's ridiculous for anybody to think that she ruined my marriage," she said. "I don't know why I'm so fortunate to have such a wonderful daughter. Margaret's never been a mean child. She's sweet, obedient and untemperamental. I've done more to hurt her than she's ever done to hurt me."[53]

Many claimed that Margaret did not want to grow up, and in that sense they may have been right. However, that attitude only reflected what the public wanted. Margaret did the one thing that the fans and the studio executives felt was unforgivable—she grew up. Child stars spend their entire lives being adu-lated and in some cases are convinced they are something they were never meant to be. As they grow older, some feel that unless they stay small, all the adulation will cease.

In 1946 while working on *Bad Bascomb*, her costar Wallace Beery told Margaret that she was getting to be a big girl. To his surprise she reacted with shock and pulled away, trying to shrink back into herself. At age 14, Margaret complained to a newspaper columnist that everybody was trying to make her grow up too fast. "I won't," she declared. "I like being young and I still play with dolls."[54]

Fortunately Margaret O'Brien was luckier than many of her show business contemporaries. Some, such as Scotty Beckett and Bobby Driscoll, were devastated when the attention ceased and their ends were tragic. But others like Dean Stockwell and Bobby Blake suffered only a temporary wane in their careers and saw their popularity return as adults.

Roddy McDowall, another popular child star who successfully made the transition to adult roles, once said: "Indeed, the successful child actor generally has a tough future in this upside down world called show business. Elizabeth Taylor and a very few others are the exceptions to this rule. Even extra-ordinarily gifted performers such as Margaret O'Brien, the most popular child actress of the early 1940s, had a rough going when the adolescent years arrived. It's a pity so much experienced talent was never allowed to shine and grow."[55]

Hedda Hopper once asked Margaret if she had a sense of loss when she learned that she was through with pictures for the time being after leaving Metro-Goldwyn-Mayer.

Margaret O'Brien celebrates her birthday with her aunt Marissa (left) and her mother Gladys.

"Yes," she told Hedda. "It became too difficult to find things for me. At first I felt bad; I'd been going to the studio since I was four, and I felt lost. A professional child works and does the usual schooling at the same time, so study alone doesn't fill his day. But soon I started occasional work in TV, and then I did stage plays. It was good training."[56]

During this time, Margaret made only two movies. *Her First Romance* (1951) made at Columbia was not a big hit and Margaret admitted she only did it because they were willing to pay her price. The second was called *Girls Hand in Hand* (1953), which was filmed entirely in Japan and costarred Hibari Misori, that country's version of Judy Garland.

That same year, Margaret was given the Sacrament of Confirmation in the Catholic Church with her sponsor, actress Loretta Young, at the Church of the Good Shepherd in Beverly Hills. Also being confirmed that evening was Margaret's good friend Marlo Thomas, the daughter of Danny Thomas.

Also at this time Margaret auditioned

for the lead in MGM's *The Actress* (1953), starring Spencer Tracy. During the film test, they were looking for someone for her to do her lines with and decided to use a kid who had been hanging around MGM's gate; that kid was Anthony Perkins.

"They called me in and I stood right in front of the camera," Perkins later recalled, "almost obliterating poor Margaret O'Brien's face and causing a director to say, 'Please move to the left.' When he said this, I turned around and said, 'Who, me?' and I was in the test."[57]

While going over the test later they decided that whoever the guy was that said, "Who, me?" would be fine for the role of the boyfriend. *The Actress* was Anthony Perkins' first film, but the lead went to Jean Simmons because they felt Margaret was too young.

During the 1950s, Margaret spent most of her time on stage and in television. "That was my training ground," she later said, "that's where I really learned my trade."[58] She also toured with Buddy Rogers' orchestra, doing, among other things, Beth's death scene from *Little Women* (1949). On television, she appeared in such landmark programs as *Toast of the Town*, *Robert Montgomery Presents* and *Studio One*. She also made her stage debut in the Clare Boothe Luce drama *Child of Morning*.

Margaret was now blossoming into a beautiful young woman. She was no longer the little moppet that most people remembered on the silver screen. Only her soft smile was reminiscent of the little girl in *Journey for Margaret*. Her warm brown eyes, long lashes, alabaster skin and auburn hair were now what captivated the photographers.

Despite her beauty, Mrs. O'Brien claimed that her daughter had no interest in boys. "I'm not rushing her either," she added. "In another six months I think she will change her mind. Right now she likes to play with her three dogs, a collie, a terrier and a dachshund, and she likes to lunch at Romanoff's. She keeps me broke taking her there. It's hard to realize she's a young lady now and only yesterday I was changing her diapers."[59]

And it was six months later that Margaret began dating Dick Bentley, a 21-year-old West Point cadet. Her mother insisted it was nothing serious, and always kept a close guard over her daughter's social life. But she swore she would not be overbearing about it. "I promise I'm not going to worry about her every time she goes out or I'll lose my mind," Gladys once said. "My mother used to wait up for me, and knowing that shadow by the window will be there when you come home can put a damper on your whole evening."[60]

Unfortunately, Mrs. O'Brien did not always live up to her promise. Margaret was now friends with Natalie Wood, another child actress whom she didn't meet until they were both teenagers. Natalie's parents were quite the opposite of Mrs. O'Brien, and gave the young actress much more free rein than Margaret had.

One night Margaret asked Natalie to spend the night at her house. At the time, Natalie was only fifteen and had an illegal driver's license, so she drove over to Margaret's Beverly Hills home by herself. Natalie had always felt her parents were very strict, but when she saw Margaret's home life, she was shocked.

"When we went to the movies, both her aunt and her mother took us," Natalie recalled. "We were not allowed

Judy Garland fixes Margaret's hair during a radio performance of *Meet Me in St. Louis* for Lux Radio Theatre.

to wait outside. We had to wait for them inside the lobby. Margaret had this extreme overprotection, which I had been rebelling against for a couple of years."[61]

Natalie was further surprised by the way Margaret accepted her situation. In fact, in her rush to get home and tell her parents that they weren't as bad as she thought, she began speeding and got into a terrible accident. Fortunately she was not hurt, but the car was demolished.

Another time, they were to go to a movie, but instead met James Dean and a few other friends at Googie's, a teen hangout on the Sunset Strip. Unfortunately for Margaret, Mrs. O'Brien happened to drive by and saw her sitting with Natalie and Dean. In front of her friends and strangers, Mrs. O'Brien walked into the restaurant, grabbed Margaret by the hair and dragged her home.

Besides Natalie Wood, Margaret spent most of her time with her childhood friend Nancy Stewart, who lived four houses down the street. Nancy was such a good friend and so faithful that the whole neighborhood called her "The Sentinel" for the way she paced the sidewalk waiting for Margaret to come out to play.

Once when they were children, Nancy went along with Margaret for a personal appearance at a Los Angeles department store. Afterward, they both climbed into the limousine and continued their conversation about their dolls or the little boys they either liked or hated.

"But then a crowd collected around the car and Mrs. O'Brien insisted that Margaret wave and smile prettily," Nancy recalled. "She told Margaret they were her public and her first duty was to be nice to them. Margaret was. She waved and smiled, but she kept looking at me as if she were being inspected and hated it."[62]

As they matured, Nancy tried to induce Margaret to spend more time with young people her own age and less with professional associates. Things improved when Margaret got her driver's license and bought a new car, a cream-colored Ford Victoria with flame-red upholstery.

"It helped get Margaret away from the old surroundings and the old ways," Nancy remembered. "When we were in it, going for a ride to the beach, it seemed silly to talk about anything but boys."

She felt that one of the most significant events in Margaret's life was when she attended a summer dance at Mount St. Mary's in Brentwood, where Nancy attended school.

"None of the kids there recognized her," Nancy said. "As soon as Margaret realized that she was just another girl to them, she started having the time of her life. It had a wonderful effect. She just

bloomed, laughing and talking like never before, dancing first with one boy, then with another. I think she learned that night that somewhere along the line in her acting life she had lost the person she actually was. But when she can find that girl, it's an awful lot of fun for her."[63]

Many people now found it hard to believe that she was actually Margaret O'Brien. Ultimately, someone would approach her and say, "Excuse me, but didn't you *used* to be Margaret O'Brien?"[64] They probably meant no harm, but were amazed that this slender young girl of seventeen could possibly have been that pert, freckled-face little kid named Margaret O'Brien. Even so, it only made her more determined to act again. That grim determination and desire to learn surprised everyone except her mother. "It's exactly what I expected from Margaret," she said. "She's going to be a great actress. It's all she lives for."[65]

But first she had to finish school. After leaving MGM, instead of going to a private or public school, Margaret continued with a tutor three hours a day at her home. At eighteen years of age, she graduated on June 19, 1955, from the University High School in West Los Angeles. Margaret O'Brien was now an adult.

"I've never seen the pictures I made in the early years," Margaret told a reporter in 1955. "Even when I was appearing regularly as a child I was kept away from my pictures. They feared I might become self-conscious about my work. Of course I remember appearing in the films while they were in the making, but that was all a childhood adventure, and always mixed with the problem of getting my schooling."[66]

Dean Stockwell and Margaret O'Brien take a break during filming of *The Secret Garden* (1949, MGM).

No longer a child actress, Margaret prepared for her first adult role. Because she had persisted in stage and television work, there was no question about her fitness for acting. So when director David Butler offered her the lead role in his new RKO picture *Glory* (1956), Margaret eagerly accepted. "My great aim is to prove myself a good dramatic actress on both stage and screen, and also in television," Margaret said. "This return to pictures in *Glory* is one of the most important things to help me realize that ambition."[67]

To complete the change, she cut off her trademark long hair into the popular Italian cut of the day, which made her look her age and appear more collegiate. *Glory* was also significant because she received her first on-screen kiss from actor John Lupton. But in real life, Margaret confessed that she had not been kissed yet. "Little short ones for goodnight," she said, "but I mean not a real, romantic kiss."[68] That first kiss came from a boy at Loyola named Don Robinson.

Margaret's film comeback made her newsworthy once again. Everyone from Hedda Hopper to Louella Parsons insisted on interviewing her. "I expect Margaret to turn into an important adult actress," Parsons said.[69]

Early in 1958, Mrs. O'Brien became ill with what was later diagnosed as heart disease. During this time, they employed a maid to help around their Beverly Boulevard house. Among the maid's responsibilities was to polish the awards in Margaret's trophy room, including the Oscar she had won in 1945. One day, the maid took the Oscar and several other awards home with her to polish. After three days, the maid failed to return to work, so Mrs. O'Brien called and told her that she was dismissed, and instructed her to return the awards, which the maid agreed to do.

Shortly after, however, Mrs. O'Brien returned to the hospital, and the maid and the awards were forgotten. Months later, Margaret tried to contact her, but found she had moved and not left a forwarding address. Margaret was certain she would never see her Academy Award again.

In mid–July, Mrs. O'Brien suffered a relapse and was admitted to St. John's Hospital in Santa Monica. At the time, Margaret was in rehearsals for a television production of *Little Women*, but would visit her mother afterward and then return home at night. After five weeks at St. John's, the doctors told Margaret that her mother was improving, and could return home soon. Then in the early morning of August 27, 1958, Gladys O'Brien awoke and couldn't get back to sleep. At a little past 2 a.m., she asked a nurse to help her to a chair by the window. "I think I'll go back to bed now," she said, after about twenty minutes.[70] However, she died suddenly without ever moving.

The end came so fast that Margaret was unable to reach her mother's side in time. Near collapse, Margaret could hardly speak. "Mother and I were very close," she tearfully told reporters.[71] After a Requiem Mass was performed at the Church of the Good Shepherd in Beverly Hills, Mrs. O'Brien was laid to rest at Holy Cross Cemetery, not far from MGM studios.

At the age of 21, Margaret was now alone. Her aunt Marissa had married many years earlier, and had a daughter of her own and was living in Fresno, California. Margaret continued to live in her Beverly Hills duplex, realizing that she had to learn to do for herself. Up to then, her mother had taken care of everything, including her contracts and finances. Margaret was uncertain whether she could make those decisions on her own.

"I didn't think I could do it," she recalled. "My mother was a tower of strength to me. After she was gone, I found myself spending more and more time alone. But then it occurred to me that I had to face up to my obligations when I realized that no one else was going to do it for me."[72]

Margaret continued to live the austere life set down by her mother. "I guess you can say I lead a very quiet, normal—and lonely—life," she said. "But I can't really say I'm unhappy." Even though she was 21, she never wanted to live a wild life. Margaret never smoked, never took drugs, nor had a problem with alcohol, which says a lot for her upbringing. "I never wanted to break loose and raise heck," she said at the time. "I've seen too much of that kind of life all around me. My few friends are not part of the Hollywood crowd."[73]

Margaret was now ready to go out on her own, and wanted to play more

Margaret O'Brien with producer Eddie Dowling rehearsing a scene from her stage debut, *Child of the Morning*.

mature roles. Within a few months, she was offered a part in *Heller in Pink Tights* (1960), a western being made at Paramount by director George Cukor. In it, she had the opportunity to show what an attractive young woman she had become. "Margaret O'Brien's new sexiness will probably astound onlookers," one critic wrote.[74]

Hedda Hopper once asked Margaret if it were true that she would not marry until she was twenty-five. "True or false," Hedda asked. Margaret laughed and said, "I really haven't any plans. It

This publicity shot was used to prove to producers that Margaret O'Brien was no longer a child.

will depend on when the right one comes along. I'm not engaged—I'm a bit young for that. I have certain requirements, however. I don't care if a man isn't handsome, so long as he's nice and understanding—and understands the business I'm in."[75]

That Christmas of 1958, Margaret felt she had found the right one and became engaged to Robert Allen, a commercial artist. Allen, who was 24, took an old-fashioned look at marriage. "Bob may want me to retire after we're married," Margaret said. "He believes a man should earn the living in a family and a wife should take care of their home."[76]

On August 8, 1959, Margaret and Robert Allen were married before Father Joseph Caldwell and 400 guests at St. Martin of Tours Catholic Church in Brentwood. Margaret wore a gown of white faille of Italian design and carried a bouquet of orchids, lilies of the valley and Easter lily petals.

She was given in marriage by Larry Sears, the man her mother was married to for three days when Margaret was an infant. Sears remained friends with Margaret and her mother all those years and would often tell people that he was the father of Margaret O'Brien.

Margaret continued in television, and on stage in such top rate productions as *Sunday in New York*, *Barefoot in the Park* and the title role in *Gigi*. But the number of her appearances dropped considerably while she took on the new role of a loving wife.

Margaret admitted that she was just now beginning to live down her past as a pigtailed little girl. Even then, many producers did not believe that the attractive brunette in front of them was actually Margaret O'Brien. "I had to start over, and make myself over," she said. "Even then I had a hard time convincing anyone. I know it sounds silly, but I think a lot of producers didn't hire me because they like to swear when they get mad, and they didn't feel right swearing at Margaret O'Brien."[77]

Even though Margaret now had earned her career as an adult, she always met people who wanted to talk about her childhood. During an interview for a television show or a stage part, the talk would invariably revert to Margaret O'Brien—child star. "I would like to forget about what I did as a child," she would sometimes say.[78]

But of course people would not allow that. She would always be little Margaret O'Brien to the public. When she appeared in the play *Love from a Stranger* with famed stripper Sally Rand, the press openly wondered why the former moppet was working with the queen of burlesque. "What are we doing in the same play?" Sally Rand replied. "Well, maybe I'm not being discreet. But we both understand it thoroughly. Margaret here is a wonderful actress and I sell tickets."[79]

Regardless of who she appeared with, one thing was certain—Margaret O'Brien loved acting. "I guess I've always liked to act since I was a very small child," she said.[80] Of course, many child actors were not as fortunate to continue their acting into adulthood. Many grumbled about their lost childhood, but Margaret refused to dwell on any regrets she may have had.

"I often see or read interviews in which these former stars complain about what the film business has done to them," she remarked. "If they don't like it so, why do they stay in it? I stay in it because I like it. I always have. I always

Margaret O'Brien costars with Pat O'Brien and Maureen O'Sullivan in "Daughter of Mine" for television's *Ford Theatre*.

felt fortunate in being able to work in movies, and I don't think I suffered for it. My mother was very careful about seeing that I lived a fairly normal life."[81]

Unfortunately, Margaret's career was partly responsible for the end of her marriage. After ten years together, she and Robert Allen were divorced. Later, in a very frank interview, Margaret explained her relationship with Allen. "We were just friends," she explained. "My mother had passed away, and I was still so young. Instead of getting a maid or butler, I got married."[82]

To help cope with her heartbreak, Margaret accepted an offer from the Panamericana Enterprises in Lima, Peru, to appear in two movies called *Diabolic Wedding* (1971) and *Annabelle Lee* (1972), which was based on the Edgar Allan Poe poem. The pictures were filmed simultaneously in English and Spanish.

To help capitalize on her name, producers of the film also signed her to appear as the host of a daily soap opera based on *Diabolic Wedding*. Her Spanish heritage and fluency in the language made this transition simple.

Margaret spent the next three years in Peru and became engaged to a wealthy socialite businessman named Julio Tijero. She collected Peruvian art and overall was quite content. Then in 1971, Margaret learned that her business manager had embezzled more than $75,000 of her earnings. Not long after, she and Julio returned to California, and settled in the San Fernando Valley in hopes of reviving her career. However, her contentment in Peru and the wonderful food of that country had a profound effect on Margaret—it made her gain weight. "It's that Peruvian food. It's so delicious," she told friends.[83]

Ironically, the extra weight allowed

her the opportunity for a television role, and the chance to be reunited with an old costar. In 1972, she appeared in an episode of *Marcus Welby, M.D.* with her friend, Robert Young. When asked about her weight gain, Margaret said, "It's true. I've been having some emotional problems over a lawsuit involving misuse of funds I earned as a child. When I get upset, I eat."[84]

However, as with past problems, Margaret persevered and with much willpower and work, recaptured her slender, youthful look. She once again became active in dinner theaters in such plays as *Star Spangled Girl*. But sadly, her relationship with Julio Tijero ended, and he returned to Peru.

On June 6, 1974, Margaret married Scandinavian steel executive Roy Thorvald Thorsen and settled in Thousand Oaks, a community outside Los Angeles. Margaret accepted stage and television roles whenever she wanted, but admitted that she did not have to. "I'd like to go on working, but I certainly don't have to," she told a reporter. "If I never perform again I wouldn't have to worry about finances."[85]

In 1976, Margaret announced that she was expecting her first child, a girl that she named Mara Tolene. When asked if she wanted her daughter to enter show business, Margaret explained, "I wouldn't mind if she became an actress. I think being a child star is much easier on girls than on boys. There's so much pampering to it. That rests easier on the girls. However, Mara will make her own decision. I will not push her into anything."[86]

Margaret continued being a homemaker and mother, and occasionally accepted acting roles such as in *Amy*, a 1981 Disney film. In non-film related

Margaret O'Brien as an adult actress.

Margaret O'Brien with her doll collection.

business, she became a civilian aide for Southern California to Secretary of the Army Clifford Alexander. One of her duties was to organize the yearly Army Ball that paid tribute to past military efforts. One year they were honoring Bob Hope for his tireless entertaining of the troops and the legendary Bette Davis for her work with the Hollywood Canteen. In order to finalize things for the ball, Margaret called Davis one afternoon. "Hello, Miss Davis, this is Margaret O'Brien," she said. But before she could finish, Davis interrupted her and said, "I do not talk at this time of the day. And please do not call again."

As she hung up Margaret was speechless and called her husband at his office to explain what had happened. During their conversation her husband received another call; it was Bette Davis. Apparently the actress had not realized that it was really Margaret O'Brien on the telephone and the only way she had of contacting her was through her husband. Bette was very apologetic and agreed to attend the ball. "She was tough and extremely professional," Margaret remembered.

Television roles continued through the 1980s in such landmark shows as *Hotel*, *Tales from the Darkside* and *Murder, She*

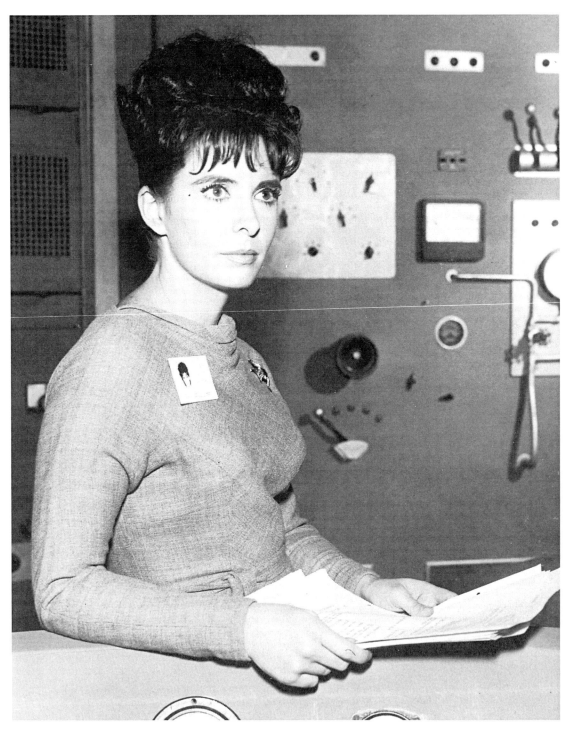

Margaret O'Brien takes a moment to study her lines for an appearance on *Bob Hope Presents the Chrysler Theater*.

Margaret O'Brien is reunited with her long lost Academy Award in a special ceremony at Academy headquarters (courtesy Michael Schwibs).

Margaret O'Brien in her latest film, *Hollywood Mortuary* (1999), with friend and costar Randal Malone (courtesy Michael Schwibs).

Wrote. However, her home life once again began to suffer, and she separated from her husband. "Divorce is very difficult," she said. "I do not recommend it. He's a very nice person, I'm a very nice person, but... "[87]

In 1996, much to the delight of her fans, Margaret appeared before the cameras in the independent film *Sunset After*

Dark with her good friend Randal Malone and silent film star Anita Page. The trio repeated the experience three years later in *Hollywood Mortuary* (1999) where Margaret played herself for the first time in a film.

In March of 1995, Margaret O'Brien was again front page news when her Oscar and other awards that disappeared in 1957 turned up at a Pasadena swap meet and were bought by two businessmen, Steve Meimand and Mark Nash. When the Oscar was spotted in a catalogue for auction, a friend of Margaret's confirmed that it was hers and the men agreed to return it and the other awards.

At a special ceremony at the Academy of Motion Picture Arts and Sciences headquarters in Beverly Hills, Margaret's miniature statuette was returned to her, ending a thirty-seven-year search. "It's amazing," Margaret said. "It was special and I did miss it. I never thought it would be returned. I had looked for it for so many years in the same type of places where it was found. I'm so thankful to both gentlemen."

Margaret O'Brien is no longer a child star, but she still continues to shine. She lives today in the San Fernando Valley and occasionally accepts acting roles. She has an impressive collection of pre–Columbian art, and is considered something of an authority on the subject. Much of her time is spent on cruises, lecturing on her film career, or attending functions in Hollywood. Many of her costars are now gone, but she still keeps in touch with George Sidney and June Allyson, among others. She also says she has no intention of ever retiring completely.

"Actresses often say that they're going to give up acting," she once remarked, "but I always stare at them open-eyed when they said it. I could never say I'll never act again. I always loved acting and I still do. I've lived a wonderful life."[88]

THE FILMS

BABES ON BROADWAY

A Metro-Goldwyn-Mayer Picture
1941

"Wait. Wait. Don't send my brother to the chair. Don't let him burn. Please, please, warden, please."
>—Margaret O'Brien to James Gleason, auditioning for a role in *Babes on Broadway*.

Opened on December 31, 1941, at Radio City Music Hall, New York City. Ad line: "Mickey and Judy Are Here Again in the Year's Biggest Musical."

Statistics

MGM production number 216.
Running time, 118 minutes; black & white; Musical.

Ratings

The Motion Picture Guide, ☆☆☆½
Leonard Maltin's Movie and Video Guide, ☆☆½
Halliwell's Film Guide, ☆☆

Credits

Produced by Arthur Freed; directed by Busby Berkeley and George Sidney (uncredited); screenplay by Fred Finklehoffe and Elaine Ryan, based on the unpublished story "Convict's Return" by Harry Kaufman; original story by Fred Finklehoffe; original music by Burton Lane; musical direction by George E. Stoll; music adaptation by Roger Edens; musical presentation by Merrill Pye; art direction by Cedric Gibbons and Malcolm Brown; set decoration by Edwin B. Willis; make-up by Jack Dawn; gowns by Kalloch; men's wardrobe by Gile Steele; sound by Douglas Shearer; cinematography by Lester White; film editing by Frederick Y. Smith; vocals and orchestration by Leo Arnaud, George Bassman and Conrad Salinger; choreography by Busby Berkeley; director: solo sequences, Vincente Minnelli (uncredited).

Songs: "How About You," "Babes on Broadway" by Burton Lane and Ralph Freed; "Chin Up, Cheerio, Carry On," "Anything Can Happen in New York" by Burton Lane and E. Y. Harburg; "Hoe Down" by Arthur Freed and Roger Edens; "Blackout on Broadway" by Roger Edens; "Mama, Yo Quiero" by Al Stillman, Jaraca and Vincent Paiva; "Franklin D. Roosevelt Jones" by Harold Rome; "By the Light of the Silvery Moon" by Edward Madden and Gus Edwards; "Albany Bound" by Buddy De Sylva, Bud Green and Ray Henderson; "Old Folks at Home" by Stephen Foster; "Waiting for the Robert E. Lee" by L. Wolfe Gilbert and Lewis

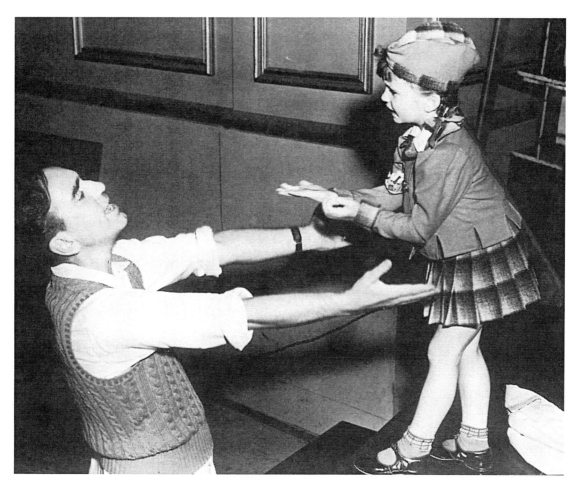

Little Maxine O'Brien rehearses her scene with director Busby Berkeley in *Babes on Broadway* (1941, MGM).

F. Muir; "Mary's a Grand Old Name," "Yankee Doodle Boy" by George M. Cohan; "She Is Ma Daisy" by Sir Harry Lauder and J. D. Harper; "I've Got Rings on My Fingers" by F. J. Barnes, R. P. Weston and Maurice Scott.

Cast

Mickey Rooney (Tommy Williams), Judy Garland (Penny Morris), Fay Bainter (Miss Jones), Virginia Weidler (Barbara Jo), Ray McDonald (Ray Lambert), Richard Quine (Morton Hammond), Donald Meek (Mr. Stone), Alexander Woollcott (Himself), Luis Alberni (Nick), James Gleason (Thornton Reed), Emma Dunn (Mrs. Williams), Frederick Burton (Professor Morris), Cliff Clark (Professor Moriarty), William A. Post, Jr. (Announcer), Dick Baron (Butch), Maxine Flores (Pit Astor Girl), William A. Lee (Waiter), Dorothy Morris (Pit Astor Girl), Maxine O'Brien (Maxine), Donna Reed (Secretary, billed as Donna Adams), Anne Rooney (Pit Astor Girl), Carl Stockdale (Man), Joe Yule (Mason, Aide to Reed), Tom Hanlon (Radio

Man), Renee Austin (Elinor), Roger Steele (Boy), Bryant Washburn (Director), Charles Wagenheim (Composer), Lester Dorr (Writer), Jack Lipson (Fat Man), Arthur Hoyt (Little Man), Barbara Bedford (Matron), Shimen Ruskin (Excited Russian), Stop, Look & Listen Trio.

Synopsis

Story of young performers who battle for their chance on Broadway and also receive some disillusionment. A sequel to *Babes in Arms* (1939), it is basically a showcase for the talents of stars Mickey Rooney and Judy Garland. The film debut of Margaret O'Brien.

Behind the Scenes

The pictures that photographer Paul Hesse made of Margaret resulted in MGM giving the four-year-old tot a small part in *Babes on Broadway*. It was in the audition for this part that Angela repeated her plea to spare her uncle from the chair, charming Arthur Freed and Vincente Minnelli into giving her a role.

Even though they would never make another picture together, Mickey Rooney and Margaret became good friends on the studio lot. During lunch at the commissary, Rooney would come over to Margaret's table and say, "How's Maggie the old Hag?" which would make the little girl laugh. "He would tease me and call me Maggie and no one else really called me that," Margaret recalled.[1]

One critic proclaimed that *Babes on Broadway* had "enough energy and enthusiasm to make older people wish they were young, and young people glad that they are."[2] It was also the beginning of a child star career that Hollywood had not seen since Shirley Tem-

ple nearly a decade earlier. "Don't send my brother to the chair!" would be the first words that Margaret O'Brien, billed as Maxine O'Brien, would utter onscreen.

Reviews

"*Babes* consumes so much celluloid at such a loud pace that it is one of the most exhausting pictures of this or any other year."—*Time*, undated.

"Here is grand entertainment; it should be enjoyed both by young and old."—*Harrison's Reports*, December 6, 1941.

Additional Reviews: *Hollywood Reporter*, 12/03/41; *Variety*, 12/03/41.

Academy Award Nominee

Ralph Freed (music) and Burton Lane (lyrics)—Best Song ("How About You?")

Costar Comments

"Maggie O'Brien was a very unique little actress. She had great dramatic abilities, truly a pint-sized pro."—*Mickey Rooney*[3]

"Margaret became my favorite actress of all time. I think she has an uncanny sense of the theater."—*Donald Meek*[4]

Comments by Margaret O'Brien

"On the set of *Babes on Broadway*, I would go around to everyone and say, 'Please don't send my brother to the chair,' for some reason. My mother originally wrote the line and the producers picked it up and used it in the film. Later, they were casting for *Journey for Margaret* and someone remembered my line from *Babes on Broadway*. That one line got me the part of Margaret and my start in movies."

JOURNEY FOR MARGARET

A Metro-Goldwyn-Mayer Picture
1942

"Oh no, that's my imagesium bomb. My very own. It came from a Germa plane."

> —Margaret O'Brien, protesting with her four year old's pronunciation not to take her incendiary bomb casing in *Journey for Margaret*.

Opened on December 17, 1942, at the Capitol Theater, New York City.
Ad line: "William White's Book Brought to the Screen
with a Charm and Beauty That Will Touch Every Heart."

Statistics
MGM production number 314.
Running time, 81 minutes; black & white; Drama.

Ratings
The Motion Picture Guide, ☆☆☆½
Leonard Maltin's Movie and Video Guide, ☆☆☆
Halliwell's Film Guide, ☆

Credits
Produced by B. P. Fineman; directed by Maj. W. S. Van Dyke, II; screenplay by David Hertz and William Ludwig, based on the book *Journey for Margaret* by William L. White (New York: Harcourt, Brace, 1941); original music by Mario Castelnuovo-Tedesco, Sol Kaplan, Franz Waxman and Eric Zeisl; art direction by Cedric Gibbons and Wade B. Rubottom; set decoration by Edwin B. Willis and Dick Pefferle; costume design by Kalloch; sound by Douglas Shearer; cinematography by Ray June; film editing by George White.

Cast
Robert Young (John Davis), Laraine Day (Nora Davis), Fay Bainter (Trudy Strauss), Margaret O'Brien (Margaret), Nigel Bruce (Herbert V. Allison), William Severn (Peter), Elisabeth Risdon (Mrs. Bailey), Doris Lloyd (Mrs. Barrie), Halliwell Hobbes (Mr. Barrie), Heather Thatcher (Mrs. Harris), Jill Esmond (Susan Fleming), G. P. Huntley, Jr. (Rugged), Lisa Golm (Frau Weber), Margaret Hamilton, Signe Hasso (Anya), Charles Irwin (Fairoaks), Herbert Evans (Man), Clare Sandars (Child), Leyland Hodgson (Censor), Anita Bolster (Woman), Matthew Bolton (Warden), Lilyan Irene (Nurse), Olaf Hytten (Manager), Ottola

Nesmith (Nurse), John Burton (Surgeon), Colin Kenny (Steward), Jimmy Aubrey (Porter), Joan Kemp (Isabel), Norbert Muller (Hans), Bea Nigro (Nora's Mother), Al Ferguson (Policeman), Cyril Delevanti (Stage Manager), Jody Gilbert (Mme. Bornholm), Craufurd Kent (Everton), Keye Luke (Japanese Statesman), David Thursby (Air Raid Warden), Henry Guttman (Polish Captain), Cyril Thornton (Man), Leslie Francis (Clerk), Vickie Campbell (Girl), George Aldwin (Boy), William O'Brien (Driver), Eric Snowden (Porter), Doris Stone (Mother), Clive Morgan (Father), Norman Ainsley (Porter), Emerson Fisher-Smith (Man), Lawrence Grossmith (Man), John Power (Man in Subway), Elizabeth Williams (Woman in Subway), Gil Perkins, Doreen Munroe, Henry Glynn, Major Douglas Francis, Jack Deery, Lotus Thompson, Jean Ransom, Allan Schute, Sybil Bacon (Bits in Subway), Frank Baker (Fireman), Art Berry, Sr. (Cab Driver), Herbert Clifton, Eric Wilton (Men at Cellar), Robert Cory (Air Raid Warden), Henry King (Service Man), Gay Bennes (Screaming Girl), Hal Welling (Tailor).

Synopsis

While covering an air raid during the World War II London blitz, John Davis, an American journalist living in London with his pregnant wife Nora, discovers an orphaned boy named Peter. When Nora loses their baby during a bombing raid on their hotel, he sends her back to the States to recuperate. Later, John visits Peter, and discovers another child named Margaret who wears an empty incendiary bomb casing around her neck. After becoming attached to the two children, he decides to adopt them and take them back home

to his wife, who agrees to the arrangement. However, he can only take one child in exchange for forty pounds of luggage. Because she is more in need of leaving the war-torn city, he decides to take Margaret. Happily, at the last moment, Peter joins them at the train station and is given permission to live in America.

Behind the Scenes

When the casting call went out for a little girl to play the title role in *Journey for Margaret*, little Angela Maxine O'Brien was one of the young hopefuls. It was in this audition that executive producer Harry Rapf said, "Stop her, she's killing me."[1]

Her first meeting with costar Robert Young was love at first sight. A friendship quickly developed between them and it continued until his death in 1998. They would make one more picture together and years later, Margaret appeared as a guest on Young's television show, *Marcus Welby, M.D.*

Actress Fay Bainter made a special impression on Margaret when she helped the young waif during a difficult crying scene. Margaret was always able to cry, but Bainter made certain that her costar had all the freedom she needed for the scene. "She was very nice to me during the crying scene," Margaret recalled, "She just let me go and told the cameras to keep rolling so they could capture what I was feeling. She was a big help."

In the film, Margaret's character carries an empty incendiary bomb casing around her neck which she lovingly called her "magnesi" bomb. The real Margaret also became attached to the prop and carried it around between scenes. "It sort of became my toy,"

Margaret O'Brien with Robert Young in *Journey for Margaret* (1942, MGM).

Margaret recalled. "It was like a doll to me. But afterwards when the movie was finished, they took it away because they thought it was best that I didn't go to sleep with a bomb at night."

During one particular scene, director Van Dyke was having some difficulty advising young Margaret on what he wanted. Coincidentally, Van Dyke's mother, Laura Winston Van Dyke, was visiting the set that day. An actress herself, Mrs. Van Dyke had experience coaching her son as a child actor on the stage. "Let me try," she offered, and of course Van Dyke stepped aside and was quite pleased with the results. "You dood it again, Ma," Van Dyke quipped, imitating comedian Red Skelton.[2]

Sadly, *Journey for Margaret* would be W. S. Van Dyke's last film. Van Dyke was a workaholic and had refused to rest, even though his mother and close friends encouraged it. Friends claimed that Van Dyke's heart was in the making of *Journey for Margaret* and he seemed to live again. "One Shot Woody," as he was called, had been with MGM for sixteen years and was responsible for such hits as *The Pagan* (1929) with Ramon Novarro, *Tarzan, the Ape Man* (1932) and *The Thin Man* (1934–41) series.

Margaret O'Brien as Margaret White in *Journey for Margaret* (1942, MGM).

Margaret attended the preview of *Journey for Margaret* under protest because she had originally been promised she could watch actress Gene Tierney in *China Girl* (1943). However, she relented and her only comment about her performance that night was, "I think I could have done that scene better."[3]

This is also the film that prompted her to legally change her name. "I really felt I was that child," she recalled.

With America in the war for less than a year, little five-year-old Margaret O'Brien became a emblem for this country's fight for freedom. Baby Peggy, another former child star from the 1920s, now known as author and historian Diana Serra Cary, said: "With her wispy voice and dark eyes that seemed to mirror the ravages of war, she symbolized the new era's vulnerable child, growing up in a world threatened by wholesale devastation."[4]

One of the studio's ad lines for the film read, "Meet Margaret O'Brien. The most amazing new child star in the history of the screen."[5] And amazing she was. Margaret's career skyrocketed after *Journey for Margaret* and she became the most beloved child star since Shirley Temple a decade earlier. The film also made a big impression on many of the little girls who watched from their seats in the audience. Comedian Joan Rivers, who became a big fan, later wrote: "When I saw Margaret O'Brien in *Journey for Margaret*, we were the same age and I was very upset that she was up there on the screen and I was sitting with my mother."[6]

Harrison's Reports said that *Journey for Margaret* was "intellectually directed and splendidly performed. This drama is one of the most appealing and highly emotional pictures yet produced of the war."[7] And most of the credit went to MGM's new discovery, little Margaret O'Brien.

Reviews

" ... a drama to stand beside the few unballyhooed classics of the screen. By the slightest and simplest of means they have created a picture of tortured childhood that will not soon be forgotten by any one who has ever loved a child. Not in recent experience has Broadway seen a film so fervent, so tender or so perceptive and true. Of little Margaret O'Brien, herself a wartime migrant, who plays the title role, one can hardly say that she gives a performance—it is too taut and true for that."—*Variety*, October 28, 1942.

"One of the least heralded and most unpretentious efforts by the screen to picture the London blitz, *Journey for Margaret* will sear your flesh with its utter truthfulness and simplicity"—*Brooklyn Citizen*, undated.

"A tot named Margaret O'Brien with no previous camera experience tears at your heartstrings like a miniature Duse."—*Collier's*, November 28, 1942.

"Margaret O'Brien and William Severn give to the picture the tug at the heart strings which sets it apart from other pictures of this kind."—*Motion Picture Daily*, October 28, 1942.

Additional Reviews: *Commonweal*, 12/25/42; *Film Daily*, 10/28/42; *Hollywood Reporter*, 10/28/42, p. 3; *The London Times*, 03/08/43, p. 8; *Motion Picture Exhibitor*, 11/04/42; *Motion Picture Herald Product Digest*, 03/28/42; *The New Republic*, 01/04/43, p. 22; *New York Times*, 12/18/42, p. 36; *PM*, 12/18/42; *Scholastic*, 01/11/43, p. 37; *Time*, 01/11/43, p. 89.

Fay Bainter, Margaret O'Brien, Laraine Day, Robert Young and William Severn in a publicity shot for *Journey for Margaret* (1942, MGM).

Awards

New York Times Annual Ten Best List. The National Board of Review Awards: Best English Language Film.

Costar Comments

"She's a young Bernhardt."—*W. S. Van Dyke*[8]

"On the first day of the picture she came to the dressing room door on the set and knocked on the door and I said, 'Come in,' and she came in and she said, 'Miss Day, my name is Margaret O'Brien and I would like to recite the Gettysburg Address for you.' And she did! And then she went to Bob Young's dressing room, knocked on the door, did the same thing."—*Laraine Day*[9]

Comments by Margaret O'Brien

"*Journey for Margaret* was very special for me not only because it was my first real film, but it was also the beginning of my friendship with Robert Young. I felt that I was that child Margaret and if I ever wanted to be adopted, I'd like to be adopted by Robert Young. That made me very close to him. I just felt at home with everyone I worked with in the movie."

DR. GILLESPIE'S CRIMINAL CASE

A Metro-Goldwyn-Mayer Picture
1943

"What's cookin'? Say, you're smart as well as good-looking.
Let's you and I go out sometime and ring some doorbells."
—Margaret O'Brien flirting
with Lionel Barrymore in
Dr. Gillespie's Criminal Case.

Opened on May 4, 1943, at the Capitol Theater, New York City.
Ad line: "Laughs, Thrills, Romance, Tears
in the Newest 'Dr. Gillespie' Film."

Statistics

MGM production number 407.
aka "Crazy to Kill."
Running time, 89 minutes; black & white; Drama/Mystery.

Ratings

The Motion Picture Guide, ☆☆½
Leonard Maltin's Movie and Video Guide, ☆☆½
Halliwell's Film Guide, 0

Credits

Directed by Willis Goldbeck; assistant director, Al Raboch; screenplay by Martin Berkeley, Harry Ruskin and Lawrence Bachmann based on characters created by Max Brand; musical direction by Daniele Amfitheatrof; art direction by Cedric Gibbons and William Ferrari; set decoration by Edwin B. Willis and Edward G. Boyle; costume design by Irene; sound by Douglas Shearer; cinematography by Norbert Brodine and Charles Lawton; film editing by Frank Hall.

Cast

Lionel Barrymore (Dr. Leonard Gillespie), Van Johnson (Dr. Randall "Red" Adams), Keye Luke (Dr. Lee Wong How), Alma Kruger (Molly Byrd), Nat Pendleton (Joe Weyman), Margaret O'Brien (Margaret), Donna Reed (Marcia Bradburn), John Craven (Roy Todwell), Michael Duane (Sgt. Patrick J. Orlain), William Lundigan (Alvin F. Peterson), Walter Kingsford (Dr. Walter Carew), Marilyn Maxwell (Ruth Edly), Henry O'Neill (Warden Kenneson), Marie Blake (Sally), Frances Rafferty (Irene), Roy Barcroft (Bit Part), Nell Craig (Nurse "Nosey" Parker), Milton Kibee (Briggs), Robert Emmet O'Connor (Samson), Boyd Davis (Mr. Coleman), Richard Crane (Sailor), Arthur Loft (Dr. Post), Aileen Pringle (Chaperone), Edna Holland (Nurse Morgan), Lorin Baker (Price), Richard Bartell (Botsford), Katherine Booth (Cashier), William Haade (Driver), Ralph Dunn, Roy Barcroft, Lee Phelps, Captain Somers (Guards), Douglas Fowley (Wallace), Barbara Bedford (Secretary), Patricia Barker (Edith), Janet Chapman (Mary), Yvette Duguay (Aggie), Irene Tedrow (Nurse Dodd), Herbert Vigran (Orderly), Gertrude W. Hoffman (Grandmother), Byron Foulger (Father), George Irving (Admiral), John Dilson (Green), Matt Moore (Harper), Edward Keane (Stiles), Edward Earle (Morris), Grant Withers (Waddy), George Lynn (Mack), Ted Adams (Stapleton), Jerry Jerome, Chick Collins (Convicts), Don Cadell (Big Marine), Helen Dickson (Dowager Hostess), Marianne Quon (Lee Ti Fang), Almeda Fowler (Nurse Trippett), Margaret Adden (Nurse).

Synopsis

The *Dr. Kildare* series continued with Dr. Gillespie, who in this episode must decide who will become his new assistant. His choices include the girl-chasing Randall Adams and the ambitious Lee Wong How from Brooklyn. Suddenly, an epidemic of erysipelas breaks out in the children's ward and Gillespie and his two budding assistants must battle to save four little girls from death. The story line is complicated even more when the good doctor tries to persuade a former flier to walk with a wooden leg, and convince a prison warden that a convicted murderer is really insane and should be transferred to a proper institution.

Behind the Scenes

Dr. Gillespie's Criminal Case was the twelfth in a series of fifteen *Dr. Kildare* films that MGM released over a ten year period. The characters were based on the novels of author Max Brand, whose first screen incarnation of Dr. Kildare appeared at Paramount with Joel McCrea playing the title role opposite Barbara Stanwyck in *Interns Can't Take Money* (1937).

The following year MGM bought the

Margaret O'Brien with legendary actor Lionel Barrymore in *Dr. Gillespie's Criminal Case* (1943, MGM).

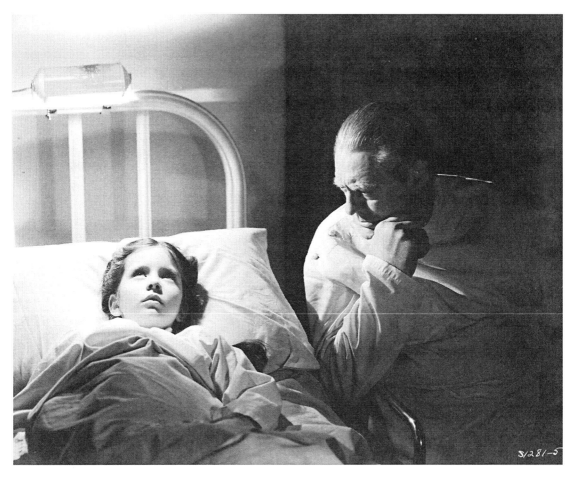

Margaret O'Brien plays a sickly child with Lionel Barrymore in *Dr. Gillespie's Criminal Case* (1943, MGM).

rights and cast Lew Ayres with Lionel Barrymore as the crusty old Dr. Gillespie. A few years later, Lew Ayres joined the army as a medic even though he was a conscientious objector. Instead of replacing Ayres, MGM continued the series with Barrymore as the star.

When filming began, young Margaret was introduced to Barrymore by director Willis Goldbeck, wearing pigtails and a long hospital gown. Margaret very politely acknowledged the elder actor and curtsied, and was then led back to her dressing room. "How bloody awful,"

Barrymore was heard to exclaim. "She'll be bringing lollipops to the set and getting them tangled in everybody's hair." As it turned out, that is exactly what happened, but Margaret also brought a lollipop for Barrymore, which softened his gruff exterior. "I managed to condone this type of refreshment," Barrymore later recalled, "and almost acquired the vice myself."[1]

Lollipops aside, Barrymore soon began to realize the extent of Margaret's talent and began falling for the little tyke. They would often have lunch

Margaret O'Brien and Lionel Barrymore in *Dr. Gillespie's Criminal Case* (1943, MGM) with
Van Johnson, Donna Reed, Nat Pendleton, Marilyn Maxwell and Keye Luke.

together, and Barrymore was sure he had made a good impression on his young costar—which he did. He soon realized, however, that with all his experience, there was no way he could compete with her scene-stealing ability. "If the magic could be accomplished," he later said, "short of slitting my throat before the camera, I should relish the miracle of lifting at least part of a scene from the enchanting Miss Margaret O'Brien."[2]

Barrymore was confined to a wheelchair because of painful arthritis and would sometimes tire very easily. Costar Keye Luke, who appeared in five episodes of the series, thought that Barrymore was a terror. "And of course no director could keep a tight rein on the old man either," Luke explained. "Although he was in a wheelchair from arthritis he still walked a bit on occasion although with great pain."[3]

There was a piano on the set, and of course, Margaret, being a child, would plunk on it to amuse herself. This form of play annoyed the elder actor until he finally had the propman tape it so it wouldn't make any sound. "Then he felt guilty," Margaret recalled, "and he made beautiful rag dolls, which he would present to me."

On the fun side, Barrymore gave nicknames to Margaret and the three other girls in the film. Patricia Barker was named "Lipstick" because she used one in a scene; Yvette Duguay obviously became "Mademoiselle," and Janet Chapman was crowned "Princess." Because of her amazing ability to cry on cue, the cast and crew dubbed Margaret "Teardrop."[4] To sum up Margaret's talent, Barrymore once said, "She is the only woman, except my sister Ethel, who made me take out my handkerchief in 30 years."[5]

Motion Picture Daily said that *Dr. Gillespie's Criminal Case* was "a picture with purpose and a lot of heart, this number in the *Dr. Gillespie* series measures up to and perhaps beyond the best of its predecessors."[6] Barrymore did two more Gillespie films before the series ended.

Reviews

"Followers of the series should find this piece readily acceptable with production studded with bright performances."—*Variety*, May 5, 1943.

"Another well thought-out comedy melodrama in the popular series. Topbilling is justifiably awarded Margaret O'Brien for a heart-wringing performance of one of the little girls, ill in the children's ward."—*Hollywood Reporter*, May 5, 1943.

"It is still Lionel Barrymore who carries the series, and fine casting of the supporting players that maintains its quality rating. This chapter is no exception in trouping ability, Donna Reed, Van Johnson and Keye Luke being the standouts in a group that also includes fine performances from Margaret O'Brien, child player."—*Box Office Digest*, May 15, 1943.

"The situation that shows children suffering from a deadly disease are too heart rending to be classed as entertainment."—*Harrison's Reports*, May 8, 1943.

Additional Reviews: *Film Daily*, 05/11/43, p. 6; *Motion Picture Daily*, 05/04/43; *Motion Picture Herald*, 05/08/43; *Motion Picture Herald Product Digest*, 05/08/43.

Costar Comments

"Next to Miss Garbo, the most awesome actress I have encountered in Hollywood is Margaret O'Brien. After my first picture with her I remarked that if she had been unfortunate enough to be born in Salem, they would have burned her as a witch. This saying has been widely quoted, and somewhat out of context; I meant it as the most envious of compliments."—*Lionel Barrymore*[7]

Comments by Margaret O'Brien

"My part was easy to play because I was suppose to be a sick little girl and got to stay in bed the whole time. I wanted to get up and play, but I couldn't. *Dr. Gillespie's Criminal Case* was also my first meeting with Lionel Barrymore. I remember he would make me rag dolls and after that movie we became very close. He became the grandfather that I never had."

THOUSANDS CHEER

A Metro-Goldwyn-Mayer Picture
1943

"I don't like tutti-frutti. What else have you got?"
—Margaret O'Brien request-
ing an ice cream sundae in
Thousands Cheer.

Opened on September 13, 1943, at the Astor Theater, New York City.
Ad line: "Stars Galore, Three Big Bands,
a Score of Hit Tunes in the Biggest Hit of the Year."

Statistics

MGM production number 413.
Running time, 126 minutes; Technicolor; Musical.

Ratings

The Motion Picture Guide, ☆☆☆½
Leonard Maltin's Movie and Video Guide,
☆☆½
Halliwell's Film Guide, ☆

Credits

Produced by Joe Pasternak; directed
by George Sidney; screenplay by Paul
Jarrico and Richard Collins; musical
direction by Herbert Stothart; art direction by Cedric Gibbons and Daniel B.
Cathcart; set decoration by Jacques
Mersereau and Edwin B. Willis;
make-up by Jack Dawn; costume design
by Irene; sound by Douglas Shearer; cinematography by George J. Folsey; film
editing by George Boemler; color con-
sultation by Natalie Kalmus and Henry
Jaffa.

Songs by: Ferde Grofe and Harold
Adamson, Lew Brown, Ralph Freed and
Burton Lane, Walter Jurmann and Paul
Francis Webster, Earl Brent and E. Y.
Harburg, Dimitri Shostakovich and
Harold Rome.

Songs: "In a Little Spanish Town"
by Sam M. Lewis, Joe Young and
Mabel Wayne, sung by Virginia O'Brien
and backed by June Allyson, Gloria
DeHaven and Bob Crosby and His
BobCats; "Honeysuckle Rose" by Andy
Razaf and Fats Waller, sung by Lena
Horne and backed by Benny Carter and
his band; "Tico Tico" by Zequinha
Abreu, danced by Don Loper and Max-
ine Barrett; "The Joint Is Really Jumpin'
Down at Carnegie Hall" by Ralph
Blane, Hugh Martin and Roger Edens,
sung by Judy Garland and accompanied
by Jose Iturbi; "Daybreak" by Harold
Adamson and Ferde Grofe, sung by
Kathryn Grayson; "Three Letters in the
Mailbox" by Paul Francis Webster and
Walter Jurmann, sung by Kathryn

Comedian Red Skelton offers to serve Margaret O'Brien an ice cream sundae in *Thousands Cheer* (1943, MGM).

Grayson; "Let There Be Music" by E. Y. Harburg and Earl Brent, sung by Kathryn Grayson; "The United Nations on the March" by Dimitri Shostakovitch, E. Y. Harburg, Harold Rome and Herbert Stothart, sung by Kathryn Grayson; "I Dug a Ditch in Wichita" by Lew Brown, Ralph Freed and Burton Lane, performed by Ben Lessy and the company, reprised by Kay Kyser's orchestra with Harry Babbitt singing and also danced by Gene Kelly; "Let Me Call You Sweetheart" by Beth Slater Whitson and Leo Friedman, danced by Gene Kelly; "Sempre Libera" from *Aida* by Verdi, sung by Kathryn Grayson; "I'm Lost, You're Lost" and "Why Don't We Try" by Walter Ruick; "Why Should I?" by Arthur Freed and Nacio Herb Brown; "Just as Long as I Know Katie's Waitin'" by Lew Brown and George R. Brown; "American Patrol" by E. H. Meacham; "Columbia, the Gem of the Ocean" (traditional); "Yankee Doodle" (traditional).

Cast

Kathryn Grayson (Kathryn Jones), Gene Kelly (Eddy Marsh), Mary Astor (Hyllary Jones), John Boles (Col.

William Jones), Ben Blue (Chuck Polansky), Frances Rafferty (Marie Corbino), Mary Elliott (Helen), Frank Jenks (Sergeant Koziack), Frank Sully (Alan), Dick Simmons (Capt. Fred Avery), Ben Lessy (Private Monks), Wally Cassell (Jack), Mickey Rooney (Guest), Judy Garland (Guest), Red Skelton (Himself), Eleanor Powell (Herself), Ann Sothern (Guest), Lucille Ball (Cameo), Virginia O'Brien (Herself), Frank Morgan (Himself), Lena Horne (Herself), Marsha Hunt (Herself), Marilyn Maxwell (Herself), Donna Reed (Guest), Margaret O'Brien (Guest), June Allyson (Guest), Gloria DeHaven (Herself), John Conte (Himself), Sara Haden (Herself), Jose Iturbi (Himself), Don Loper (Himself), Maxine Barrat (Herself), Sig Arno (Uncle Algy), Lionel Barrymore (Announcer), Monte Blue (Bit Part), Daisy Bufford (Maid), Georgia Carroll (Herself), Cyd Charisse (Bit Part as Lily Norwood), Connie Gilchrist (Taxi Driver), Myron Healy (Soldier), Betty Jaynes (Girl at Train Station), Willy Kaufman (Papa Corbino), Marta Linden (Nurse), Odette Myrtil (Mama Corbino), Bea Nigro (Woman), Carl Saxe (Sergeant Major), Paul Speer (Dancer), Harry Strang (Captain Haines), Don Taylor (Soldier), Ray Teal (Ringmaster), Florence Turner (Mother at Train Station), Bryant Washburn, Jr. (Lieutenant Colonel Brand), Pierre Watkin (Alex), Kay Kyser and his orchestra, Bob Crosby and his orchestra, and Benny Carter and his band.

Synopsis

Kathryn Jones, a colonel's daughter, becomes romantically involved with Eddy Marsh, a hotheaded circus acrobat, now soldier. After some close calls with the colonel, their relationship comes into jeopardy when Kathryn's mother disapproves of their budding new romance. Also, during a concert held at the army camp, Eddy is taught the meaning of teamwork during his family's trapeze act. The star-studded musical production becomes an excuse to highlight MGM's top talent, hosted by Mickey Rooney.

Behind the Scenes

Thousands Cheer was a huge all-star extravaganza featuring more than thirty of MGM's biggest stars. This was Margaret's first film for producer Joe Pasternak, whom she described as "overwhelming." Russian-born Pasternak had a very gregarious personality, which slightly intimidated the young actress. "I always wanted to make sure I didn't make a mistake," Margaret recalled. "I was afraid he'd get mad at me or something. I didn't have to worry though, because all in all, he was very nice to me."

Originally titled "Private Miss Jones," the film was assigned to director George Sidney and was the first of his many lavish musicals. "When I got in," Sidney said, "I kept getting more ideas to expand it and expand it." Impressed by his suggestions, Mayer and Pasternak put everything behind the film and changed it to Technicolor. Sidney improvised scenes, dialogue and whole musical numbers and some scenes were shot before they were written. "It was creatively exciting; everything was spontaneous, exhilarating," Sidney recalled.[1]

Margaret shared her scene in *Thousands Cheer* with comedian Red Skelton, who played a soda jerk that is allergic to ice cream. At the end of the scene she stands offstage and reminds host Mickey Rooney to thank her while holding an ice cream cone. She enjoyed the ice cream so much that she purposely forgot her lines so they would have to shoot the scene over. Skelton caught on to her ploy, and played along. "He was great to me," Margaret said. "I thought he was so funny."

The hat she wore in the scene was designed by her mother and became one of her trademarks. In *Lost Angel* (1944) she wore a different version of the same hat and later added it to the Margaret O'Brien line of hats that she endorsed.

The premiere of *Thousands Cheer* at the Astor Theater in New York City doubled as a War Bond rally and earned $534,000 for the war effort. "It's been a long time since Metro spread itself so lavishly," wrote the *New York Times*. "And it's been longer than that since the screen provided such a veritable grab-bag of delights."[2]

Reviews

"These cavalcades of the stars are getting to be quite the thing—MGM's *Thousands Cheer* is one of the biggest and best of the lot."—*Family Circle*, October 29, 1943.

"When a filmmusical can hold an audience's absorbed attention for a full two hours and five minutes the way *Thousands Cheer* does, that attraction may be adjudged an unqualified success."—*Hollywood Reporter*, September 15, 1943.

"Paramount keynote of this expert filmmusical is the tiptop manner in which George Sidney has marshaled his multiple talents so that none trips over the other. It's a triumph for Sidney on his first major league effort."—*Variety*, September 15, 1943.

"A lavish production, photographed in Technicolor, an appealing story, good comedy, romance, dancing and delightful music—popular and classical—make *Thousands Cheer* extremely enjoyable."—*Harrison's Reports*, September 18, 1943.

Additional Reviews: *New York Times*, 09/14/43.

Academy Award Nominees

Daniel B. Cathcart, Cedric Gibbons, Jacques Mersereau, Edwin B. Willis—Best Art Direction-Interior Decoration, Color; George Folsey—Best Cinematography, Color; Herbert Stothart—Best Music, Scoring of a Musical Picture.

Costar Comments

"I made four pictures with Margaret O'Brien. In some people's opinion she is perhaps the most gifted of all the children who ever played before the motion picture cameras, dramatically, that is. She was certainly a skillful actress. Nor was she limited to portrayals of adorable saccharine youngsters."—*Joe Pasternak*[3]

"That darling little Margaret O'Brien was a giant talent; one of the all time greats of the movies."—*Red Skelton*[4]

Comments by Margaret O'Brien

"*Thousands Cheer* was directed by George Sidney, who was one of our finest directors. He directed some wonderful musicals and I only regret I wasn't able to make more pictures with him. I'm still friends with him today."

MADAME CURIE

A Metro-Goldwyn-Mayer Picture
1943

"All right Daddy, my eyes are closed."
—Margaret O'Brien to Walter Pidgeon, who is about to tell her a bedtime story in *Madame Curie*.

Opened on December 16, 1943, at Radio City Music Hall, New York City. Ad line: "One of the Best Films of All Time with Top Performances by Greer Garson and Walter Pidgeon in *Madame Curie*."

Statistics

MGM production number 490.
Running time, 124 minutes; black & white; Biographical Drama.

Ratings

The Motion Picture Guide, ☆☆☆☆
Leonard Maltin's Movie and Video Guide, ☆☆☆
Halliwell's Film Guide, ☆

Credits

Produced by Sidney Franklin; directed by Mervyn LeRoy; screenplay by Paul Osborn and Paul H. Rameau, based on the book *Madame Curie* by Eve Curie (New York: Doubleday, Doran, 1939); narration by James Hilton; music direction by Herbert Stothart; art direction by Cedric Gibbons and Paul Groesse; set decoration by Edwin B. Willis and Hugh Hunt; make-up by Jack Dawn; women's costume design by Irene Sharaff; men's costume design by Gile Steele; sound by Douglas Shearer; cinematography by Joseph Ruttenberg; film editing by Harold F. Kress; special effects by Warren Newcombe.

Cast

Greer Garson (Madame Curie), Walter Pidgeon (Pierre Curie), Henry Travers (Eugene Curie), Albert Basserman (Professor Jean Perot), Robert Walker (David Le Gros), C. Aubrey Smith (Lord Kelvin), Dame May Whitty (Mme. Eugene Curie), Victor Francen (President of University), Elsa Basserman (Mme. Perot), Reginald Owen (Dr. Becquerel), Van Johnson (Reporter), Margaret O'Brien (Irene, age five), James Hilton (Narrator, Voice), Ruth Cherrington (Swedish Queen), Ray Collins (Lecturer), Howard Freeman (Professor Constant), Lisa Golm (Lucille), Ilka Gruning (Seamstress), Lumsden Hare (Professor Roget), Gene Lockhart (Bit Part), Miles Mander (Businessman), George Meader (Singing Professor), Dickie Meyers (Master Michaud), Leo Mostovoy (Photographer), Alan Napier (Dr. Bladh), Moroni Olsen (President of Businessman's

Walter Pidgeon and Greer Garson read a bedtime story to Margaret in *Madame Curie* (1943, MGM; courtesy of the Academy of Motion Picture Arts and Sciences).

Board), Gigi Perreau (Eve, at age eighteen months), Francis Pierlot (Monsieur Michaud), Almira Sessions (Madame Michaud), Arthur Shields (Businessman), Wyndham Standing (King Oscar), Ray Teal (Driver), Charles Trowbridge (Board Member), Marek Windheim (Jewelry Salesman), Frederick Worlock (Businessman), Eustace Wyatt (Doctor).

Synopsis

Biography of the famed scientist, who at first is a young Polish student studying in Paris where she eventually meets and marries Pierre Curie, whose laboratory she shares. During their experiments, Marie becomes aware of some new element contained in pitchblende and chronicles their years of research to discover its secret. One evening, after many disappointments, they find a residue of radium glowing in the bottom of a dish, which brings the couple national attention and respect. After Pierre is tragically killed in an accident, Marie continues to lecture and share her secrets with the French scientific community.

Behind the Scenes

Universal Studios had bought the rights to Eve Curie's book about her famous mother in the late 1930s, hoping to create a vehicle for Irene Dunne. When that fell through, the studio sold the rights to MGM, which had Aldous Huxley and F. Scott Fitzgerald write a screenplay. Mayer's hope was to star Greta Garbo as *Madame Curie*, but unfortunately she retired before it could be arranged and the script was shelved.

In 1943, the script was rediscovered when the studio was searching for a vehicle for Greer Garson and Walter Pidgeon, who were a hit in *Blossoms in the Dust* (1941) and the Academy Award–winning *Mrs. Miniver* (1942). Paul Rameau and Paul Osborn were assigned to polish the Huxley-Fitzgerald script while Sidney Franklin produced and Mervyn LeRoy directed.

At the time, the studio was in the midst of preparing *Lost Angel* for Margaret, which took a year to write and rewrite the script. To fill the time, they put her in supporting roles in several major films including *Madame Curie*, where she played Irene, the scientists' daughter. Margaret, who had just turned six, was in awe of Greer Garson. "I thought Greer Garson was beautiful, just beautiful," Margaret exclaimed. "She was lovely to work with and Walter Pidgeon was a very nice person also."

Margaret spent most of her time with Gigi Perreau, who played her sister Eve in the film. At the age of two, this was Gigi's first film and she would become a well-known child star herself, although her career would never equal Margaret's. When Margaret left MGM in 1949, the studio was grooming Gigi Perreau as her replacement, but it never happened. "Gigi and I were mostly together," Margaret recalled. "On a lot of my movies there was never another child on the set so we spent a lot of time together."

Although *Madame Curie* did not garner the same success as *Mrs. Miniver*, it was critically acclaimed and was nominated for five Academy Awards including Best Picture. The *New York Herald-Tribune* proclaimed the film "a staunch and brilliant motion picture account of things which are generally considered outside the realms of dramatic revelation."[1]

Reviews

"It is seldom that Hollywood makes much of intellectual adventure per se or that it dares to discover excitement in the pure exercise of the mind. But that it has done in this case—and done with dramatic effect."—*Variety*, November 24, 1943.

"In *Madame Curie*, Margaret O'Brien plays Irene, the older daughter of Marie and Pierre Curie. Although this is one of her shortest roles, she lends it a remarkable validity, and is able to hold her own with such polished performers as Greer Garson and Walter Pidgeon."—*Life*, December 13, 1943.

"Excellent entertainment! Splendidly produced, directed, and acted, this is a highly dramatic and absorbing account of the lives of Marie and Pierre Curie."—*Harrison's Reports*, November 20, 1943.

Additional Reviews: *Commonweal*, 12/31/43; *Film Daily*, 11/22/43, p. 7; *Hollywood Reporter*, 11/19/43, p. 3; *Motion Picture Herald Product Digest*, 11/20/43; *New York Times*, 12/17/43, p. 23; *New York Times Magazine*, 09/26/43, p. 18; *The New Yorker*, 12/18/43, p. 53; *Newsweek*, 12/27/43, p. 82; *Time*, 12/20/43, p. 54.

Academy Award Nominations

Sidney Franklin—Best Picture; Walter Pidgeon—Best Actor; Greer Garson—Best Actress; Cedric Gibbons, Paul Groesse, Hugh Hunt, Edwin B. Willis—Best Art Direction-Interior Decoration, Black-and-White; Joseph Ruttenberg—Best Cinematography; Herbert Stothart—Best Music Scoring of a Dramatic or Comedy Picture; Douglas Shearer—Best Sound, Recording.

Comments by Margaret O'Brien

"During *Madame Curie* I became friends with Gigi Perreau who played my little sister. Remarkably we have remained friends throughout the years. I always envied her because she had many brothers and sisters—two of which also became actors. I was an only child so with Gigi on the set there were always lots of kids to play with."

YOU, JOHN JONES

A Metro-Goldwyn-Mayer Picture
1943

"When I step out on the platform you must applaud me because the children in school will applaud me—'cause they like me. I think. I hope."

> —Margaret O'Brien preparing to recite the Gettysburg Address for James Cagney and Ann Sothern in the wartime short *You, John Jones.*

Opened January 14, 1943, nationwide.

Statistics

Distributed and exhibited under the auspices of the War Activities Committee—Motion Picture Industry.

Running time, 8 minutes; black & white; Drama/Short/Documentary.

Credits

Produced by Carey Wilson; directed by Mervyn LeRoy; screenplay by Carey Wilson.

Cast

James Cagney (John Jones, uncredited), Ann Sothern (Mary Jones, uncredited), Margaret O'Brien (Their Daughter, uncredited).

Synopsis

War time story of a normal American, John Jones, who works in an aircraft plant. He performs his patriotic duty by being an air raid warden and believes he understands what atrocities America's allies in the war must live with. One day he comes home from work and listens to his young daughter recite the Gettysburg Address for a school play when the phone rings and a "blue alert" is announced. Taking his gas mask and helmet, John Jones leaves for his post where he thanks God for keeping the enemy's bombs away from his family and beloved America. Suddenly he hears the voice of God, who asks him what his family would be like if they were not in America. From then, John Jones is taken from one war-torn country to another to see how the war affects children. In each country he is shown his own daughter going through the horror that the children of that country must be experiencing. Without warning, the sound of the sirens scream their alarm and bombs begin to fall around

John Jones. He rushes home to find his house destroyed and his daughter running among the ruins, crying hysterically. He then finds himself back at his post and realizes that he has had a vision. Looking up at the sky, he hears the "all clear" whistle and returns home to the family he loves.

Behind the Scenes

In 1943, the country was in the middle of a world war. Every studio did their part, including the actors and actresses who gave of their time to sell War Bonds and entertain the troops at the Hollywood Canteen, which was founded by Bette Davis. Even though she was only six, Margaret did her part to help the war effort. The studio issued shorts that would not only educate the public about the war but would let them know how fortunate all Americans were. One such short was *You, John Jones*.

You, John Jones was produced and written by Carey Wilson, who had been with MGM since its formation in 1924. It was the story about a man, played by James Cagney, who was shown how lucky he was to be an American. Cagney, who had just won an Academy Award as Best Actor for *Yankee Doodle Dandy*, was loaned out from Warner Bros. His flag-waving sentimentality made him an obvious choice for the part. "James Cagney was wonderful," Margaret said. "He was very warm and understanding."

Margaret played Cagney's daughter. Ann Sothern portrayed her mother. "*You, John Jones* was where I first did the Gettysburg Address," Margaret recalled. "I used it in a lot of things during the war when I made public appearances before the soldiers."

In the short, Margaret got the chance

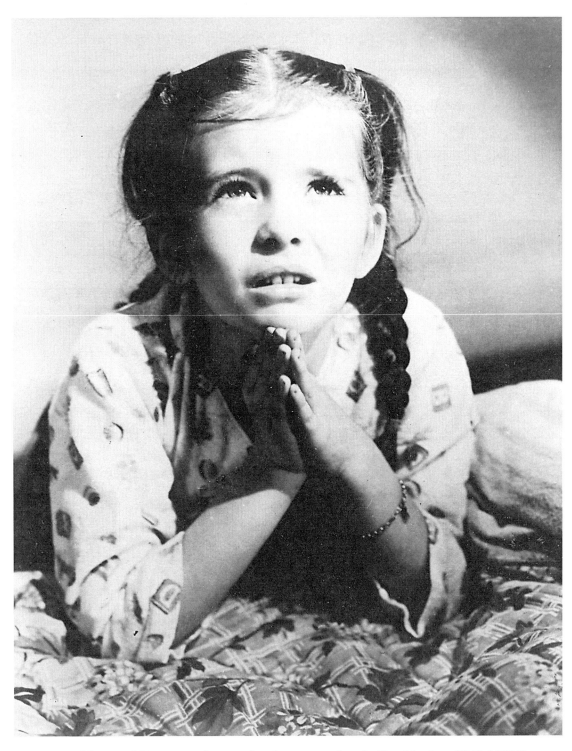

Margaret O'Brien prays for an end to the ravages of war in *You, John Jones* (1943, MGM).

to play eight different characters— among them French, Russian and Chinese. In one scene she plays a shell-shocked victim in a concentration camp. She is so convincing that many in the audience worried about her mental state. Margaret gives all the credit to director Mervyn LeRoy. "Mervyn's the one who really got me to look like I was shell-shocked," she recalled. "It wasn't easy to get a child to play a realistic death scene like that."

Fortunately, playing such violent scenes did not upset the little six-year-old. She was easygoing and wasn't the type of child to react to such things. Margaret could play a death scene and then go out and jump rope on the back lot. However, playing the role did give her a sense of patriotism and the realization that the war was a real thing, and not just play acting.

"It brought such a realistic feeling to me about the war that I wanted to help in the effort," Margaret said. "I really felt for some of those children just as I had learned to feel about the war orphans during *Journey for Margaret*. The war was something real to me."

Reviews

"The horror as he (James Cagney) sees his wife and his child (Margaret O'Brien) repeatedly bombed in the various parts of the United Nations is heart-rending. Excellent!"—*The Exhibitor*, January 13, 1943.

Comments by Margaret O'Brien

"*You, John Jones* was my mother's favorite. I think she felt my acting was the best in that one, especially the scene where I'm in the concentration camp. And I enjoyed doing it because I got to play all the different characters from the little Russian to the Chinese girl."

LOST ANGEL

A Metro-Goldwyn-Mayer Picture
1944

"You said there were dragons and flying carpets and witches. Well, magic. And you said not everybody could, but you knew how to find it. That's what you said."
—Margaret O'Brien reminding James Craig about the meaning of magic in *Lost Angel*.

Opened on April 8, 1944, at Loew's Criterion, New York City.
Ad line: "The Starlet of *Journey for Margaret* ...
Margaret O'Brien ... Is Back Again."

Margaret O'Brien as Alpha in *Lost Angel* (1944, MGM; author's collection).

James Craig and Margaret O'Brien in *Lost Angel* (1944, MGM).

Statistics

MGM production number 415.

Running time, 91 minutes; black & white; Drama.

Ratings

The Motion Picture Guide, ☆☆☆

Leonard Maltin's Movie and Video Guide, ☆☆½

Halliwell's Film Guide, ☆

Credits

Produced by Robert Sisk; directed by Roy Rowland; screenplay by Isabel Lennart, based on an idea by Angna Enters; original music by Daniele Amfitheatrof; art direction by Cedric Gibbons and Lynden Sparhawk; set decoration by Edwin B. Willis and Helen Conway; costume design by Irene; sound by Douglas Shearer; cinematography by Robert Surtees; film editing by Frank E. Hull.

Cast

Margaret O'Brien (Alpha), James Craig (Mike Regan), Marsha Hunt (Katie Mallory), Philip Merivale (Professor Peter Vincent), Henry O'Neill (Professor Pringle), Donald Meek (Professor Catty), Keenan Wynn (Packy), Alan Napier (Dr. Woodring), Sara Haden (Rhonda Kitterick), Kathleen Lockhart (Mrs. Catty), Walter Fenner (Professor Endicott), Howard Freeman (Professor Richards), Elizabeth Risdon (Mrs. Pringle), Bobby Blake (Jerry), Bobby Driscoll (Boy on Train), Jack Lambert (Lefty Moran), William Bishop (Reporter), Naomi Childers (Matron), Ava Gardner (Hat Check Girl), Russell Gleason (Reporter), Gloria Grafton (Operator), Edward Hearne (Reporter), Al Hill (Mug), Mike Mazurki (Fighter), Edward McWade (Old Man), Kay Medford (Operator), Lee Phelps (Reporter), Allen Wood (Tough Kid), Joe Yule (Tenant), Donald Curtis (Mounted Cop), Paul Fung, Sai King, Sam Young, Tom Yuen (Chinamen), Eddie Acuff (Cop), Nolan Leary (Manager), Ray Walker (Trainer), Fred Beckner (Man), Ray Teal (Man in Full Dress), William Fox (Tough Kid), Hooper Atchley (Pepi), Bert Roach (Man with Spaghetti), Robert Emmet O'Connor (Cop), John Maxwell (Detective), Barbara Bedford (Operator), Mary Elliott (Cigarette Girl), Charles D. Brown (Ed Vincent, Editor), Gerald Pierce (Delivery Boy), Pauline Starke (Boy's Mother), Charles Sullivan (Referee), George Levine, Mickey Golden (Fighters).

Synopsis

Alpha, a child prodigy, is raised by a group of scientists and thinks she is happy until a young reporter named Mike Regan enters her life and captures her imagination with a promise to show her magic. When Alpha challenges him for proof, he steals her away and shows her the joys of a normal childhood—a world she never imagined. The young girl becomes attached to Regan, who cannot find it in his heart to return her to the scientists. Alpha is also instrumental in developing the romance between Regan and Katie, his torch-singer girlfriend. When Regan goes to Washington on assignment, his feelings for Alpha are too great and he returns and adopts her.

Behind the Scenes

Because of the phenomenal success that Margaret O'Brien achieved in her first picture, *Journey for Margaret*, MGM studio head Louis B. Mayer ordered a script to be written exclusively for the moppet. Finally, after a year of writing and rewriting, *Lost Angel* was ready to go before the cameras. In the film, Margaret plays a child prodigy who can speak Chinese and talk philosophy. What surprised everyone was that she could do all of these things, and that commanded the respect of everyone working with her.

Henry O'Neill, who played Professor Pringle, marveled at Margaret's ability to run the gamut of emotions with such ease, and the minute the scene was over, become her own uncomplicated self. He once asked her how she could so quickly become a normal six year old. "Well," she began, "Mommie tells me the story. I go over it with her and learn the lines. Then I just do it for the picture." O'Neill nodded and muttered, "Yes, I understand Margaret. You make it very simple. I had to learn the hard way."[1]

Lillian Burns, Margaret's dramatic coach, was responsible for helping her master the many accents she would perform over the years. Whenever Margaret finished a film, Burns would give her young student a gold charm for her bracelet. By now she already had three charms for her work in *Journey for Margaret* (1942), *You, John Jones* (1943) and *Dr. Gillespie's Criminal Case* (1943). When *Lost Angel* completed filming, Burns presented Margaret with a tiny gold locomotive to add to her bracelet.

The romantic leads were handled deftly by James Craig and Marsha Hunt. Craig and Hunt had costarred together in what was said to be Mayer's favorite film, *The Human Comedy* (1943). Because of his resemblance to Clark Gable, Craig was to be the studio's replacement for the star, who had recently joined the army. Even though

Craig was a very talented actor and immensely popular with the fans, he was never quite able to fill The King's shoes.

None of this mattered to little Margaret, who developed her first crush on the actor. Even though Marsha Hunt was very nice to her, Margaret became just a little jealous when she saw the actress play love scenes with Craig, thinking she was trying to steal her "boyfriend." However, Marsha knew of Margaret's crush on Craig, so she understood her jealousy.

Marsha Hunt felt that Margaret O'Brien was what all families wanted for Christmas in the 1940s. "She was a great, great and underrated actress," Marsha recalled. "I really enjoyed doing *Lost Angel* with Margaret. My favorite wardrobe piece was from that film and was designed by Irene."[2]

James Craig noticed Margaret's infatuation for him and gave his young costar a beautiful doll as a gift. In return, Margaret personally picked out the loudest tie she could find and proudly presented it to Craig, who promised to cherish it forever. "I also had a secret crush on Bobby Blake," Margaret recalled. "Except he had to be mean to me in one of the scenes. But it was fun because I got to push him in a fight."

Bobby Blake, who was nine years old, was another popular child star at the time. Once playing in *Our Gang* comedy shorts, he appeared as Little Beaver in Republic Studio's *Red Ryder* series. He eventually made his mark as an adult actor, winning an Emmy for his television series *Baretta* (1975–1978).

Keenan Wynn, who played Packy in the film, would sometimes bring his four-year-old son Ned to the studio. To pass the time, young Ned would watch *Tom and Jerry* or *Woody Woodpecker* cartoons in one of the screening rooms. One day as Ned was waiting in the corridor, Margaret saw him and gave him a piece of candy. Ned immediately became awestruck at the vision before him. In his biography, *We Will Always Live in Beverly Hills*, Ned Wynn recalls that moment with much emotion.

"She was so beautiful, at eight years of age," he wrote, "that I at four was dumb struck. She smiled at me and blushed as she gave me the candy. For a moment she leaned against the wall. She had on a brown coat. Her smile was so radiant it seemed to tug at my neck, to warm my ears. I thought that I would like to follow her like a puppy, stay very near to her, to yip and beg for candy. I wept when her mother took her away."[3]

In one scene, Margaret had to eat spaghetti and purposely forgot her lines so she could eat more, just as she had done with the ice cream cone in *Thousands Cheer*. However, this time no one could figure out why there had to be so many retakes. "They caught on fast with the ice-cream cones in *Thousands Cheer*," Margaret said, "But they didn't catch on with the spaghetti. I was a little craftier by then."

With the release of *Lost Angel,* fans all over the country began inundating the studio with requests for pictures of the youngster, including men in the armed forces. One letter from a serviceman read, "I have a little girl I've never seen, and I'd like to have Margaret's picture so I can get some idea of how she might look when she is six."[4]

Another serviceman, Major Clark Gable, had just returned to MGM from active duty overseas. Gable had been at war since his wife, actress Carole Lombard, was tragically killed in a plane crash during a War Bond drive in 1942.

Lost Angel was one of the first films the highly decorated officer saw upon his return. The next day, he saw Margaret on the lot and asked her to have lunch with him. "I'm very sorry," she said. "I would like to very much, but I'm full."[5] This was one young lady who did not fall easily for the Gable charm.

Critics all over the country applauded *Lost Angel* and again praised Margaret's acting abilities with such headlines as "A New Child Wonder"[6] and "O'Brien Child Amazing."[7] The *Showmen's Trade Review* said, "This is the happiest tear jerker that I ever want to see. When you're not filling up with sentiment you're howling with laughter—there is no mid-path."[8]

Reviews

"A new Hollywood star of the first magnitude has come out of the making of Metro-Goldwyn-Mayer's *Lost Angel*. The magnitude, of course, refers to the ability, not the size, of this new personality; she is little Margaret O'Brien, who played in *Journey for Margaret* and is now appearing in her first starring role."—*New York Herald-Tribune*, April 10, 1944.

"In *Lost Angel*, MGM's saucy little scion, Margaret O'Brien, steps smartingly and winningly into a movie milieu where only Shirley Temple has heretofore dared to tread."—*New York Newspaper PM*, April 10, 1944.

"Little Margaret O'Brien, the wistful heroine of *Journey for Margaret*, is now officially a star."—*New York Sun*, April 10, 1944.

"Six-year-old Margaret O'Brien's performance ... is sheer magic. Her natural ability transcends acting, and she is always an amazingly realistic dramatic figure. Her appearance in *Lost Angel*

Robert Blake and Margaret O'Brien in *Lost Angel* (1944, MGM).

makes her a brilliant star."—*Hollywood Reporter*, November 5, 1943.

"But top honors go to little Margaret for her natural and unaffected performance."—*Motion Picture Daily*, November 5, 1943.

"No small factor in the success of the picture is the appearance in the cast of little Margaret O'Brien. The young miss is fully up to the tough assignment given her in *Lost Angel*. The child gives such a touching account of herself in the number one role of the picture that she steals your heart."—*Film Daily*, November 10, 1943.

Additional Reviews: *Box Office*, 11/06/43; *Brooklyn Eagle*, 04/10/44; *The Exhibitor*, 11/17/43; *Independent*, 11/13/43; *Los Angeles Daily News*, 03/03/44; *Motion Picture Herald*, 11/06/43; *The Nation*, 01/15/44; *The New Yorker*, 04/15/44; *New York Daily News*, 04/09/44; *New York Journal-American*, 04/10/44; *New York Mirror*, 04/10/44; *New York Post*, 04/10/44; *New York Times*, 04/10/44; *New York World-Telegram*, 04/08/44; *Showmen's Trade Review*, 11/06/43; *Variety*, 04/12/44.

Costar Comments

"What got to me and the public, was that as a tot, Margaret was so true. Her acting was completely true. She has such a simple instinctive talent which was able to present the truth. And this seared right through the camera lens into the hearts of the moviegoing public."—*Marsha Hunt*[9]

"In the part of a professor, I found it difficult to appear as though I knew more than Margaret did, and after watching her act, I'm inclined to think she taught me more tricks of the trade than I did her."—*Philip Merivale*[10]

"She was my first leading lady, and wow what a talent! A real trouper."—*Robert Blake*[11]

Comments by Margaret O'Brien

"I developed a big crush on James Craig. I kept following him around because I thought he was so handsome. And then I would get jealous when he had his scenes with Marsha Hunt, because I thought she was taking away my boyfriend."

JANE EYRE

A 20th Century–Fox Picture
1944

"We live always in Paris. But then Mama had to go to the Holy Virgin. Mr. Rochester came and took me across the sea in a great ship with a chimney that smoked. And I got sick."

—Margaret O'Brien to Joan Fontaine in *Jane Eyre*

Opened on February 3, 1944, at Radio City Music Hall, New York City.
Ad line: "The Strangest Love Story Ever Lived by a Woman."

Statistics

20th Century–Fox production number 470.
Running time, 96 minutes; black & white; Drama.

Ratings

The Motion Picture Guide, ☆☆☆☆
Leonard Maltin's Movie and Video Guide, ☆☆☆
Halliwell's Film Guide, ☆☆☆

Credits

Produced by William Goetz, Kenneth McGowan and Orson Welles (uncredited); directed by Robert Stevenson; screenplay by Aldous Huxley, Robert Stevenson, John Houseman and Henry Koster (uncredited) from the novel *Jane Eyre* by Charlotte Brontë (New York: Harper, 1848); scenario assistant, Barbara Keon; original music by Bernard Herrmann; production design by William L. Pereira; art direction by Wiard B. Ihnen and James Basevi; set decoration by Ross Dowd and Thomas Little; make-up by Guy Pearce; costume design by René Hubert; sound by W. D. Flick and Roger Heman; cinematography by George Barnes; film editing by Walter Thompson; special effects by Fred Sersen.

Cast

Orson Welles (Edward Rochester), Joan Fontaine (Jane Eyre), Margaret O'Brien (Adele Varens), Peggy Ann Garner (Jane as a Child), John Sutton (Dr. Rivers), Sara Allgood (Bessie), Henry Daniell (Brocklehurst), Agnes Moorehead (Mrs. Reed), Aubrey Mather (Colonel Dent), Edith Barrett (Mrs. Fairfax), Barbara Everest (Lady Ingram), Hillary Brooke (Blanche Ingram), Harry Allen (Guard), Billy Bevan (Bookie), Ruth Brady (Girl at Party), Colin Campbell (Proprietor), David Clyde (Guard), Charles Coleman (Guard), Alec Craig (Footman), Alan Edmiston (Dealer), Jean Fenwick (Guest), Mary Forbes (Mrs. Eshtor), Arthur Gould-Porter (Young Man), Ethel Griffies (Grace Poole), Brandon Hurst (Trustee), Adele Jergins (Girl at Party), George Kirby (Old Gentleman), Bud Lawler (Guest), Gwendolyn Logan (Dowager), Thomas Loudon (Sir George Lynn), Moyna MacGill (Dowager), Barry Macollum (Trustee), Eily Malyon (Mrs. Scatcherd), Mae Marsh (Leah), John Meredith (Guest), Roseanne Murray (Guest), Tempe Pigott (Fortune Teller), Nancy June Robinson (Girl), Marion Rosamond (Guest), Erskine Sanford (Mr. Briggs), Billie Seward (Girl at Party), Yorke Sherwood (Beadle), Ivan F. Simpson (Mr. Woods), John Abbott (Mason), Ronald Harris (John), Charles Irwin (Auctioneer), Gerald Oliver Smith (Footman of Gateshead), Elizabeth Taylor (Helen Burns), Leslie Vincent (Guest), Dan Wallace (Guest), Frederick Worlock (Waiter), Eustace Wyatt (Dr. Carter).

Synopsis

Set in Victorian times, it is the story of a young girl named Jane Eyre, an unfortunate orphan who has a sad childhood growing up at Lowood School. When she is grown, she becomes a governess for a wealthy brooding Englishman named Rochester at his mansion in Yorkshire called Thornfield Hall. While there, she is in charge of Rochester's young French ward, Adele Varens, and becomes involved in mystery and romance.

Behind the Scenes

In her career, Margaret O'Brien appeared in several films adapted from literary classics. *Jane Eyre* would be her first and was the fifth filming based on the forbidding novel by Charlotte Brontë. MGM loaned its child prodigy to another studio for the first and only time. "Filming at 20th Century–Fox was very exciting to me," Margaret remembered. "Fox was a beautiful studio and since I was always at Metro, you very seldom got loaned out. It made me feel like a grown-up star."

Even though she was only six years old and could not read, Margaret was well versed in all the literary classics that her mother read to her. One of her favorite authors was Robert Louis Stevenson, so when she was introduced to *Jane Eyre's* director, Robert Stevenson, she extended her hand in awe and proclaimed, "The famous author?"[1]

On her first day of filming, she was

Margaret O'Brien as Adele in *Jane Eyre* (1944, 20th Century–Fox).

greeted by the film's star, Orson Welles, who had made a big impact in the industry just two years earlier in the now-classic *Citizen Kane* (1941). Welles, who was in make-up, leaned his large frame over the six-year-old to give her a hug. After returning to his dressing room, Margaret turned to her mother and said, "He's much older than I thought."

"That's just make-up for this part," her mother explained. "He's only about 25."

"Why he's really just a baby, isn't he?" Margaret replied.[2]

Even though Welles gave her a cordial greeting, he never became close to her or any of the children on the set, which included Peggy Ann Garner and Elizabeth Taylor; in fact, he held some contempt for her. Welles was always the type who made his presence known whether he was on or off the set; however, he had never met Margaret O'Brien, who naturally attracted everyone to her, young and old alike.

One day Margaret arrived on the set dressed in a frilly white gown she was to wear for her scene that day. She was thrilled to be dressed up so elegantly and everyone enjoyed seeing her so happy. "I loved wearing the costumes," she said. "Usually I would get the poor bedraggled costumes, but on *Jane Eyre* I got to be dressed up and wear the pretty clothes."

While she was standing in front of a mirror admiring her dress, Welles noticed how everyone was watching her. He turned to his secretary and grumbled, "That kid's nothing but a little scene stealer."[3] Fortunately at the time, Margaret never knew how Welles felt.

"He was nice, but he was a little more distant than the others," she recalled. "The only thing with Orson Welles was that he would take about a hundred takes for one line, and that got real boring to me and I would tire out. And other times he would mumble and they couldn't get the clarity and had to do several takes."

Bosley Crothers, film critic for the *New York Times*, found the film "grimly fascinating," but agreed with Margaret's assertion about Welles' speaking ability. "He so mumbles and macerates his words that half the time we were unable to tell what he was talking about," the critic wrote.[4]

The rest of the cast was a joy for Mar-

garet to work with. She admired costar Joan Fontaine, who appeared to her as very soft-spoken and dignified. "Joan was easy to get along with," she recalled, "but wasn't someone you'd romp around in the dirt with. She was very sweet, and to me was almost like a schoolteacher."

Margaret enjoyed roaming through the gigantic sets that were built for *Jane Eyre*. Like MGM, Fox had a huge back lot where the castle for the film was constructed. "I was always fascinated by antiques and ancient times," Margaret said. "It was really fun wandering around the large stone castle they built and seeing all the authentic furniture."

The critics liked *Jane Eyre*, with the exception of Orson Welles' performance. One journalist noted that the film was "a fine picture production, with Joan Fontaine contributing an enchanting performance in the title role. But for Orson Welles, who overplays Rochester, the balance of the cast is excellent."[5]

Of Margaret O'Brien, *Life* magazine said, "not since Shirley Temple stole into people's hearts with her endearing waifishness in 1934's *Little Miss Marker* has any child actress shown as much promise as Margaret O'Brien."[6]

Reviews

"In *Jane Eyre*, Margaret O'Brien plays the role of Adele Varens, a lively French girl who is the moody Rochester's ward. Her beautifully disciplined performance is in sharp contrast to the ludicrous overacting of Orson Welles' Rochester. In this movie she shows a Gallic volubility."—*Life*, April 3, 1944.

"Little Margaret O'Brien is completely engaging as Rochester's ward, Adele."—*New York Daily News*, February 4, 1944.

"Little Margaret O'Brien gives her

Orson Welles looks on Joan Fontaine and Margaret O'Brien in *Jane Eyre* (1944, 20th Century-Fox; courtesy of the Academy of Motion Picture Arts and Sciences).

usual astonishing account in an exacting assignment."—*Hollywood Reporter*, February 2, 1944.

"Margaret O'Brien is appealing as Rochester's French ward."—*Harrison's Reports*, February 5, 1944.

Additional Reviews: *Commonweal*, 10/29/43, pp. 36–37; *Film Daily*, 02/03/44, p. 14; *Hollywood Motion Picture Review*, 02/07/44, p. 6; *The London Times*, 12/24/43, p. 6; *Motion Picture Exhibitor*, 02/09/44; *Motion Picture Herald Product Digest*, 02/05/44; *The Nation*, 02/12/44; *The New Republic*, 03/13/44; *New York Herald-Tribune*, 02/04/44; *New York Journal-American*, 02/04/44; *New York Newspaper PM*, 02/04/44; *New York Post*, 02/04/44; *New York Sun*, 02/04/44; *New York Times*, 02/04/44, p. 12; *New York Times*, 02/13/44, sec. 2, p. 3; *New York World-Telegram*, 02/04/44; *Newsweek*, 02/14/44, p. 88; *Photoplay*, 08/43, pp. 40–41; *Rob Wagner's Script*, 02/19/44, p. 18; *Saturday Review*, 02/19/44, p. 18; *Scholastic*, 12/13/43, p. 27; *Time*, 02/21/44, p. 96; *Variety*, 02/02/44, p. 18.

Costar Comments

"My recollections of Margaret are of a sweet, modest and talented child."—*Joan Fontaine*[7]

Comments by Margaret O'Brien

"Although we knew each other at Metro, I didn't have any scenes with Elizabeth Taylor. However I would see her on the Fox lot and I was just happy I could put my nose in the air and go past her and Peggy Ann [Garner] because they had to wear the raggedy clothes and I had the pretty clothes for a change. We were only kids, but Elizabeth was envious of me for once."

THE CANTERVILLE GHOST

A Metro-Goldwyn-Mayer Picture
1944

"Cuffy, you're not a coward, you're not a coward. Cuffy, you were doing a brave deed, don't you see. You can do it. You don't have to be afraid because you're a Canterville. You only think you do."

—Margaret O'Brien giving encouragement to Robert Young in *The Canterville Ghost*.

Opened on July 28, 1944, at the Globe Theater, New York City. Ad line: "When an English Ghost and a Gang of American Rangers Mix—Look Out."

Statistics
MGM production number 430.
Running time, 95 minutes; black & white; Comedy.

Ratings
The Motion Picture Guide, ☆☆☆
Leonard Maltin's Movie and Video Guide, ☆☆☆
Halliwell's Film Guide, ☆

Credits
Produced by Arthur Field; directed by Jules Dassin; screenplay by Edwin Harvey Blum, based on a story by Oscar Wilde (Vienna: Steyrermahl Pub.); music by George Bassman; art direction by Cedric Gibbons and Edward Carfagno; set decoration by Edwin B. Willis and Mildred Griffiths; dance direction by Jack Donahue; make-up by Jack Dawn; costume design by Irene; men's costumes by Valles; sound by Douglas Shearer; cinematography by Robert Planck; film editing by Chester V. Schaeffer.

Songs: "Ye Who Would" by George

Margaret O'Brien as Lady Jessica de Canterville in *The Canterville Ghost* (1944, MGM).

Bussman; "Gertie from Bizerte" by James Cavanaugh, Walter Kent and Bob Cutter.

Cast

Charles Laughton (Sir Simon de Canterville), Robert Young (Cuffy Williams), Margaret O'Brien (Lady Jessica de Canterville), William Gargan (Sgt. Benson), Reginald Owen (Lord Canterville), Rags Ragland (Big Harry), Una O'Connor (Mrs. Umney), Donald Stuart (Sir Valentine Williams), Elizabeth Risdon (Mrs. Polverdine), Frank Faylen (Lieutenant Kane), Lumsden Hare (Mr. Potts), Mike Mazurki (Metropolis), William Moss (Hector), Bobby Readick (Eddie), Marc Cramer (Bugsy McDougle), William Tannen (Jordan), Peter Lawford (Peter de Canterville), Frank Reicher (Bit Part), Brent Richards (Bit Part).

Synopsis

Based on the story by Oscar Wilde, it concerns the ghost of Sir Simon de Canterville who haunts his ancestral castle for more than 300 years. When he decides to scare a group of American servicemen who are using the castle as a barracks during World War II, he runs into a soldier named Cuffy who befriends him in order to prove to young Lady Jessica that the old ghost is harmless. Cuffy discovers that Sir Simon, who was a coward, was sealed up in the castle's walls in 1604 and doomed to haunting until a descendant performs a brave deed and therefore sets him free. To date all of Sir Simon's descendants have been cowards, which has doomed him to his 300 years of restlessness. When it is discovered that Cuffy has the Canterville birthmark and is a relative of Sir Simon, the old ghost tries to convince him to do

a brave deed. Unfortunately the young soldier is indeed a Canterville and possesses the same cowardly trait. Only through Lady Jessica is Cuffy able to come to grips with the reality of his honor and perform a brave deed and thus free Sir Simon.

Behind the Scenes

In *The Canterville Ghost*, Margaret was reunited with Robert Young. She knew and loved Young and felt comfortable with him, but her other costar proved to be a little more formidable. Margaret had heard of Charles Laughton, the great English actor, and for some reason assumed that he did not like children. However, that proved not to be the case, because Laughton succumbed to the young lady's charm and the two became great friends.

Norman Z. McLeod was originally assigned to direct the picture, but after an argument with the studio over which Tartan plaid Margaret was to wear, he was replaced with Jules Dassin. McLeod, being Scottish himself, wanted to use his own plaid but producer Arthur Field refused. Ironically, they ended up using McLeod's plaid anyway.

Charles Laughton played the part of the ghost and was always in white powdery make-up. Concerned about how his appearance would affect his six-year-old costar, Laughton took great care not to scare her on the first day of filming. "She was startled, it's true," Laughton later said. But from behind his macabre mask, he reassured little Margaret. "It's only me, darling," he told her. "Just a silly old man trying to scare people—but not you!"

"To look at you," she replied, "people would never know how nice you really

Charles Laughton mugs for Margaret O'Brien in *The Canterville Ghost* (1944, MGM).

are."[1] To Margaret, Laughton was the perfect ghost.

"He really gave me the impression that he was a ghost," she said. "While I was working with him I felt he was from another world. And he had a very Renaissance look anyway. I didn't look at him as a modern person."

Having two of Hollywood's biggest scene stealers on the same picture proved to be hectic at times. Even young Margaret was concerned with such things. "All they had to do to make me cry was to tell me that Charles Laughton was going to steal the scene," she would say. Laughton, who was very

insecure with his talent, once became very agitated with his younger costar and complained to Robert Young. "He was ready to jump out the window," Young recalled. "He was storming and climbing the walls."

"Robert, I think she's stealing my scenes," Laughton told him. "What do you *do* about that child?"

"Listen Charles," Young said, "you have a marvelous part. You wear an outlandish costume. You're invisible. You walk through walls. You're bound to get attention. So just relax. Play your own scenes, and when you're in a scene with her, don't try to compete. If you stand there and make faces or pick your nose, people will be looking at her anyway. You'll look like a fool if you try to compete with a seven-year-old child who wears an elfin hat and can make tears roll down her face at a look."[2]

This seemed to placate the older actor, but even Margaret could tell that Laughton was unsure of himself. "He was very insecure," Margaret recalled. "And he really worried that he wouldn't be good in the scene, but of course he was always marvelous."

Highlights of working on *The Canterville Ghost* for Margaret were doing her first jitterbug dance and riding a horse. "I got to ride," she recalled. "They had a pony I really liked. But I fell off once and they didn't let me ride anymore."

But of course the main highlight was working with Charles Laughton, who always treated Margaret as if she were an adult. Sometimes they would argue about a scene, but in the end they would make up and be the best of friends again. Until the day he died, Margaret O'Brien was always one of Charles Laughton's favorite actresses.

When the film opened, critics and audiences alike were delighted with *The Canterville Ghost*. The *New York Sun* proclaimed that "Movies have at last discovered the fun of a good ghost story."[3]

Reviews

"The variable characteristics which are generally manifest by spooks are equally evident in the picture Metro has made about one in *The Canterville Ghost*, a genial whimsy ... Robert Young, in those scenes which permit him, is winning as the hero, and Margaret O'Brien radiates childish sweetness as Lady de Canterville. Naturally

the script permits her to run a gamut, from prayers to jumping jive."—*New York Times*, July 29, 1944.

"Margaret O'Brien, who seems to become more enchanting with her every appearance, is seen in an entirely new type of characterization ... (and) walks away with every scene in which she appears and is positively thrilling in the crucial moment when she frantically inspires Young with her own courage."—*Hollywood Reporter*, May 26, 1944.

"Margaret O'Brien, in a less demanding role than usual, plays the youngest of the de Cantervilles with charm and a nice sense of comedy."—*New York Sun*, July 29, 1944.

"For it is Charles Laughton's brilliant and flamboyant portrayal of the title role, the nicely modulated characterization of an American Ranger by Robert Young and the pertly serious acting of little Margaret O'Brien which keeps a rather random continuity spinning briskly along."—*New York Herald-Tribune*, July 29, 1944.

"Margaret O'Brien, as six-year-old Lady Jessica de Canterville, is as winsome and appealing as ever. Her performance is one of the brilliant spots."—*Harrison's Reports*, June 3, 1944.

Additional Reviews: *Commonweal*, 08/11/44; *Film Daily*, 05/31/44; *The London Times*, 07/26/44, p. 7; *Motion Picture Exhibitor*, 05/31/44; *Motion Picture Herald Product Digest*, 05/27/44; *The Nation*, 07/22/44; *New York Daily News*, 07/29/44; *New York Journal-American*, 07/29/44; *New York Newspaper PM*, 07/30/44; *New York Post*, 07/29/44; *New York World-Telegram*, 07/28/44; *The New Yorker*, 08/05/44, p. 32; *Newsweek*, 07/31/44, p. 82; *Time*, 08/14/44, p. 96; *Variety*, 05/31/44, p. 20.

Charles Laughton, Margaret O'Brien and Robert Young in *The Canterville Ghost* (1944, MGM).

Costar Comments

"I never felt nervous working with anyone else but Margaret. Does she like me?"—*Charles Laughton*[4]

"No matter what anyone else says—I saw her first! Anyone working with Margaret might just as well wear King beards and overalls."—*Robert Young*[5]

Comments by Margaret O'Brien

"*The Canterville Ghost* was lots of fun because I was back with Robert Young. And of course working with Charles Laughton—I was afraid to be working with this great English actor. I thought of all people he probably doesn't like working with children, but he was wonderful, just wonderful. I guess I liked him because he treated me like an adult actress. We'd fight for each other's scenes and then he would get mad and of course so would I, but then we'd make up and we really became good friends. He was always one of my favorite actors."

MUSIC FOR MILLIONS

A Metro-Goldwyn-Mayer Picture
1944

"The stork doesn't bring babies, Mr. Andrews. No it doesn't. Only children think the stork brings babies. You're big—you should know better!"
>—Margaret O'Brien explaining the facts of life to Jimmy Durante in *Music for Millions.*

Opened on December 21, 1944, at the Capitol Theater, New York City. Ad line: "*Music for Millions* ... It Will Have You Laughing ... It Will Bring Tears to Your Eyes."

Statistics
MGM production number 515.
Working title, "Dear Barbara."
Running time, 117 minutes; black & white; Comedy/Musical.

Ratings
The Motion Picture Guide, ☆☆
Leonard Maltin's Movie and Video Guide, ☆☆½
Halliwell's Film Guide, ☆

Credits
Produced by Joe Pasternak; directed by Henry Koster; screenplay by Myles Connolly; musical direction by Georgie Stoll; incidental music by Michel Michelet; orchestration by Joseph Mussbaum, Ted Duncan and Calvin Jackson; art direction by Cedric Gibbons and Hans Peters; set decoration by Edwin B. Willis and Helen Conway; costume design by Irene and Kay Dean; sound by Douglas Shearer; cinematography by Robert Surtees; film editing by Douglas Biggs.

Jose Iturbi conducting and playing the music of Dvorak, Grieg, Herbert, Debussy, Tchaikovsky, Liszt, Handel and Chopin.

Songs: "Toscanini, Stokowski and Me" by Jimmy Durante, Walter Bullock and Harold Spina; "Umbriago" by Jimmy Durante and Irving Caesar; "At Sundown" by Walker Donaldson; "Clair de Lune" by Debussy.

Cast
Margaret O'Brien ("Mike"), Jose Iturbi (Himself), Jimmy Durante (Andrews), June Allyson (Barbara Ainsworth), Marsha Hunt (Rosalind), Hugh Herbert (Uncle Ferdinand), Harry Davenport (Doctor), Marie

Margaret O'Brien as Mike in *Music for Millions* (1944, MGM).

Wilson (Marie), Larry Adler (Larry), Connie Gilchrist (Traveler's Aid Woman), Ben Lessy (Kickebush), Ethel Griffies (Mrs. McGuff), Katharine Balfour (Elsa), Helen Gilbert (Helen), Mary Parker (Anita), Madeleine Lebeau (Jane), Eddie Jackson (Singer), Jack Roth (Drummer), Lillian Yarbo (Jessie), Robert Emmet O'Connor (Policeman), Jean Bayless, Roberta Ridley, Tanis Chandler, Lorraine Page, Linda Deane, Sybil Merritt, Danna McGraw, Helen

Pender (Orchestra Members), Lottie Harrison (Kate), William "Bill" Phillips (Stooge), Robert Homans (Railroad Conductor), Lottaine Miller (Girl), Dick Crockett (Soldier), Willie Best (Red Cap), Sarah Edwards (Third Woman), Edith Leach (Second Woman), Geraldine Wall (First Woman), Joel Friedkin, Earl Schenck, George Carleton, Ronnie Rondell (Men), Broderick O'Farrell (Stage Doorman), Al Ferguson, Capt. Somers (Workmen), Jody Gilbert (Burley Woman Cab Driver), Lee Phelps, Charles Sullivan (Expressmen), Frank Darien (Old W. U. Messenger), Sam Finn (Taxi Driver), Harry Burns (Louie, Waiter), Ed Agresti (Headwaiter), Sam McDaniel (Col. Pullman), Arthur Space (Colonel), Garry Owen (Soldier Waiter), Tim Murdock (Captain), Wally Cassell (Soldier), Mary Gordon (Woman Hotel Proprietor), Paul E. Burns (Hiram), Frank Gagney (Policeman), Nestor Paiva (Willie, Bartender), Ed Gargan, Eddie Dunn (Cops), Robert Dudley (Rafferty, Postman), Jane Green (Nurse), Byron Foulger (Elevator Girl), Ruth Lee (Nurse), Kenneth Scott (Soldier on Street), Effie Laird (Wardrobe Woman), Volta Boyer (Nurse), Stanley Andrews (Doctor in Hospital), Josephine Allen (Old Lady), Doris Stone (Bit Mother), Ned Dobson, Jr. (Bit Boy), Lyle Clark (Bit Sailor), Ava Gardner (Bit Part).

Synopsis

Because of the increasing number of men being taken by the war, Barbara Ainsworth, a girl bass viol player, joins Jose Iturbi's orchestra. Heartsick with worry over the failure to hear from her husband who is fighting in the Pacific, and facing the prospect of having a child, Barbara has all but lost faith. One day her young sister "Mike" joins her and gradually instills in her the unshakable faith in God the child herself possesses. Yet this does not in itself solve the problem. There are complications and moments of despair, with all the orchestra girls coming to the rescue in a curious manner of their own that paves the way for a dramatic and delightful twist at the end.

Behind the Scenes

World War II was in full swing and war-themed films with classical music and sentimentality were what the public wanted. *Music for Millions* gave the audience this and more. Margaret was the star of this flag-waver about an all-girl orchestra, and was surrounded by quite an array of talent. June Allyson played her big sister who is a member of Jose Iturbi's orchestra and Jimmy Durante provided the laughs. This was Margaret's first picture with June Allyson and the two fell in love with each other from the beginning. "June was very nice to me," Margaret recalled. "Always very sisterly, and we've been friends ever since."

During one scene, June is crying because her husband is overseas in the war and she doesn't know whether he is dead or alive. Comforting her, Margaret tells her he will be coming back. "He promised to bring me a Japanese *saw-ward*," she tells her.

Because June kept hearing Margaret say "saw-ward," she also began to pronounce it the same way in her scenes. The director, Henry Koster, would stop filming and the crew would break up with laughter. "Sometimes I started talking like Maggie even on dates," June said.[1]

Jimmy Durante entertains Margaret O'Brien in *Music for Millions* (1944, MGM).

Once Margaret was carefully looking at her face in a mirror. After a few moments she turned to her mother and said, "Mother, do you think I'll grow up to look like Hedy Lamarr?"

"No, I don't think so," her mother said.

"That's fine," Margaret replied, "because I'd rather look like June Allyson."[2]

Her other costar, Jimmy Durante, was like an uncle to her. He would tell her jokes or advise her on her hats, which was Margaret's passion. Between takes he would always go to the piano and sing songs. Sometimes a crowd would gather around and everyone would join in a sing-along. Other times it would just be Jimmy and Margaret alone, singing a melody that Durante wrote just for her.

"Margaret O'Brien, I love you!" Jimmy would croon while Margaret hummed along. Sometimes they would get so involved, they would forget to return to the set and the irritated assistant director would have to send someone to look for them.

One day Margaret was signing an autograph for a soldier in the South Pacific who had named his plane "Lost Angel" after one of Margaret's films. "He's flying those big silver ones, isn't he?" she commented while very carefully writing her name. "I think I'll draw one and put Mr. Durante in it."[3]

Jose Iturbi also became close to Margaret and her mother, since both were Spanish. Iturbi would bring his two daughters on the set to play with Margaret and she would usually take them and any visitor that dropped by to her new dressing room. It was presented to her the month before to celebrate MGM's twentieth anniversary.

The new dressing room had blue gingham walls and a peppermint-striped ceiling. But the one feature Margaret liked best was the concealed bathroom that looked more like a closet. "My last one," she explained, "was right out in the open. I only used it in emergencies because it embarrassed me. This one nobody can tell about 'less they're in on it."[4]

Music for Millions was director Henry Koster's first film for MGM. Koster felt that the studio interfered with the production style of their films by overprogramming everything. "They had a coach for this, an aide for that, a department for this," he complained.[5] Although he sensed that it may have been right in some cases, in the long run it was not always good for the picture.

One day Koster took Margaret aside for some direction on one particular scene. Larry Adler was to play "Clair de Lune" on a harmonica, which was supposed to make June Allyson cry. Koster thought it appropriate that Margaret should weep also. "You're so happy," Koster explained, "that you cry." Margaret listened intently to the director. She paused for one moment and then asked, "Mr. Koster, do you want the tears just visible in my eyes or rolling down my cheeks?"

"What do you mean?" Koster replied.

"Well, I can control that," Margaret explained. "I think of something very sad when I have them roll down my cheeks, or just a little sad when you just want my eyes to get wet."

"And she actually did that," Koster later said. "She could control her acting and her emotions through her own will."[6]

Music for Millions became a big moneymaker and a critical success for the studio. The *Hollywood Reporter* said, "*Music for Millions* has been aptly

Jimmy Durante, Marsha Hunt, Margaret O'Brien, June Allyson and Jose Iturbi in *Music for Millions* (1944, MGM).

named, for many, many millions are going to see and hear it and enjoy a grand experience."[7]

Reviews

"It has Margaret O'Brien—which is all any picture needs. She is the completely captivating, flawless performer she always is."—*Hollywood Reporter*, December 13, 1944.

"Furthermore—and probably above all else in the long run—little Margaret O'Brien is present to lend the human element to all proceedings."—*Los Angeles Times*, March 7, 1945.

"Little Margaret O'Brien wandering around with her sister, is as cute a trick as she has ever been."—*New York Herald-Tribune*, December 22, 1944.

"*Music for Millions* never fails to come up with a moment of delight when Margaret gets before the camera."—*New York World-Telegram*, December 21, 1944.

"Margaret O'Brien is a delightful, diminutive person, and her conversation with Durante concerning the facts of life are something for the ear."—*New York Post*, December 22, 1944.

"Miss O'Brien, as the younger sister, has a lot of cute moments—and a lot of dramatic ones too, that she puts over very forcefully. It's easily her finest screen performance yet."—*Hollywood Citizen-News*, March 7, 1945.

Additional Reviews: *Daily News*, 03/07/45; *Los Angeles Examiner*, 03/07/45; *The Nation*, 01/06/45; *The New Yorker*, 12/23/44; *New York Daily News*, 12/22/44; *New York Journal-American*, 12/22/44; *New York PM*, 12/22/44; *New York Sun*, 12/22/44; *New York Times*, 12/22/44; *New York World-Telegram*, 12/21/44; *Time*, 01/05/45; *Variety*, 12/13/44.

Academy Award Nominee

Myles Connolly—Best Writing, Original Screenplay.

Costar Comments

"And dat's not all. Dis little O'Brien dame. She's terrific! When she opens a door, somebody walks into a room. And Lord help us if we don't know our lines. She's got 'em all memorized an' she just looks at us if we forget 'em. I'm skeered to deat' of her."—*Jimmy Durante*[8]

"But for me the picture's greatest thrill was playing with Margaret O'Brien. This was the first time we had played together, and I fell in love with her immediately. During the filming of *Music for Millions*, little Maggie O'Brien's picture was the only one I kept on my dresser."—*June Allyson*[9]

Comments by Margaret O'Brien

"*Music for Millions* was filled with a wonderful cast and wonderful music. There was June Allyson and Marsha Hunt—all the adult women which made me feel grown-up. And of course Jimmy Durante was fabulous. He sort of became an uncle to me just as Lionel Barrymore became my grandfather. In between scenes Jimmy would play the piano and he even made up a song about me. I couldn't wait to finish a scene so I could go and hear Jimmy play."

MEET ME IN ST. LOUIS

A Metro-Goldwyn-Mayer Picture
1944

"I bet she won't live through the night. She has four fatal diseases."

> —Margaret O'Brien fussing about her doll to Chill Wills in *Meet Me in St. Louis*.

Opened on December 31, 1944, at the Astor Theater, New York City.
Ad line: "'Meet Me in St. Louis' and Have the Time of Your Life."

Chill Wills with Margaret O'Brien as Tootie in *Meet Me in St. Louis* (1944, MGM).

Statistics

MGM production number 512.
Running time, 113 minutes; Technicolor; Musical.

Ratings

The Motion Picture Guide, ☆☆☆☆☆
Leonard Maltin's Movie and Video Guide, ☆☆☆☆
Halliwell's Film Guide, ☆☆☆

Credits

Produced by Arthur Freed; directed by Vincente Minnelli; assistant director, Al Jennings; 2nd assistant director, Al Alt; screenplay by Irving Brecher and Fred F. Finklehoffe, from *The New Yorker* stories and the novel *Meet Me in St. Louis* (New York: Random House, 1942) by Sally Benson; musical direction by Georgie Stoll; musical adaptation by Roger Edens; orchestration by Conrad Salinger; art direction by Cedric Gibbons, Lemuel Ayers and Jack Martin Smith; set decorations by Edwin B. Wills and Paul Huldchinsky; make-up by Jack Dawn; costume supervision by Irene; costume design by Irene Sharaff; sound by Douglas Shearer; cinematography by George Folsey and Henri Jaffa; film editing by Albert Akst; assistant film editor, Frank Capacchione; color consultant, Natalie Kalmus; associate color direction by Henri Jaffa; choreography by Paul Jones; dance direction by Charles Waters.

Songs: "The Boy Next Door," by Hugh Martin and Ralph Blane, sung by Judy Garland; "Skip to My Lou," traditional, sung by Judy Garland; "I Was Drunk Last Night," traditional, sung by Margaret O'Brien; "Under the Bamboo Tree," by J. Rosamond and Bob Cole, sung and danced by Judy Garland and Margaret O'Brien; "Over the Banister," by Hugh Martin and Ralph Blane, sung by Judy Garland; "The Trolley Song," by Hugh Martin and Ralph Blane, sung by Judy Garland and chorus; "Have Yourself a Merry Little Christmas" by Hugh Martin and Ralph Blane, sung to Margaret O'Brien by Judy Garland; "Meet Me in St. Louis" by Andrew B. Sterling and Kerry Mills, sung by Joan Carroll, Harry Davenport, Henry H. Daniels, Judy Garland and Lucille Bremer; "You and I" by Arthur Freed and Nacio Herb Brown, sung by Arthur Freed (on-screen Leon Ames).

Cast

Judy Garland (Esther Smith), Margaret O'Brien (Tootie Smith), Mary Astor (Mrs. Anna Smith), Lucille Bremer (Rose Smith), Tom Drake (John Truett), Marjorie Main (Katie), Leon Ames (Mr. Alonzo Smith), Harry Davenport (Grandpa), June Lockhart (Lucille Ballard), Henry H. Daniels, Jr. (Lon Smith, Jr.), Joan Carroll (Agnes Smith), Hugh Marlowe (Colonel Darly), Robert Sully (Warren Sheffield), Chill Wills (Mr. Neely), Sidney Barnes (Hugo Borvis), Joe Cobb (A Clinton Badger), Victor Cox (Driver), Donald Curtis (Doctor Terry), Kenneth Donner (A Clinton Badger), Mary Jo Ellis (Ida Boothby), Helen Gilbert (Girl on Trolley), Buddy Gorman (A Clinton Badger), Sam Harris (Mr. March), Darryl Hickman (Johnny Tevis), Victor Killian (Baggage Man), Belle Mitchell (Mrs. Braukoff), Mayo Newhall (Mr. Braukoff), Robert Emmett O'Connor (Motorman), John Phipps (Mailman), William Smith (Bit Part), Myron Tobias (George), Dorothy Tuttle (Singing Waitress), Leonard Walker (Conductor), Ken Wilson (Quentin).

Margaret O'Brien and Judy Garland in the cakewalk scene from *Meet Me in St. Louis* (1944, MGM).

Synopsis

Charming story of the Smith family living in St. Louis, Missouri, at the time of the 1903 World's Fair. The excitement of the fair affects the entire family until Mr. Smith informs everyone that they are moving to New York, where he has been offered a promotion. At first very upset, the family eventually concedes to the elder Smith's decision and goes about tying up loose ends and relationships. Finally, Mr. Smith sees the error of moving his family from St. Louis and decides to decline the promotion, which allows everyone to attend the World's Fair.

Behind the Scenes

Meet Me in St. Louis was based on a series of articles by Sally Benson called "The Kensington Stories," which originally appeared in *The New Yorker* magazine. Producer Arthur Freed fought for several years to have Benson's stories of life in St. Louis at the time of the World's Fair made into a film, but was always met with opposition.

Freed knew if he was to ever get the film made, he had to convince Louis B. Mayer, the head of MGM. He also knew that Mayer never read any scripts but would have a reader tell him what the story was about. One of Mayer's favorite readers was Lillie Messinger, whom Freed convinced to describe the story to her boss. "I think I understood Mr. Mayer very well, and the things he would like in a story," Lillie said, "and that helps you in telling it."

During a conference with all the production heads, each member voiced their dissatisfaction with the story. Their opposition to *Meet Me in St. Louis* was that there was no plot, no action and no conflict. "What's the matter with you

guys?" Mayer asked. "I think the story is very exciting, there's a lot of action! And what about those girls who have to leave their home and their sweethearts? I tell you, it broke my heart."

Now that Freed had Mayer's backing, he had the script written, and instructed the art department to design the sets. However, what began to form was not the movie Freed envisioned. "I want to make this into the most delightful piece of Americana ever," Freed told Mayer. "Sets, costumes … it'll cost a bit, but it'll be great. And I'll get a great score."

"Well Arthur," Mayer said, "go ahead. Either you'll learn or we'll learn."[1]

Freed originally chose George Cukor to direct but he went into the army shortly before filming began. Instead Freed decided on Vincente Minnelli and the two began casting the picture. Judy Garland was on the rise at MGM at the time and was assigned the role of Esther Smith. Surprisingly, Judy did not want the part. Director Joseph Mankiewicz, a close friend, had told her that she would not have the starring role. The starring role in Mankiewicz's eyes was that of Tootie, the youngest sister. Judy went to Minnelli with her doubts. "This is awful! Isn't it?" she asked.

"No," Minnelli replied. "I think it's marvelous."[2]

After answering her questions and having Freed read her the script, Judy finally agreed to do the film. It was decided to film it in Technicolor and to build a whole new St. Louis street on the back lot instead of using the Andy Hardy Street, which was originally suggested. Margaret O'Brien loved the new street. "I used to go out and walk up and down that street and pretend I was in Victorian times," Margaret recalled. "Years later I would look for a similar street and have always wanted a house like the one in *Meet Me in St. Louis*."

After Judy agreed to do the film, the rest of the casting did not pose much of a problem except for the role of Tootie, the youngest girl. Minnelli wanted Margaret O'Brien and later claimed responsibility for discovering her, even though this was her ninth film. However, Margaret's popularity was at an all-time high and her mother insisted on a larger salary. Freed refused, so Mrs. O'Brien took Margaret to New York without telling anyone and another girl was cast as Tootie. "MGM would have had me working for a hundred and fifty a week if my mother hadn't pulled me out of the film," Margaret recalled.

After doing wardrobe tests, Mayer relented and agreed to Mrs. O'Brien's salary demands. Finally they found Margaret and her mother in New York and they returned to Culver City to begin filming. The father of the little girl Margaret replaced was furious that his daughter had been taken off the film. Margaret had replaced the same little girl in *Journey for Margaret* and this was a second rejection.

The rest of the cast included veteran actors Mary Astor, Leon Ames and Harry Davenport along with Lucille Bremer, Tom Drake and Joan Carroll. Filming began on November 11, 1943, and the opening sequence was shot first.

The shooting schedule became very erratic from the beginning. Schedules had to be changed numerous times when several cast members became sick. Most of the time it was because of Judy's real and imagined ailments, but the rest of the cast also contributed to the picture's setbacks. Mary Astor had a sudden attack of sinusitis and was out for three weeks. Harry Davenport came down with a viral infection and Joan Carroll had to have an emergency appendectomy.

One day Margaret's mother informed the producer that her daughter had to have braces on her teeth and she would be out for ten days. Gladys O'Brien was also concerned about the grueling work schedule that Margaret was being put through. On January 30, Margaret's aunt Marissa called and said that they were leaving for Arizona in the morning because Margaret had developed a cold and sinus condition.

Of course the head of production, Walter Strohm, felt her ailment was imaginary and insisted that they stay, but Mrs. O'Brien refused. Two days later an MGM public relations man saw the O'Briens in Chicago where it was explained that Margaret was feeling better and they had decided to go to New York. Shortly after, they returned to the studio and filming began on the Halloween sequence.

The Halloween sequence was of special interest to Minnelli. In the original story, that particular incident had happened to Agnes; instead, Minnelli gave the scene to Tootie. "I changed it to express the horror of that little child," Minnelli said, "because she was always talking about blood."[3]

Margaret loved filming that sequence because Halloween was always one of her favorite times of the year. Also, working at night made her feel grown up. She arrived at the studio at four o'clock and usually worked until midnight without having to go to school, so during her spare time she could play. That time was usually spent playing with the other kids and with the dog from the scene, who was tamer than he appeared on screen because he was so well trained.

Margaret O'Brien takes a break with a costar during filming of the Halloween sequence in *Meet Me in St. Louis* (1944, MGM).

"That dog looked fierce but he really wasn't," she recalled.

Margaret remembers Judy Garland with great awe and respect. Judy was herself a child actress, and could relate to her young costar and felt compassion for her role. "You know that little girl is not having a life," she told girls on the set. "I've been there and I know what I'm talking about."[4]

Garland knew the hardships that she endured while growing up and didn't want to see the same fate befall young Margaret. Fortunately, there was no need to worry because it was a different time and there were many people looking out for Margaret's well-being, including her mother. But that didn't stop Judy from taking a special interest in her. "She really was like a big sister to me," Margaret remembered.

When it came time to film the scene with the snowmen, Judy once again thought about her young costar. They planned for Judy to sing "Have Yourself a Merry Little Christmas" to Margaret. However, when she heard the song, she was appalled at the lyrics.

> *Have yourself a merry little Christmas.*
> *It may be your last.*
> *Next year we will all be living in the*
> *   past...*

"I love the melody, but those lyrics!" Judy exclaimed. "If I sing that to little Margaret O'Brien, people will think I'm a monster."[5] The song's authors, Martin and Blane, at first did not agree with Garland but changed the words to the version that is sung in the picture.

Because Margaret was playing such a bratty character as Tootie, it was sometimes hard for her not to fall into that character herself when the cameras were not rolling. Minnelli made sure that the

sets were meticulous in their design, down to the most minute detail. One of the things that most fascinated her was the ornate doorknobs. On several occasions she tried to take them off but was not successful.

Another time, during the filming of the dinner scene, Margaret changed the place settings during a break. The change was not noticed until after filming had resumed and the scene had to be shot again. Costar Mary Astor, who truly acted like the mother of the brood, chastised young Margaret. "Margaret, you can't do that," Astor scolded. "No more changing of the silverware."[6]

It seemed Mary Astor did not have much patience with Margaret. In her autobiography, *A Life on Film*, Astor wrote, "She was a quiet, almost too well behaved child, when her mother was on the set. When Mother was absent, it was another story and she was a pain in the neck."[7]

When the film was finally finished, a preview was arranged for June 5, 1944. At the last minute, Freed decided to cut the Halloween sequence, much to Minnelli's objections. Everyone on the staff was appalled and felt it was one of the best sequences in the film. Because of previous problems he had with the producer, Minnelli asked Irving Brecher, one of the screenwriters, to intervene. "Arthur, I hear you're dropping the Halloween sequence," Brecher said to the producer.

"Yeah, what about it?" Freed snapped. "It's out!"[8] Brecher convinced Freed that it was only a preview and he could always take it out later if the audience didn't like it. When the movie previewed that night, the Halloween sequence was intact and remained in the picture when it was released.

The legendary Judy Garland and Margaret O'Brien in *Meet Me in St. Louis* (1944, MGM).

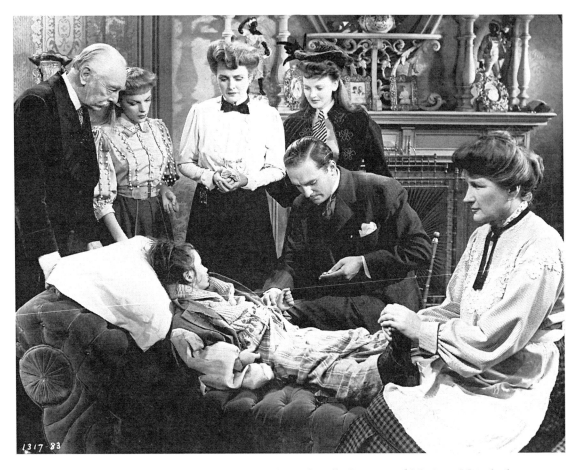

Harry Davenport, Judy Garland, Mary Astor, Lucille Bremer and Marjorie Main look on as
Donald Curtis attends to Margaret O'Brien in *Meet Me in St. Louis* (1944, MGM).

Today the film is just as entertaining as it was when it was first released. Many consider *Meet Me in St. Louis* one of the best musicals ever made, and much of the film's success can be attributed to Margaret O'Brien's performance. Del Reisman, a screenwriter and former president of the Writers Guild of America, said, "Watch *Meet Me in St. Louis* today. Sally Benson's charming story, under Vincente Minnelli's direction, plays beautifully more than half a century later, in large part due to Margaret O'Brien's performance as 'Tootie.' She proved that child actors don't have to pose and preen in the film tradition of cute kids; they can let the actor and the written part become one, like all the great adult actors."[9]

Harrison's Reports wrote that the film was "a tuneful, merry comedy-drama, which is so wholesome and heartwarming that few will be able to resist its appeal."[10] *Meet Me in St. Louis* cost the studio $1,707,561 and in spite of all the delays it only exceeded its budget by ten percent. It grossed more than $7,500,000 in its initial release, making it the number two box office hit that year. Today the film is considered a classic and Margaret's performance earned her a special Academy Award for Outstanding Child Actress of 1944.

Reviews

"Little Margaret O'Brien makes a wholly delightful imp of Satan as Tootie."—*New York Times*, November 29, 1944.

"Excellent performances are the rule in *Meet Me in St. Louis*, but there is no question that Margaret O'Brien calmly walks away with the show."—*Hollywood Reporter*, November 1, 1944.

"These triumphs are credible mainly to the intensity and grace of Margaret O'Brien and to the ability of director Minnelli and company to get the best out of her. Her song ("Drunk Last Night") and her cakewalk, done in a nightgown at a grown-up party, are entrancing little acts."—*Time*, November 27, 1944.

"There is Tootie (Margaret O'Brien), who swipes the picture right out from under her elders' noses and has a Halloween sequence, which involves probably the most desperate practical joke in the world, that is an almost perfect combination of humor and pathos."—*The New Yorker*, December 9, 1941.

"In point of performance, it is probably inevitable that little Margaret O'Brien packages the picture neatly under her own label. She is practically resistant-proof, but anyway, this reviewer didn't even try."—*Motion Picture Daily*, November 1, 1944.

Additional Reviews: *Film Daily*, 11/01/44, p. 6; *Life*, 12/11/44, pp. 68–70; *The London Times*, 02/26/45, p. 8; *Motion Picture Exhibitor*, 11/01/45; *Motion Picture Herald Product Digest*, 11/04/44; *The Nation*, 11/25/44; *The New Republic*, 12/18/44; *New York Daily News*, 11/29/44; *New York Herald-Tribune*, 11/29/44; *New York Journal-American*, 11/29/44; *New York PM*, 11/29/44; *New York Post*, 11/29/44; *New York Sun*, 11/29/44; *New York World-Telegram*, 11/28/44; *Newsweek*, 12/11/44, p. 104; *Rob Wagner's Script*, 01/06/45, p. 2; *Variety*, 11/01/44, p. 10.

Academy Award Nominations

Irving Brecher and Fred F. Finklehoffe—Best Screenplay.

George Folsey—Best Color Cinematography.

Georgie Stoll—Best Scoring of a Musical Picture.

Hugh Martin and Ralph Blane—Best Song ("The Trolley Song").

Awards

Academy Award Winner: Margaret O'Brien, Outstanding Child Actress of 1944.

New York Times Annual Ten Best List.

National Board of Review Awards: Best English Language Film.

National Board of Review Awards: Best Acting, Margaret O'Brien.

National Film Preservation Board, USA, 1994.

Costar Comments

"I hope they don't do to her what they did to me."—*Judy Garland*[11]

"Margaret O'Brien was a huge success as Tootie, the youngest child. I found her performance—and the lengths one had to go to achieve it—engrossing but enervating."—*Vincente Minnelli*[12]

"Margaret O'Brien was at her most appealing (I might say 'appalling') age. And she could cry at the drop of a cue. Real tears, an endless flow, with

apparently no emotional drain whatso-
ever."—*Mary Astor*[13]

Comments by Margaret O'Brien

"In *Meet Me in St. Louis* I got to play
a bratty part. In real life I didn't get into
too much trouble, but as Tootie I could

say and do all the things that I wouldn't
have done myself. And I loved the people I worked with. We were all like a big
family. I don't think the picture would
have worked if we hadn't all liked each
other."

OUR VINES HAVE TENDER GRAPES

A Metro-Goldwyn-Mayer Picture
1945

"But it isn't what you mean to do Pa—it's what you do."
—Margaret O'Brien to
Edward G. Robinson in *Our
Vines Have Tender Grapes.*

Premiered on September 6, 1945, at Radio City Music Hall, New York City.
Ad line: "A Simple Tale of Simple Americans."

Statistics

MGM production number 600.
Running time, 105 minutes; black &
white; Drama.

Ratings

The Motion Picture Guide, ☆☆☆☆
Leonard Maltin's Movie and Video Guide,
☆☆☆½
Halliwell's Film Guide, ☆

Credits

Produced by Robert Sisk; directed by
Roy Rowland; assistant director, Horace
Hough; screenplay by Dalton Trumbo,

based on the novel *For Our Vines Have
Tender Grapes* by George Victor Martin
(New York: W. Funk, Inc., 1940); musical direction by Bronislau Kaper; art
direction by Cedric Gibbons and
Edward Carfagno; set decoration by
Edwin B. Willis and Hugh Hunt; costume design by Irene and Kay Carter;
make-up by Jack Dawn; sound by Douglas Shearer; special effects by A. Arnold
Gillespie and Danny Hall; cinematography by Robert Surtees; second cameraman, A. Lindsley Lane; film editing
by Ralph E. Winters.

Cast

Edward G. Robinson (Martinius Jacobson), Margaret O'Brien (Selma Jacobson), James Craig (Nels Haverson), Frances Gifford (Viola Johnson), Agnes Moorehead (Bruna Jacobson), Morris Carnovsky (Bjorn Bjornson), Jackie "Butch" Jenkins (Arnold Hanson), Sarah Haden (Mrs. Bjornson), Greta Granstedt (Mrs. Faraassen), Dorothy Morris (Ingeborg Jensen), Arthur Space (Pete Hanson), Elizabeth Russell (Kola Hanson), Louis Jean Heydt (Mr. Faraassen), Charles Middleton (Kurt Jenson), Francis Pierlot (Minister), John Berkes (Circus Driver), Abigal Adams (Girl), Arthur Hohl (Dvar Svenson), Rhoda Williams (Marguerite Larsen).

Synopsis

The joys and sorrows of life in a small Norwegian farming settlement in Wisconsin are examined with the Jacobson family. Martinius, the father, dreams of building a new barn and making ends meet for his family. His small daughter Selma, along with her cousin Arnold, goes about getting in trouble and astonishing the town folks when she encourages them to contribute to a well-to-do farmer who lost his barn and livestock in a tragic fire.

Behind the Scenes

Our Vines Have Tender grapes was based on the best-selling novel by George Victor Martin and told the story of life on a Wisconsin farm. MGM selected an all-star cast that included Edward G. Robinson, Agnes Moorehead and James Craig.

The role of Martinius Jacobson was originally offered to Wallace Beery, but he rejected it and Robinson stepped in.

This film was a change for the actor who was used to playing the gangster and tough-guy roles. Margaret had seen most of his films and was expecting someone totally different from the Edward G. Robinson she met on the set. "I didn't think of him as the gangster-type at all," Margaret recalled. "I had difficulty connecting the gangster to the loving father. He was playing such a different role and he played it so well. I became really close with him, I really thought of him as my father on the farm."

During one particularly trying scene, Robinson was to slap the young actress, but had difficulty pulling it off. "I can't do it," he said, looking at that moppet face. "I can't slap her."[1] It finally took three takes before he could do it.

By this time Margaret's crush on James Craig had diminished but her affections were not transferred to costar Butch Jenkins. Even though Margaret admitted that Butch did not have much time for her, he was always quite a flirt with the young ladies. "How about this O'Brien dame?" director Roy Rowland asked the youngster.

"Oh boy," he exclaimed, "she's the one."[2] Unfortunately nothing ever came of the romance. Margaret did fall in love, but it was not with a human. When it came time to film the scene with the elephant, director Rowland intended to use a double, but Margaret insisted on doing the scene herself.

"The most exciting part of the film was riding the elephant," she recalled. "Even though it was a trained elephant, they were going to use a double but I told them that I wanted to do it. That's something I'll always remember."

Another fun part was riding the bathtub during the flash flood. Filmed in a

Margaret O'Brien and Edward G. Robinson in *Our Vines Have Tender Grapes* (1945, MGM).

Agnes Moorehead, Margaret O'Brien and Edward G. Robinson celebrate Christmas in *Our Vines Have Tender Grapes* (1945, MGM).

big vat on the back lot, both Margaret and Butch insisted on doing the scene over and over. During the more dangerous angles doubles were used, much to their dismay.

A slightly embarrassing moment occurred for the seven year old during the scene when her father awakens her at three o'clock in the morning so she can see the circus animals at the train station. In the scene, Robinson begins to unbutton her nightgown so she can change into street clothes. As he opens the second button, director Roy Rowland was to stop the scene—but the cameras kept running, so Robinson con-

tinued to undo her buttons. Not hearing the director yell "cut," Margaret reached up and grabbed Robinson's hand when he started on the fourth button. "I'm sorry I spoiled it, Mr. Rowland," Margaret said. "But you waited so long and I was getting very worried."[3]

Dalton Trumbo wrote the screenplay for *Our Vines Have Tender Grapes*, which proved to be his last film before he was labeled a Communist and sentenced to jail for refusing to testify before the House Un-American Activities Committee. Known as one of the "Hollywood Ten," Trumbo fought his way back by writing scripts using a pseudonym until Kirk

Douglas insisted that his name appear in the screen credits of *Spartacus* (1960).

After his arrest, *Our Vines Have Tender Grapes* was banned from being shown on the basis that it had Communist overtones. In the opening scene, Selma and Arnold argue about whether girls can fight as well as boys. To prove her point Selma throws a rock in the direction of a red squirrel sitting on a tree stump and inadvertently kills it. In horror, she cradles the dead animal in her hands. "I didn't mean to kill you, little squirrel," she sobs. "It was only pretend."

"Shucks, it's only a *red* squirrel," Arnold tells her. "They're bad."

This supposed reference to Communism was enough for the McCarthyites to prove their point. Sharing similar viewpoints, Edward G. Robinson and Trumbo talked openly about politics, and their desires for America, much to the dismay of many onlookers. "I'd known Trumbo for a long while," Robinson later recalled. "I knew he was hot-headed, wildly gifted, inordinately progressive, and, it seemed to me, intensely logical. My relationship with him professionally and socially became, not very many years later, a subject for official concern of the Congress."[4]

Dalton Trumbo and his wife Cleo also became good friends with Gladys O'Brien. After serving a ten-month jail sentence at the federal penitentiary in Ashland, Kentucky, Trumbo sold his home and moved to Mexico. "My mother was very good friends with Dalton," Margaret said. "In fact we saw them off when they left town on the train. Everyone was waving a flag. People warned my mother not to go down to the train station because it would ruin her and me, but we went anyway because

they were our friends. That was a terrible time during the McCarthy era. So many of those writers were not Communists."

Critics compared Dalton Trumbo's screenplay to *The Human Comedy*, calling it a "smooth, engaging continuity that never lets the interest drag."[5] John McManus wrote that the film was "one of the best of a healthy trend in the last several years—the trend toward characteristic American life as a film theme."[6]

Reviews

"This is one of the most charming, delightful and heartwarming pictures of this or any other year. [Robinson] gets some pretty stiff competition from La O'Brien, who not only has the advantage of being a child but a really superior actress. Frankly, she's this reviewer's dream princess."—*Hollywood Reporter*, September 10, 1945.

"The cast is superb, with the appealing team of Jenkins and O'Brien lighting the way for fine performers."—*Liberty*, October 20, 1945.

"Both youngsters are well-equipped with what it takes to steal scenes. Dalton Trumbo's adaptation notably catches the satisfactions and the drudgery of an R.F.D. address. And on the whole, *Our Vines Have Tender Grapes* is considerably more appealing than its syrupy title."—*Newsweek*, September 10, 1945.

"A deeply appealing drama. It is a heart-warming, wholesome entertainment, excellent for all the family. Both [O'Brien and Jenkins] of them give splendid performances."—*Harrison's Reports*, July 21, 1945.

Additional Reviews: *Commonweal*, 09/14/45; *Independent*, 07/21/45; *Motion Picture Herald*, 09/01/45; *The Nation*,

Butch Jenkins and Margaret O'Brien go rowing in *Our Vines Have Tender Grapes* (1945, MGM).

09/29/45; *The New Yorker*, 09/15/45; *New York Herald-Tribune*, 09/07/45; *New York Times*, 09/07/45; *PM*, 09/09/45; *Time*, 09/10/45; *Variety*, 07/18/45.

Costar Comments

"The studio kept telling me to get some acting tricks. It was just as I began thinking maybe I'd go to a drama coach for additional technique that they cast me with Margaret O'Brien. Now that little girl can't even read, so what could she know about technique? But she's an actress, a very great actress and a very great star. So I decided if I could keep the simplicity and sincerity of Maggie, I'd do okay."—*James Craig*[7]

"That turned out to be a lovely picture, I thought. It wasn't wildly successful, but it was a very sweet, honest, decent picture of farm life, and that's because it came from a lovely novel."—*Dalton Trumbo*[8]

Comments by Margaret O'Brien

"*Our Vines Have Tender Grapes* was a very sweet story and it was one of my favorite films to make. My costar on that picture was Butch Jenkins. He wasn't too much of a companion because he was more interested in playing ball than being with me so my stand-in and I stayed more together. But I loved roller skating so I got a chance to do that."

VICTORY IN EUROPE

A Metro-Goldwyn-Mayer Picture
1945

Opened May 1945, nationwide.
Note: Film unavailable for viewing.

Statistics

Made for distribution on or after "Victory in Europe Day."

Running time, 5½ minutes; black & white; Drama/Short/Documentary.

Credits

Produced by Carey Wilson.

Cast

Agnes Moorehead (Mother), Margaret O'Brien (Daughter).

Synopsis

A woman receives a wire that her husband is "missing in action" and her daughter prays for the safe return of her father.

Behind the Scenes

Unfortunately not much is known of this short produced by MGM. Margaret O'Brien remembers little of the making of this film, which was probably shot in a day or two to quickly take advantage of the recent victory. It has also been reported that O'Brien made a short in 1943 called *Three Sisters of the Moors*, however there is no evidence to back this up nor does she remember making it.

Reviews

"The audience is reminded that there is still a tough job ahead, namely the licking of Japan, before the victory will be complete and final, and the peace secured." — *The Exhibitor*, May 16, 1945.

Comments by Margaret O'Brien

"I vaguely remember this short, and could not comment on it other than to say that Agnes Moorehead was a dear to work with. You have to understand that I was seven or eight years old at the time, and something like this was probably a day's work. It was just routine for me."

BAD BASCOMB

A Metro-Goldwyn-Mayer Picture
1946

"Why does your nose run when your feet gets wet? You feet don't run when your nose gets wet!"
> —Margaret O'Brien posing a question to Marjorie Main in *Bad Bascomb*.

Opened on May 22, 1946, at Loew's Criterion, New York City. Ad line: "Beery and O'Brien … Together for the First Time."

Statistics
MGM production number 619.
Running time, 110 minutes; black & white; Western.

Ratings
The Motion Picture Guide, ☆☆½
Leonard Maltin's Movie and Video Guide, ☆☆
Halliwell's Film Guide, ☆

Credits
Produced by Orville O. Dull; directed by S. Sylvan Simon; assistant director, Earl McAvoy; original story by D. A. Loxley; screenplay by William Lipman and Grant Garrett; musical direction by David Snell; orchestration by Wally Heglin; art direction by Cedric Gibbons and Paul Youngblood; set decoration by Edwin B. Willis and Jack Ahern; costume design by Irene; men's costumes by Valles; sound by Douglas Shearer; cinematography by Charles Edgar Shoenbaum; second cameraman, Irving Glassberg; film editing by Ben Lewis; special effects by Warren Newcombe; transparency projection shots, A. Arnold Gillespie.

Songs: "Climb Up the Ladder;" "Wait, Wait, Brother."

Cast
Wallace Beery (Zeb Bascomb), Margaret O'Brien (Emmy), Marjorie Main (Abbey Hanks), J. Carrol Naish (Bart Yancey), Frances Rafferty (Dora), Marshall Thompson (Jimmy Holden), Russell Simpson (Elijah Walker), Warner Anderson (Luther Mason), Donald Curtis (Annie Fremont), Connie Gilchrist (Annie Fremont), Sara Haden (Tillie Lovejoy), Renie Riano (Lucy Lovejoy), Wally Cassell (Curly), Jane Green (Hannah), Henry O'Neill (Governor Winton), Frank Darien (Elder Moab McCabe), Joseph Crehan (Governor Ames), Clyde Fillmore (Governor Clark), Arthur Space (Sheriff), Eddie Acuff (Corporal), Stanley Andrews (Colonel Cartright).

Margaret O'Brien and Wallace Beery in *Bad Bascomb* (1946, MGM.)

Synopsis

An adventure story about a gang of desperadoes terrorizing the post–Civil War West. Zeb Bascomb, the leader, attempts an unsuccessful bank holdup before he and his lieutenant are forced to seek aliases and sanctuary in a Mormon wagon train heading for Utah. During the trip he runs into the soulful endearments of little Emmy and her grandmother Abbey Hanks, which causes him to turn a deaf ear to his sidekick. In the course of the trip there are many opportunities for the occasional fights and shoot-outs and Bascomb saves the wagon train and surrenders to the law.

Behind the Scenes

The filming of *Bad Bascomb* was the first and only time that Margaret O'Brien worked on location during her MGM career. To reproduce the post–Civil War West, the cast and crew traveled to the rugged terrain of Jackson Hole, Wyoming. Margaret was thrilled to be off the back lot and to be on what was, to her, a big camping trip. "That was a really wild rugged town," she recalled. "You were out in the wilder-

Margaret O'Brien and Marjorie Main in *Bad Bascomb* (1946, MGM; author's collection).

ness. There were cowboys and western saloons and even bears would come up on our cabin porch at night and search for food."

Mosquitoes were also a big problem, which upset Marjorie Main, who played Margaret's grandmother in the film. To combat the nasty bugs, Main would wrap toilet paper around her arms between shots, much to the delight of young Margaret and the giggles of the cast and crew.

The studio paired their million-dollar moppet with Wallace Beery, who had several successes with youngsters in the past including his Academy Award–winning performance in *The Champ* (1931) opposite another child performer, Jackie Cooper. Remarkably, with all his accomplishments with children, he was not very fond of them, which fortunately did not show on the screen. "Wallace Beery was very hard to work with," Margaret recalled. "Thank goodness for the crew, because he did not like children at all."

Many times the cast and crew would come to Margaret's rescue whenever Beery decided to torture her. "He didn't like children," she recalled. "He was a tyrant. They had to put a wooden box between us so he couldn't turn me away from the camera." When that didn't work, he began pinching her. "He'd pinch me so I'd say the lines the way he wanted," she said.

Fortunately his behavior did not last long once Mrs. O'Brien saw what was happening and insisted something be done. Trying to be as diplomatic as possible, the director finally decided on using the blocks to keep Margaret out of arm's reach. After that, the actor continued his cruel treatment in other ways such as stealing her hot lunch. "We had just enough lunches for the cast and crew and he'd steal mine. But he had a marvelous way. He could look like he adored you."

Beery's meanness was not limited to his child costars. Margaret recalled that Beery's adopted daughter, who was about eleven at the time, worked on the film as an extra. One day she broke her glasses and Beery made her work extra hours to pay for them.

Margaret's experience with Marjorie Main was much more enjoyable. They knew each other from working on *Meet Me in St. Louis* and got along very well. Unlike their previous film, they actually had to live and eat together during *Bad Bascomb* and Margaret had the opportunity to witness Marjorie's little eccentricities. During the evening meal, Main would set a place for her dead husband and carry on a conversation with him as if he were there. "She was a lot of fun and she was very nice," Margaret recalled. "And I enjoyed riding in the covered wagon with her. It was pretty wild and woolly and rugged up there."

On her days off Mrs. O'Brien would take her daughter into town to the restaurant-saloon that had a slot machine, where Margaret would try her luck. One day, however, she decided to stay at the film site and got into a fist-fight with director Sylvan Simon's daughter, who was working as an extra. Members of the crew had to pull them apart and to this day Margaret does not remember what the fight was about, but does remember the spanking her mother gave her. Simon was a little more progressive and instead of a spanking, sent his daughter to a boarding school. "We became real good friends years later," Margaret said. "And she turned out to be one of the sweetest girls I ever met."

Margaret became fascinated with the Native Americans who were extras in the film. There was one particular little boy near her age whom she fell in love with. She was invited to spend several days with his family and they taught her their traditions and showed her how to ride horses. Margaret's fascination with American Indians began when she saw a screening of the film *Geronimo* (1939). She would periodically ask Louis B. Mayer to get it and run it for her in a screening room at the studio. Then she learned that the Hitching Post Theater on Hollywood Boulevard would run requests so she sent in a letter asking for *Geronimo*.

One day, to prove what she had learned, Margaret insisted on riding Wallace Beery's horse. Beery, of course, let her ride it knowing that the horse was not gentle. After a few steps, the horse took off across the canyons with Margaret holding on for dear life. Hearing Margaret's screams, everyone went into a panic and several Native American extras took off on their horses after her. They finally were able to catch up and rescue her, much to the relief of everyone on the set. "I never asked to ride Wallace Beery's horse again," Margaret said. The Apaches,

Margaret O'Brien joins in a taffy pull with Wallace Beery during filming of *Bad Bascomb* (1946, MGM).

however, were very impressed with Margaret's courage during the incident and made her an Indian princess, much to her delight.

The teaming of Margaret O'Brien and Wallace Beery was considered inevitable, although not entirely enjoyable for all concerned. *Bad Bascomb* was met with mixed reviews. The *New York Times* called it a "cheerful if somewhat lumbering and familiar Western,"[1] but all agreed that it was a film that children would love more than adults.

Reviews

"Little Miss O'Brien, a winner in the 1945 *Motion Picture Herald-Fame* exhibitors poll, is the perfect foil for Beery's portrayal of a rough, tough outlaw with a heart of gold."—*Motion Picture Herald*, February 9, 1946.

"The child who now shares top billing with him [Beery] has never ceased to amaze by her completely natural delivery."—*Hollywood Reporter*, May 28, 1946.

"He [Beery] has an apt sparring

Margaret O'Brien is made an honorary Indian princess during filming of *Bad Bascomb* (1946, MGM).

partner in little Miss O'Brien, who's no slouch even against such a scene-stealer as her costar."—*Variety*, February 6, 1946.

"Little Margaret O'Brien is as winsome as ever."—*Harrison's Reports*, February 9, 1946.

Additional Reviews: *Cue*, 05/25/46; *Hollywood Citizen-News*, 08/17/46; *New York Times*, 05/23/46; *Time*, 06/17/46.

Costar Comments

"Margaret's a great trouper. A wonderful little actress."—*Wallace Beery*[2]

Comments by Margaret O'Brien

"On *Bad Bascomb* I worked on location for the first time at Jackson Hole, Wyoming. We used many members of the Apache tribe as extras which was a wonderful experience for me. I came to admire Native Americans very much. I thought they were strong, wonderful riders and of course very handsome. I even developed a crush on a young Indian brave and spent several days with his family learning their traditions and legends."

THREE WISE FOOLS

A Metro-Goldwyn-Mayer Picture
1946

"They're the very next things to angels. They whisper good things in your ear at night when you're asleep, so you can't help but doing good things during the day."

> —Margaret O'Brien trying to convince Lionel Barrymore, Lewis Stone and Edward Arnold of the existence of Leprechauns in *Three Wise Fools*.

Opened on September 27, 1946, at the Capitol Theater, New York City.
Ad line: "You'll Cry and Laugh When You See Margaret O'Brien
Warm the Hearts of the 'Three Wise Fools.'"

Statistics
MGM production number 628.
Running time, 90 minutes; black & white; Comedy.

Ratings
The Motion Picture Guide, ☆☆
Leonard Maltin's Movie and Video Guide, ☆☆
Halliwell's Film Guide, 0

Credits
Produced by William H. Wright; directed by Edward Buzzell; assistant director, Marvin Stuart; screenplay by John McDermott and James O'Hanlon, based on the play *Three Wise Fools* by Austin Strong, as staged by Winchell Smith and presented by John Golden (Ottawa, 1919); musical score by Bro-nislau Kaper; art direction by Cedric Gibbons and Edward Imazu; set decoration by Edwin B. Willis and Hugh Hunt; make-up by Jack Dawn; costume supervision by Irene; costume design by Valles; sound by Douglas Shearer; cinematography by Harold Rosson; second cameraman, Robert Martin; film editing by Gene Ruggiero and Theron Warth.

Cast
Margaret O'Brien (Sheila O'Monahan), Lionel Barrymore (Dr. Richard Gaunght), Lewis Stone (Judge Thomas Trumbull), Edward Arnold (Theodore Findley), Thomas Mitchell (Terence Aloysius O'Davern), Ray Collins (Judge Watson), Jane Darwell (Sister Mary Bridgid), Charles Dingle (Paul Badger), Harry Davenport (The Ancient), Henry

Margaret O'Brien and Lionel Barrymore in *Three Wise Fools* (1946, MGM).

O'Neill (Horace Appleby), Cyd Charisse (Rena Fairchild), Warner Anderson (The O'Monahan), Billy Curtis (Dugan), Gary Gray (Willie the Squeak), Marissa O'Brien (Sister Veronica), Jerry Maren (Sir Boulder), Michael Kirby (Jimmy Trumbull), Tim Murdoch (Dick Gaunght), John Carlyle (Ted Findley), Henry Sylvester (Corby), Teddy Infuhr (Johnny, the Grunt), Charles Bates (Eddie Oakleaf), Bob Alden (O'Davern, as a Youth), George McDonald (Tumbleweed), Emmet Vogan (Bailiff), William Tannen (Prosecutor), Olin Howlin (Witness), Marjorie Davies (Secretary), Cameron Grant (Assistant), Hans Hopf (Pixie), John Sheehan (Murphy), Bud Harrison (Bailiff), Betsy Stoddard (Miss Emert), Lee Phelps (Policeman), Barbara Billingsley (Sister Mary Leonard), Ray Teal (Foreman), Robert Emmet O'Connor (Chief of Police), Ernie Adams (Man), Garry Owen (Man), Martin Ashe (Photographer), Nit Krebs (Bit Part), Mary Ellen St. Aubin (Bit Part).

Synopsis

Sheila O'Monahan arrives in America from Ireland in 1910 with her faithful servant, Terence Aloysius O'Davern, a good man though a bit fond of the bottle. She is searching for the three men who once courted her grandmother, whose beauty has kept these men together as they sought their fortune as a doctor, a judge and a banker. Little Sheila's unexpected arrival coincides with the gift of property these three men are making to a university to be used for the building of a Greek stadium. A search of the deed leads to the discovery that Sheila, not they, owns the land. To avoid embarrassment, they take the young girl into their home and attempt to talk her out of the deed. The only reason that she won't give it up is that she believes little people live in an old oak tree on the property. She will not let anything disturb or possibly hurt them. When everything else fails, they hire a troupe of midgets to impersonate the little people. But the deception backfires and she streaks off to a convent. Finally, they realize that they truly love Sheila and they do everything in their power to win her back. The doctor and judge finally chain themselves to the tree to prevent its destruction and the banker donates a million dollars so the property can be turned into a park. Sheila then realizes that the three old men do believe in the little people and she returns to live with them.

Behind the Scenes

Three Wise Fools was based on an Austin Strong play and was a remake of a 1923 Goldwyn film of the same name. This time around, Margaret played Sheila O'Monahan, a little Irish girl sent to America after her mother's death. The producers surrounded Margaret with a vast array of seasoned leading men including Lionel Barrymore, with whom she had worked in *Dr. Gillespie's Criminal Case*. Lewis Stone and Edward

Arnold filled the roles of the remaining two fools and were equally amazed at Margaret's abilities. Arnold was astounded at Margaret's knack for memorizing long speeches. "She rattles them off like a veteran," he said in awe.[1]

Margaret fell in love with her costars and immediately adopted them all as grandfathers. "The three older men were wonderful," Margaret recalled. "I loved working with Lionel Barrymore again, he was like my grandfather. And Lewis Stone was real gentle and sweet." Edward Arnold was a bit more fussy with his young costar. On occasion, if Margaret was daydreaming, he would look her in the eye and give her a stern warning. "Margaret, you're not listening," Arnold would snap. "Pay attention."

"Of course he was right," she admitted.

Margaret's Aunt Marissa had a small part as a nun along with Jane Darwell. "My aunt was under contract with MGM," she said. "She was sort of the look-alike for Lucille Bremer and Donna Reed. It was fun working with her."

Film veteran Thomas Mitchell played Margaret's servant and guardian and was a source of enjoyment for her. He always made sure she was having fun and made her wish she had a manservant of her own just like him.

The premise of the story of *Three Wise Fools* concerns little Sheila's belief that leprechauns inhabit an old tree that the three men want to destroy so they can build a Greek amphitheater and find favor with the community. For the part of the leprechauns, the studio hired actors who had previously worked at MGM as Munchkins in *The Wizard of Oz* (1939), including Jerry Maren, who was the presenter from the Lollypop Guild. *The Wizard of Oz* had always been a favorite of Margaret's and she was in awe of seeing the little men and truly believed they were real leprechauns. In all, twenty-three were in the film.

Housing presented a problem and only eighteen of them found rooms in a hotel at Seventh and Broadway in downtown Los Angeles. The remaining five stayed on the MGM lot in converted dressing rooms. Billy Curtis, who played the leprechaun named Dugan, was the spokesperson for the group. "We don't mind being small," Curtis said. "The only thing that is really tough is this matter of shaving for the men."

Hotel chairs would not fit through the bathroom door, so in order for the men to shave, they had to stand on each other's shoulders in order to see into the mirror, which was originally designed for a man of average height. "It's a none too steady perch," Curtis admitted. "Sure—we cut ourselves."[2]

Each morning as they left the hotel, onlookers would gaze in amusement as the hotel doorman hailed a taxi and eighteen little people would pile in for the trip to Culver City. Margaret was fascinated and was convinced that the small, doll-like people were far outside the realm of reality. During lunch, she would watch them march into the MGM commissary and devour full-sized meals in nothing flat. "I thought they lived on dew out of bluebells," she told her mother.[3]

When director Edward Buzzell discovered that a real-life lunar eclipse was expected to occur during their shooting schedule, he immediately worked it into the script. On the night of the event,

Buzzell assembled the cast and positioned a camera directly on the moon while another caught the action of Margaret watching the leprechauns exit the old oak tree.

Everything seemed perfect until Buzzell called "action," and a fog began to roll in just as the cameras began to roll. Fortunately, the next day when the rushes were viewed, they discovered that all the elements, including Margaret's wide-eyed expression, combined to make a perfect scene. "It was really scary," she told a friend. "Even the moon had to hide his eyes."[4]

Surprisingly, years later, the miracle of the lunar eclipse had lost its effect on the actress. "I don't know why it didn't make a bigger impression on me," she wondered. "I guess I was more busy playing with the Leprechauns." Unfortunately the footage never made it into the final print of the film.

Margaret spent a lot of time with Lionel Barrymore on the set of *Three Wise Fools*. She was fascinated with the Barrymore family, and the stories he would tell of his life in the theater. He also told her about a pin that belonged to his mother that had been worn by all the Drew women on opening nights. He called it the "crown jewels of the theater" and was looking for someone worthy to pass it on to. After working with Margaret in *Dr. Gillespie's Criminal Case*, Barrymore began to consider that she might be the girl for "Mum Mum's pin."

"I was certain sometime later when she did *Meet Me in St. Louis*," Barrymore wrote in his memoir, "and no one was happier than I when she won a special Academy Award for it."

When filming for *Three Wise Fools* was completed, everyone attended a wrap

Margaret O'Brien lectures Lionel Barrymore, Edward Arnold, Lewis Stone and Thomas Mitchell in *Three Wise Fools* (1946, MGM; author's collection).

party on the sound-stage. When the ice cream cake was cut, Margaret was of course given the first piece. Instead of eating it herself, she gave it to Barrymore. "Mr. Barrymore," she told him, "this is the first piece and it is for you because I love you." Barrymore was so touched by Margaret's unselfish gesture that he gave her his mother's pin right there. "She deserved it," he said, "with all the sentimental implications I attach to it."[5]

Critics were unanimous in their praise for *Three Wise Fools*. *Film Daily* wrote: "MGM is to be complimented on the filming of this property, and releasing it at a time when world conditions are so entangled and provoking, that its effect can do much toward arousing those human qualities, which each of us possess, to greater activity."[6]

Reviews

"If there was ever a child actress whose dramatic ability could parallel the finest of the adult Academy Award winners, Margaret O'Brien is rightfully entitled to that recognition. Her faultless expression, emotion, and delivery of lines in Irish brogue—in a part which requires the intelligence of a well-seasoned player—is astounding."—*Film Daily*, June 14, 1946.

"Miss O'Brien, who has thoroughly mastered all the juvenile attitudes intended to pulverize fond parents, puts them all to full use in this film and adds the prodigious accomplishment of speaking in a winsome Irish brogue."—*New York Times*, September 27, 1946.

"*Three Wise Fools* is a brilliant setting for the talents of that angelic genius, Margaret O'Brien."—*Motion Picture Herald*, June 15, 1946.

"Words often seem inadequate in trying to describe a talent as astounding as the one possessed by Margaret O'Brien. Again her performance is not something tricked by the deft intercutting of scenes. She reaches each of her climaxes in a master shot, building from the opening passages to a peak of magnificent emotion. There is no explaining how she does it, merely our privilege to admire the way of her accomplishments."—*Hollywood Reporter*, June 11, 1946.

"The astonishing and competent Margaret O'Brien walks away with the show in *Three Wise Fools*."—*Motion Picture Daily*, June 13, 1946.

Additional Reviews: *Box Office*, 06/15/46; *Brooklyn Eagle*, 09/27/46; *Daily Mirror*, 09/27/46; *Daily News*, 09/27/46; *The Exhibitor*, 06/24/46; *Film Bulletin*, 06/24/46; *Independent*, 06/21/46; *Journal American*, 09/27/46; *Los Angeles Herald-Tribune*, 09/27/46; *Los Angeles Times*, 10/02/46; *Motion Picture Daily*, 06/13/46; *New York Post*, 09/27/46; *New York Sun*, 09/27/46; *PM*, 09/27/46; *Time*, 09/23/46; *Variety*, 06/12/46; *World Telegram*, 09/26/46.

Costar Comments

"I soon realized that Margaret could perform like no youngster I or anybody else had ever seen. When she takes over, you might as well imagine yourself a design on the wallpaper. You could stand on your head and no audience would notice you."—*Lionel Barrymore*[7]

"I thought the script writers were slightly touched in the head to give her such long speeches. But apparently I was the one who was touched. She rattles them off like a veteran. And I've never come in contact with such a memory or such a gift for just the right interpretation of lines."—*Edward Arnold*[8]

"Yes, I thought Mickey Rooney was pretty wonderful—and he was and is. And I've never seen an actor or an actress who could hold his own with that mighty mite. But I'd love to see the Mick and Margaret get together. That would be worth watching."—*Lewis Stone*[9]

Comments by Margaret O'Brien

"*Three Wise Fools* was a great film because I loved playing the little girl with the Irish accent. I also loved working with the Leprechauns—a lot of them were from *The Wizard of Oz*, which was one of my favorite movies. I really felt they were real and could fix everything."

THE UNFINISHED DANCE

A Metro-Goldwyn-Mayer Picture
1947

"Suppose the lights went out, and the theater was dark like it was the other day. How the people in the theater would laugh at her. They'd walk out on her."

—Margaret O'Brien scheming with Elinor Donahue in *The Unfinished Dance.*

Opened on October 30, 1947, at the Capitol Theater, New York City.
Ad line: "Her Greatest Role in Her Screen Career ...
Margaret O'Brien in the Unforgettable *The Unfinished Dance.*"

Statistics

MGM production number 802.
Running time, 101 minutes; Technicolor; Musical Drama.

Ratings

The Motion Picture Guide, ☆☆
Leonard Maltin's Movie and Video Guide, ☆☆½
Halliwell's Film Guide, 0

Credits

Produced by Joe Pasternak; directed by Henry Koster; screenplay by Myles Connolly based on the story "La Mort du Cygne" by Paul Morand; musical direction by Herbert Stothart; art direction by Cedric Gibbons and Daniel B. Cathcart; set decorations by Edwin B. Willis and Hugh Hunt; choreography by David Lichine; costume design by Irene and Helen Rose; sound by Douglas Shearer; cinematography by Robert Surtees; film editing by Douglas Biggs.

Songs: "Watch Song" by Lothar Perl and Herbert Stothart; "Minor Melody" by Ray Jacobs and Danny Thomas and sung by Danny Thomas; "I Went Merrily Merrily on My Way" by Irving Kahal and Sammy Fain; "Holiday for Strings" by David Rose; "Liebesfreud" by Kreisler; "Symphony No. Two" by Beethoven; "Swan Lake" by Tchaikovsky; parts of "The Bartered Bride" by Smetana.

Cast

Margaret O'Brien ("Meg" Merlin), Cyd Charisse (Mlle. Ariane Bouchet), Karin Booth (La Darina), Danny Thomas (Mr. Paneros), Esther Dale (Olga), Thurston Hall (Mr. Ronsell), Harry Hayden (Murphy), Mary Eleanor Donahue (Josie), Connie Cornell (Phyllis), Ruth Brady (Miss Merlin), Charles Bradstreet (Fred Carleton), Connie

Margaret O'Brien gets ready to pull the switch in *The Unfinished Dance* (1947, MGM).

Gilchrist (Mrs. Devore), Wilson Wood (Photographer), Ann Codee (Mme. Borodin), Gregory Gaye (Jacques Lacoste), Dorothy Neumann (Betsy), Jimmy Dietrich (Richard Ping), Tim Ryan (Moose), George Zoritch (Dancing Partner), Jane Loofbourrow (Classic Pianist), Paul Newland (Electrician), Norman Leavitt (Joe), Sid D'Albrook (Gallagher), Edward Kilroy (Old Doorman), Tom Dillon (Detective Sergeant), Robert Emmet O'Connor (Mr. Brown), Dutch Schlickenmeyer (Chauffeur), Rose Langdon (Old Wardrobe Woman), Celia Travers (Pretty Nurse), Ann O'Neal (Head Nurse), Addison Richards (Doctor), Nella Walker (Miss Hendricks), Barbara Billinsley (Miss Hogan), Rhea Mitchell (Seamstress), Lola Deem, Pat Emery, Alice Wallace (Fashion Models), Marie Windsor (Saleslady), Freda Stoel (Audition Accompanist), Max Linder (Announcer), John Hamilton (Doctor), Eloise Hardt (Asst. Ballet Instructor), Phil Dunham (Watchman), Jessie Grayson (Maid), Edward Keane (Customer), Polly Bailey (Wardrobe Woman), Dick Earle (Dignified Man), Paul Kruger (Cop), Mary Stuart (Girl at Opera), Margaret Bert (Hairdresser).

Synopsis

Young Meg Merlin, who is devoted to the star of the big ballet, plots to ruin the routine of a visiting dancer whom she regards as a rival of her favorite. She plans to turn off the lights at the point that the dancer's ballet "Swan Lake" is at its height. Instead Meg pulls the wrong switch, and a trap door opens on stage causing the dancer to fall and seriously injure herself. Meg is sorry for what she has done, but is afraid to tell anyone.

Behind the Scenes

Dance had always been an important part of Margaret's life. Gladys O'Brien had at one time been a Spanish dancer for Eduardo Cansino, father of actress Rita Hayworth. Gladys even taught young Rita several dance steps herself. Years later Margaret met Rita during the filming of *Jane Eyre* at a pool party hosted by Orson Welles, who was Rita's husband at the time.

Margaret's aunt, Marissa Flores, was also a dancer and performed for many years with Xavier Cugat during his shows at the Waldorf-Astoria in New York City. So together, both women were a big influence on Margaret, who also loved to dance and quickly learned the flamenco at a very early age.

Margaret was thrilled to have a chance to do the ballet in *The Unfinished Dance*. At first the studio was going to use a double for the ballet sequences, but when they saw how well Margaret could dance, they decided against it. She had such a natural ability for dancing that she learned most of her steps within minutes from choreographer David Lichine.

Lichine, who was a protégé and later a partner of the great ballerina Anna Pavlova, created the choreography for the picture. For eight years he had toured the world with the famous Ballet Russe and gave command performances before the king and queen of England, the king of Denmark and other notable royals.

Lichine was so impressed with Margaret's dancing that he asked her to join the Ballet Russe. However, Mrs. O'Brien knew how difficult the dancer's life was and politely refused. "Even though my mother said no," Margaret recalled, "I was really into the ballet. I carried my toe shoes everywhere because there was a lot of competition going on among the girls on set. I thought the ballet dancers were beautiful, but their life was just too hard."

The statistics on *The Unfinished Dance* were remarkable in themselves. It was the first 100 percent all–American ballet comprising 110 dancers from 46 states. And with 40 child ballerinas, along with 40 mothers and the staff of schoolteachers that were needed, director Henry Koster had his hands more than full.

Unfortunately Koster did not hold this film in very high regard. *The Unfinished Dance* was his last film for MGM (another Margaret O'Brien film, *Music for Millions*, was Koster's first film for the studio). Near the end of his life when an interviewer questioned him about *The Unfinished Dance*, his response was, "Don't look at it."[1]

One day Margaret twisted her ankle during one of the dance scenes and Koster told her to go home for two days and recover. Margaret did as she was told but secretly felt that the director was devising some plot against her. After several hours in bed, a distraught Margaret called producer Joe Pasternak. "Oh Mr. Pasternak," she sobbed, "they're trying to take my picture away from me. Why can't I come in and do my sitting down scenes?"[2] And of course, Pasternak agreed with his young starlet and made the necessary arrangements.

This picture also gave Margaret the chance to wear her hair in curls instead of in pigtails. Also the make-up department allowed her to wear lipstick and rouge on her face for the first time. "Afterward I hated to take it off because I felt so plain without it," she recalled.

Cyd Charisse, herself a veteran of the Ballet Russe, appeared as Margaret's idol in the film. After doing her previous film for MGM called *Fiesta* (1947), she received thousands of letters from fans hailing her as a great Mexican actress. Even though she was an all–American girl from Amarillo, Texas, she was authentic enough in the part to convince people otherwise. During the eight months of rehearsals and shooting for *The Unfinished Dance*, she estimated that she was on her toes at least 600 hours during which she wore out more than 100 pairs of dancing slippers.

"I really admired Cyd Charisse," Margaret said. "I thought she was gorgeous and such a talented dancer. They had these fabulous dresses for her besides the ones she wore for the ballet scenes. She was so beautiful that I wanted to wear all the clothes she wore. I would be in awe of the costumes and declared that I was going to have them copied when I grew up. And some of them I did."

Elinor Donahue was cast in this film as Margaret's best friend. Donahue had always been a huge fan of Margaret's and was thrilled to be working in a film with her. On their first day at the studio, Elinor and her mother were in the commissary when Margaret and Mrs. O'Brien walked in. "Look Mom, there she is," whispered Elinor, who began staring. "I was like a deer caught in headlights. You know how it is when you see a big movie star." Margaret noticed her staring at her and went over to their table and said, "Hi. I hear you're cast as my friend. I'm looking forward to working with you."[3]

The Unfinished Dance was also the film debut of comedian Danny Thomas, who had made it big on the nightclub

Margaret O'Brien and Danny Thomas in *The Unfinished Dance* (1947, MGM).

Cyd Charisse, Margaret O'Brien and Karin Booth in *The Unfinished Dance* (1947, MGM).

circuit. He accepted the part in the film because of his mother. It seems she had never seen him perform his nightclub routine and did not know how talented Danny was. "If you're so good," she continuously asked her son, "why aren't you in pictures?"

When producer Joe Pasternak saw Thomas perform at Chez Paree, he offered him the role of Paneros. "I've got to have that face in my next picture," Pasternak exclaimed. In the film, Pasternak included a song that Thomas wrote called "Minor Melody." "I sang it to a distraught Margaret O'Brien on a rooftop, while playing a concertina," Thomas later wrote in his memoirs.[4] During the filming, Thomas would often bring his daughter Marlo on the set.

"This was Danny Thomas' first film, and he was wonderful," Margaret said. "He was great with kids, and of course he had kids of his own. His daughter Marlo was my age and many times she would be on the set with him. Later Marlo and I graduated our first communion and confirmation together. So we really knew each other as we were growing up."

The *Unfinished Dance* was one of Margaret's favorite roles because of the dancing. Even though she received much praise for her skill in the film, she was also proud of the fact that she was promoted to the fifth grade an entire year ahead of schedule, and grew a whole two inches during filming. When asked by a reporter what she wanted to be when she grew up, she said, "Before playing this picture, I had planned to be a dog trainer when I grew up. But dancing is a lot of fun, and now I think maybe I'll be a ballet dancer."[5] Of course Margaret also wanted to be a nun after seeing *The Song of Bernadette* (1944), so it seems her ambitions changed with whatever was popular at the time, just like any child.

Upon its release, many critics were impressed with *The Unfinished Dance* and the *Los Angeles Times* wrote, "This picture is an eyeful, without the slightest question."[6]

Reviews

"Now the amazing Margaret O'Brien adds ballet to her other towering screen achievements."—*Hollywood Reporter*, July 29, 1947.

"Margaret O'Brien is made to be something of a delinquent type, which is a new development for her."—*Los Angeles Times*, September 20, 1947.

"Producer Joe Pasternak and director Henry Koster have come very close to fashioning a work of art in *The Unfinished Dance*. Very likely it may be a popular, modern work too. That Miss O'Brien applied herself to learning intricacies of ballet steps is very evident in her performance which easily matches her conviction in dramatic parts."—*Film Daily*, July 30, 1947.

"Removed as the ballet is from the average person, Miss O'Brien's drawing power, the beauty of the two ballerinas, the music and the sets should nevertheless make this effective box-office fare."—*Motion Picture Daily*, July 30, 1947.

Additional Reviews: *Cue*, 11/01/47; *Daily News*, 09/19/47; *Esquire*, 09/47; *Hollywood Citizen-News*, 09/20/47; *Los Angeles Herald-Express*, 09/20/47; *The New Yorker*, 11/08/47; *New York Times*, 10/31/47, p. 29; *Time*, 11/17/47; *Variety*, 07/30/47.

Costar Comments

"Margaret was marvelous! Just marvelous! I know a lot of people don't mean marvelous when they say it, but I really mean it. She was my favorite actress."—*Elinor Donahue*[7]

"Margaret O'Brien was a born actress, and very talented, technically so experienced that she couldn't be compared with Deanna [Durbin]."—*Henry Koster*[8]

Comments by Margaret O'Brien

"I liked the role of Meg Merlin in *The Unfinished Dance* because there was a lot of dancing in it and there were a great many beautiful costumes. I never did any dancing in a picture before. My mother and my aunt used to take me to see the Ballet Russe, and I enjoyed that. But I enjoyed dancing far more after I had taken ballet lessons and had a chance to dance myself."

TENTH AVENUE ANGEL

A Metro-Goldwyn-Mayer Picture
1948

"I don't know who to believe. I don't know what to believe.
Everybody lies to me. Even the ones I love the most."
                                    —Margaret O'Brien to Phyllis
                                    Thaxter in *Tenth Avenue
                                    Angel.*

Opened on January 7, 1948, in wide release.
Ad line: "This Will Tug at Your Heart Strings, and Never Let Go."

Statistics
MGM production number 816.
Running time, 74 minutes; black &
    white; Drama.

Ratings
The Motion Picture Guide, ☆
Leonard Maltin's Movie and Video Guide,
    Bomb
Halliwell's Film Guide, 0

Credits
Produced by Ralph Wheelwright;
directed by Roy Rowland; screenplay by
Harry Ruskin and Eleanore Griffin,
based on a story by Angna Enters and a
radio sketch titled "Miracle at Midnight" by Craig Rice; musical direction
by Rudolph G. Kopp; special effects
by Warren Newcombe; art direction
by Cedric Gibbons and Wade Rubottom; set decoration by Edwin B. Willis
and Mildred Griffiths; costume design by Irene; sound by Douglas
Shearer; photographed by Robert

Surtees; edited by Ralph E. Winter and
George Boemler.

Cast
Margaret O'Brien (Flavia Mills),
Angela Lansbury (Susan Bratten),
George Murphy (Steve Abbutt), Phyllis Thaxter (Helen Mills), Warner Anderson (Joseph Mills), Rhys Williams
(Blind Mac), Barry Nelson (Al Parker),
Connie Gilchrist (Mrs. Murphy), Tom
Trout (Daniel Oliver Madson), Marissa
O'Brien (Jane Lighton), Dickie Tyler
(Jimmy Madson), Henry Blair (Rad
Arley), Walter Soderling (Mr. Cassetto), Cameron Mitchell (Ted Foley),
Charles Cane (McKay, Parole Officer),
Richard Lane (Street Vendor), Mary
Eleanor Donahue (Cynthia), Cy Kendall (Higgins), Paul Burns (Pop), Robert
Emmet O'Connor (O'Callan), Della
Clark (Mrs. Klein), Charles Bates
(Child), Garry Gray (Child), Nolan
Leary (Fruit Vendor), Tom Dillon
(Doctor), Charles Wagenheim (Fussy

Margaret O'Brien as Flavia Mills in *Tenth Avenue Angel* (1948, MGM).

Man), Larry Wheat (Mr. Challupski), Andy Pomeroy (Bat), Ben Mosselle (Smile), Lee Phelps (Police Officer), Ray Teal (Cowboy), George Magrill (Brakeman), Mike P. Donovan (Engineer), Lane Chandler (Doorman), Jane Greer (Doorman), Ruth Cherrington (Overdressed Woman), George Travell (Taxi Driver), Barbara Billingsley (Salesgirl), Margaret Bert (Woman at License Bureau), Monte M. Singer (Fat Man), Teddy Infuhr (Bit Boy), Henry Sylvester, John W. Dillon, Howard Mitchell, Heine Conklin (Aldermen),

Jesse Arnold (Woman at Block Party), Bruce Fernald (Police Officer), Edna May Wonacott (Violinist), Jon Gilbreath (Policeman).

Synopsis

Flavia Mills is a young girl brought up on New York's West Side during the Depression. She is especially fascinated by Tenth Avenue and calls it "her" street. Her attention is centered on her parents and creating a love affair between her Aunt Susan and a young man named Steve who was just paroled from prison. Steve was implicated in a bank robbery but was not directly involved. Because he refused to testify against the true thieves, he was put in jail for eighteen months. Once at home, Steve is disillusioned when he must take a job washing taxi cabs instead of driving them. Through a misunderstanding, Flavia is accused of stealing money, and she loses faith in her loved ones. Soon, her mother is told she is pregnant, and must take it easy. On Christmas Eve, she tells Flavia that all the cows bow to receive a blessing from Jesus, so when her mother falls, complications set in and Flavia attempts to find a cow. She meets Steve at the stockyard and he takes her through a cattle car. There she sees a cow kneel as the church bells strike midnight. Flavia sees this miracle and knows that she will receive the blessing of Jesus. Once she returns home, she sees her mother is well and that she has a new little brother. Flavia's faith returns, Steve and Susan are reunited and Tenth Avenue becomes the most beautiful street in the world again.

Behind the Scenes

Tenth Avenue Angel was another screenplay written especially for Margaret O'Brien. It was based on a story by Angna Enters who was a famous painter, sculptress, actress and writer. The theme of the script was the old axiom, "Beauty is in the eye of the beholder."

Margaret had just finished *Three Wise Fools* when she was read the script for *Tenth Avenue Angel*; however she was a little bewildered. "But where is Tenth Avenue?" she asked her mother. "I've seen Fifth Avenue, and the Statue of Liberty and Grant's Tomb and the Empire State Building, but I must have missed Tenth Avenue. I must see it to study for the role."[1]

Because Margaret was so enthusiastic about the part, Mrs. O'Brien took Margaret to New York to visit Tenth Avenue. While there, she met with Lillian Burns, her dramatic coach, and spent several days sightseeing and talking to residents on the street. She even visited a pawn shop and bought the one roller skate that she uses in the film.

When she returned to Culver City, she found that the studio had dressed their "New York Street" on the back lot to resemble Tenth Avenue. MGM's "New York Street" had been on the back lot for many years and was used any time a New York location was needed in a film. Old timers called it "Lucky Street" because many big stars worked on it in films before they made it to stardom.

Judy Garland ran through the street in her first film, *Every Sunday* with Deana Durbin. In 1935, Mickey Rooney played marbles on the sidewalk in *Hide Out*, and Van Johnson drove a car down it in *The War Against Mrs. Hadley*, one of his first films.

Now that Margaret was thoroughly indoctrinated to "Lucky Street," she began filming on March 11, 1946. Her

Angela Lansbury, Margaret O'Brien and George Murphy in *Tenth Avenue Angel* (1948, MGM).

costars were just as fascinating to her as the old back lot street. The cast included George Murphy in a non-dancing role and Phyllis Thaxter—television's Lois Lane—wife of future MGM president James Aubrey.

Another costar was Angela Lansbury, who was only in the second year of a career that is still going strong today. By this time, Lansbury had already been nominated for two Academy Awards for *Gaslight* (1944) and *The Picture of Dorian Gray* (1945). "Angela was very nice," Margaret recalled. "I remember I was always envious of her because she got to appear in *National Velvet* which was one of my favorite films."

Angela Lansbury's mother was the famous British stage and screen star Moyna MacGill. Shortly before production began, Miss MacGill signed a long-term contract with MGM. The year before she had won praise for her role with Judy Garland in *The Clock*. Both mother and daughter were thrilled when they discovered that they were cast to play a scene together in *Tenth Avenue Angel*.

As was usual in a Margaret O'Brien film, crying was part of the script in *Tenth Avenue Angel*. Fortunately for her it was easy to do, so she did not mind doing it. "I could cry easily," Margaret recalled. "A lot of people asked how they got me to cry. A story went around during the making of *Meet Me in St. Louis*, that Vincente Minnelli told me my dog had died, but that just wasn't true. Vincente told that story in his book, but it never happened. Besides, my mother would have never let them tell me my dog had died. She knew how much I loved him."

At the studio, Margaret and June Allyson were called the "Town-Criers of MGM." Every time Margaret had a hard time crying, her mother would tell her that she was sure that June would be able to do it with no problem. "Maybe we need the make-up man to put the false tears on," Mrs. O'Brien would tell her.[2]

To Margaret that meant that she wasn't as good as June, so before long the tears would flow. However, this unique ability could not be put to good use to get her way at home, since her mother always knew when she was faking it.

After crying in so many films, some critics of *Tenth Avenue Angel* felt that Margaret needed a change. *Variety* said, "as a weeper, film fulfills all aims, but the young actress' suffering is beginning to wear."[3]

Unfortunately, problems arose during the filming including retakes and cutting. The film was not released until eighteen months after it began—and after the release of Margaret's next film, *The Unfinished Dance*. "They seemed to be having problems with that movie," recalled costar Elinor Donahue. "It seemed that it was just not gelling."

In fact, since Margaret and Elinor had such good chemistry in *The Unfinished Dance*, the screenwriters wrote a new scene for them in this film. "To be honest it didn't make any sense," Donahue recalled. "But I loved working with Margaret again."

In one scene they had to eat shaved-ice cones, and character actor Billy House kept blowing his lines. Because of the retakes Margaret and Elinor had to eat lots of shaved-ice cones, which was fine with them. "Poor Billy was at the end of his career," said Donahue. "Quite heavy, the poor man had a sunstroke. He was replaced by Richard Lane who was like a surrogate father to me. He was wonderful in the scene."[4]

Reviews were mixed for *Tenth Avenue Angel*. Many critics felt that everyone was miscast, but Margaret still fared quite well. One critic declared that the film's success "will be decided by Margaret O'Brien's draw in the family and neighborhood houses."[5]

Reviews

"Miss O'Brien pulls all the stops in her display of oratory and tears for *Tenth Avenue Angel*."—*Daily News*, March 17, 1948.

"Margaret O'Brien, on hand for virtually every scene of the picture, works with the zeal of a trouper to make her characterization believable."—*Hollywood Reporter*, January 13, 1948.

"It is a pretty heavy burden to give Miss O'Brien, but she shoulders it admirably. Others in the cast just go along."—*Motion Picture Daily*, January 13, 1948.

"The film is, for the most part, a showcase for the talents of O'Brien, and the youngster makes the most of her opportunities."—*The Exhibitor*, January 21, 1948.

Additional Reviews: *Variety*, 01/21/48.

Costar Comments

"This movie was filmed in 1946, then held up for two years before it was

Margaret O'Brien in *Tenth Avenue Angel* (1948, MGM).

released which probably tells you every-thing you need to know about it. I do however, have fond memories of Margaret. When I started at MGM, there was still gas rationing due to World War II. So I rode to work every-day on the bus with Margaret and her mother."—*Angela Lansbury*[6]

"Margaret O'Brien was by far, the greatest child actress of all time—bar none! Nobody could touch her. The ability she has is tremendous. I don't think that MGM knew what an amazing talent she really was."—*George Murphy*[7]

Comments by Margaret O'Brien

"*Tenth Avenue Angel* was a great movie for me to work on because I got to roller skate again. It was not my favorite script, but it was a lot of fun working with George Murphy and Angela Lansbury."

BIG CITY

A Metro-Goldwyn-Mayer Picture
1948

"Send me away. It's the only thing to do."
—Margaret O'Brien telling
Edward Arnold how to
solve the controversy with
her three fathers in *Big City*.

Opened May 15, 1948, at Lowe's Sheridan, New York City.
Ad line: "If You Want to See a Picture to Buoy Your Spirits and Provoke Laughs by the Dozen, Don't Miss 'Big City.'"

Statistics
MGM production number 827.
Running time, 103 minutes; black & white; Drama.

Ratings
The Motion Picture Guide, ☆☆½
Leonard Maltin's Movie and Video Guide, ☆☆½
Halliwell's Film Guide, 0

Credits
Produced by Joe Pasternak; directed by Norman Taurog; screenplay by Whitfield Cook and Anne Norrison Chapin, with additional dialogue by Aben Kandel, based on a story by Mik-lós László as adapted by Nanette Kut-ner; musical direction by Georgie Stoll; orchestral arrangement by Leo Arnaud; choreography by Stanley Donen; art

direction by Cedric Gibbons and Preston Ames; set decoration by Edwin B. Willis and Alfred E. Spencer; costume design by Helen Rose; hair styles designed by Sydney Guilaroff; make-up created by Jack Dawn; sound by Douglas Shearer; photographed by Robert Surtees; edited by Gene Ruggiero; sound specialties by the Page Cavanaugh Trio.

Songs: "I'm Gonna See a Lot of You" by Al Spielman and Janice Torre; "Shoo Shoo Baby" by Phil Moore; "Ok'l Baby Dok'l" by Sidney Miller and Inez James; "Yippee-O, Yippee-Ay" by Jerry Seelen; "Kol Nidre" and "Traumerei" by Schumann; "Kerry Dance" by Malloy; "God Bless America," "What'll I Do" by Irving Berlin; "Don't Blame Me" by Jimmy McHugh and Dorothy Fields.

Cast

Margaret O'Brien (Midge), Robert Preston (Rev. Phillip Y. Andrews), Danny Thomas (Cantor David Irwin Feldman), George Murphy (Patrick O'Donnell), Karin Booth (Florence Bartlett), Edward Arnold (Judge Martin O. Abercrombie), Jackie "Butch" Jenkins (Lewis Keller), Betty Garrett ("Shoo-Shoo" Grady), Lotte Lehmann ("Mama" Feldman), Connie Gilchrist (Martha), Page Cavanaugh, Al Viola, Lloyd Pratt (Trio), Marles Noie (Little Girl), Peter Roman (Stooge), Robert Emmett Keane (Man Bit), Brick Sullivan, Jack Worth (Cops), Hank Mann, Heine Conklin (Drunks), Ben Moselle, Bobby Barber, Sailor Vincent, Clarence Hennecke (Fighters), Charles Sullivan (Brawler), Stanley Blystone (Bartender), David Leonard (Rudy), Lottie Stein (Rudy's Wife), Arthur Walsh (Jitterbug Boy), Joy Ames (Jitterbug Girl), George Davis (Florist), Skeets Noyes (Cleaning Man), Patricia Vaniver (Bride), Maynard Holmes (Groom), Wilson Wood (Best Man), Doris Kemper (Mrs. Crouse), Jerry Michelson, David Bair (Boys' Voices), Frank Mayo, Colin Kenny (Lawyers), Sherry Hall (Court Clerk), Irene Seidner (Woman Guardian), Donald Gordon (Bit Boy), George Calliga (Rabbi).

Synopsis

Story of a foundling who is adopted by a Protestant minister, a Jewish cantor and an Irish Catholic cop. The child, whom they name Midge, grows up in the Jewish home with many years of multi-parental bliss until a misunderstanding arises when the cop marries and threatens to break up the friendship by providing the young girl with a mother's care. Only through the wisdom of a judge and young Midge are the hurdles overtaken, but not before many tears and much romantic confusion.

Behind the Scenes

"This Picture is dedicated to people who like people," is how the film *Big City* opens. It is the story of three very unlikely men who find an abandoned baby and decide to raise her together. The story stressed tolerance at a time in history when it was most needed.

In the film, Margaret was rejoined with some very familiar faces from her past films. Danny Thomas and Karin Booth both appeared in *The Unfinished Dance*; Edward Arnold was one of the *Three Wise Fools*; Butch Jenkins was her cousin and playmate in *Our Vines Have Tender Grapes* and George Murphy was in *Tenth Avenue Angel*. Robert Preston was cast as the Protestant

Margaret O'Brien dances with Betty Garrett in *Big City* (1948, MGM).

Margaret O'Brien as Midge in *Big City* (1948, MGM).

minister and newcomers Betty Garrett and Lotte Lehmann each made their film debuts.

"Even though I enjoyed working with such a wonderful cast, *Big City* did not leave too much of an impression on me," Margaret recalled. "I did enjoy per-

forming with Betty Garrett who was very talented. I liked the way she sang and danced."

Margaret imitated one of Betty Garrett's songs in a scene, which thrilled her. In her biography, Garrett recalled that experience: "I sang one of the

Margaret O'Brien joins Karin Booth, Lotte Lehmann, Robert Preston, Danny Thomas and George Murphy in *Big City* (1948, MGM).

world's truly silly songs in the picture, 'Ok'l Baby Dok'l.' Later in the movie, Margaret O'Brien sang it, too, and I had to laugh when I saw she had hammed it up more than I did."[1]

Margaret did sing, but her voice was dubbed by newcomer Marni Nixon, who would later dub Natalie Wood's voice in *West Side Story* (1961). "The studio never let me sing because they didn't think my singing voice was that good," Margaret said.

Someone who did not need dubbing

was opera singer Lotte Lehmann, who played Margaret's grandmother. Lehmann was an accomplished singer who sang with the Metropolitan Opera. "Miss Lehmann was a wonderful opera singer and was very, very famous," Margaret said. "She wasn't really an actress and didn't do many movies so it was a great honor to work with her."

There was one incident that stood out to Margaret, but it occurred after *Big City* had completed filming. Six months after the film wrapped, they found something wrong with some of the footage, so they recalled Margaret and Butch Jenkins to refilm them. What no one thought about was how much children that age grow in six months. "The cameraman, Robert Surtees, took one look at us and almost fainted," Margaret recalled. "What happened was that Butch had his teeth fixed and we both had grown. He didn't know how he was going to match us."

Big City was met with mixed reviews. *The Motion Picture Guide* wrote, "Good production values, charming musical numbers, and standout performances by the principals keep this somewhat hokey material from being too maudlin."[2]

Reviews

"Margaret O'Brien troupes with her usual vigor, carving an appealing characterization."—*Hollywood Reporter*, March 23, 1948.

"The entire cast performs very well, with Margaret O'Brien, in the pivotal role, given ample opportunity to display her versatile talents."—*Harrison's Reports*, March 27, 1948.

"Little Margaret O'Brien is excellent and unaffected."—*Los Angeles Times*, undated.

"Little Miss O'Brien, who is growing apace and whose precocity has been noted before, is not only properly dewy-eyed but manages to maintain a running feud with her freckled sidekick, Butch Jenkins, and also do a traditional chant in a synagogue and an imitation of a torrid cafe songstress."—*New York Times*, May 21, 1948.

Additional Reviews: *Daily News*, 07/10/48; *Film Daily*, 03/29/48, p. 7; *Motion Picture Herald Product Digest*, 04/03/48; *Newsweek*, 05/31/48, p. 72; *Variety*, 03/24/48, p. 8.

Costar Comments

"Margaret O'Brien was the sweet little girl with the big, big talent. All of us at MGM admired her."—*Betty Garrett*[3]

"Margaret was an actress, born to the craft. Was she as happy as the poodles in the dog act? Did she prefer play-acting before the camera rather than among the dolls and toys of her own room? I can't answer that of course. By the way, little Miss O'Brien was a jewel, an angel."—*Joe Pasternak*[4]

Comments by Margaret O'Brien

"*Big City* was great because I got to work with Danny again and with George Murphy, who was wonderful to me. Although it was pleasant to work on, it wasn't as memorable to me as some of my other films."

LITTLE WOMEN

A Metro-Goldwyn-Mayer Picture
1949

"I'm not afraid anymore Jo. I've learned that I won't lose you. That nothing can really part us, though it seems to. Now we'll always be a family, even though one of us is gone. But Jo, I think that I will be homesick for you, even in heaven."

—Margaret O'Brien telling June Allyson that she is aware that her sickness is incurable in *Little Women*.

Opened on March 10, 1949, at Radio City Music Hall, New York City. Ad line: "A Book That Has Been Read and Loved by Millions Returns Triumphantly to the Screen in Gorgeous Technicolor."

Statistics
MGM production number 922.
Running time, 122 minutes; Technicolor; Drama.

Ratings
The Motion Picture Guide, ☆☆½
Leonard Maltin's Movie and Video Guide, ☆☆½
Halliwell's Film Guide, ☆

Credits
Produced by Mervyn LeRoy; directed by Mervyn LeRoy; screenplay by Andrew Solt, Sarah Y. Mason and Victor Heerman, based on the novel *Little Women* by Louisa May Alcott (Boston: Little, Brown, 1912); musical direction by Max Steiner and Adolph Deutsch; special effects by Warren Newcombe; art direction by Cedric Gibbons and Paul Groesse; set decoration by Edwin B. Willis and Jack D. Moore; make-up by Jack Dawn; costume design by Walter Plunkett; hairstyles by Sydney Guilaroff; sound by Douglas Shearer; color direction by Natalie Kalmus and Henri Jaffa; cinematography by Robert Planck and Charles Schoenbaum; film editing by Ralph E. Winters.

Song: "At Christmas Time" by Alberto Columbo.

Cast
June Allyson (Jo), Peter Lawford (Laurie), Margaret O'Brien (Beth), Elizabeth Taylor (Amy), Janet Leigh (Meg), Rossano Brazzi (Professor Bhaer), Mary Astor (Marmee March),

Lucille Watson (Aunt March), Sir C. Aubrey Smith (Mr. Lawrence), Elizabeth Patterson (Hannah), Leon Ames (Mr. March), Harry Davenport (Dr. Barnes), Richard Wyler (John Brooke), Connie Gilchrist (Mrs. Kirke), Ellen Corby (Sophie), Will Wright (Mr. Grace, the Storekeeper), Harlan Briggs (Old Crony) and Frank Darian (Old Crony), Lisa Golm (Mrs. Hummel), Scott Hungenbert, Stewart Torres, Maria Torres, Patty Henry, Melinda Plowman (Children), Norman Rainey (Servant), Marci Booth (First Girl), June Hedin (Second Girl), Gloria Moore (Third Girl), Marylyn Thorpe (Fourth Girl), Dorothy Abbott (Girl), Rosalie Calvert (Girl), Arthur Walsh (Young Man), Eloise Hardt (Sally Gardiner), Isabel Randolph (Mrs. Gardiner), Olin Howlin (Schoolteacher), Diane Nance (Kitty), Clara Jane Karnback (Tina), Ralph Peters (Hackman).

Synopsis

During the Civil War, the four March sisters, Jo, Meg, Amy and Beth, stay with their mother while their father is away. The four girls are busy lending their support to the war by helping those in the community who are in need. Jo, the eldest, is an aspiring writer who moves to New York when her father returns from the war. While there, she meets a German professor who makes a fanciful impression on her. Meg finds love, marries and gives birth to twins. Amy marries Laurie, who previously dated Jo, and Beth, who has been sickly her entire life, eventually dies from scarlet fever.

Behind the Scenes

"Good pictures are always difficult to make," Mervyn LeRoy once said.[1] He should know because he produced or directed several including *Tugboat Annie* (1933), *Madame Curie* (1943) and the perennial favorite, *The Wizard of Oz* (1939).

However, the one film he always wanted to make was an adaptation of Louisa May Alcott's *Little Women*. It had been fourteen years since David O. Selznick produced the RKO version with Katharine Hepburn, so LeRoy persuaded Louis B. Mayer to buy the rights from him.

Selznick had attempted to produce a Technicolor remake himself a few years earlier and planned to star his wife, Jennifer Jones. However, several postwar problems and a threatened craft workers' strike forced him to abandon his plans. So when MGM bought the rights to the film, they also bought all the sets that Selznick had built. One night during production, LeRoy's wife Kitty was reading some of the dialogue from the script when she began to cry. "I can't finish this," she told her husband.

"My God," he exclaimed. "Is it that good?"[2]

LeRoy chose some of the finest actresses at MGM to play the March sisters. Each one had experience with big screen success: Elizabeth Taylor in *National Velvet*, June Allyson in *The Stratton Story*, Janet Leigh in *The Forsythe Saga* and Margaret O'Brien in *The Secret Garden*, which LeRoy described as "one of her finest pictures."[3]

LeRoy had directed two of Margaret's films: *You, John Jones* with James Cagney, and the Greer Garson classic, *Madame Curie*. He also directed Elizabeth Taylor's screen test for *National Velvet*. "And like everybody else who saw her," he said, "I was struck by her potential beauty." When she began filming on *Little Women*, Elizabeth was seventeen and her beauty was at its peak. "There was no bad side, no good side," LeRoy said. "All sides were fantastically beautiful."[4]

During the filming, Elizabeth turned eighteen and no longer had to go to school, something which made Margaret very envious. "We had a party on the set for Elizabeth's eighteenth birthday," Margaret recalled, "and I remember her throwing away all her school books. She really disliked the schoolteacher and was happy that she would no longer be following her around every minute."

Walter Plunkett, of *Gone with the Wind* fame, designed the costumes for *Little Women*, which thrilled all the actresses. "Oh my goodness," Elizabeth exclaimed. "I get to wear Walter Plunkett clothes!"[5]

For her part as Beth, Margaret had to learn everything she could about Louisa May Alcott, and even visited her house in Boston. The film gave her a new appreciation of the author and got her interested in Civil War memorabilia.

The four actresses became good friends on the set of *Little Women*. At lunch, they would go to the studio commissary together and gossip—mostly about Louis B. Mayer. Elizabeth detested him, but June admired the fact that he had risen from the ranks as a junk dealer to one of the most powerful moguls in the business.

Margaret recalled that all three of her costars had crushes on Peter Lawford. "I was out of the competition," Margaret said, "because they were all older and I was only eleven. I sort of felt like an outcast because all three had a crush

on him. Peter had a wonderful time on that movie."

One person who did not have a wonderful time was Mary Astor, who played their mother, Marmee. Astor later recalled this period of her career as "Mothers for Metro" and did not always speak of it very fondly. "My approach to the part of Marmee was not an enthusiastic one," Astor later wrote. "Everybody else had fun."

She would complain because the girls were always laughing and fooling around during every scene. She criticized Elizabeth for talking on the phone to Nicky Hilton all the time and became irritated when June snapped her gum. Her experience in *Meet Me in St. Louis* had not endeared her to Margaret and things had not changed. "Maggie O'Brien looked at me as though she were planning something very unpleasant," Astor wrote.[6]

During the scene when Jo cuts off her hair, Peter Lawford's character sees her and is supposed to say, "What have you done? You look like a porcupine!" Instead, Peter would pronounce it "porky-pine." "We must have shot that scene a hundred times," Margaret recalled. "And then Peter and June would laugh every time she took off the hat and he saw her hair."

On every take, he would say "porky-pine" and everyone would burst out laughing, including Mervyn LeRoy. Unfortunately, Mary Astor did not see the funniness in it. "My sense of humor, my sense of fun, had deserted me long ago," she said. "And it just wasn't all that funny."

Eventually, everyone would pull themselves together and start the scene again. "Okay. I've got it now! I've got it now!" Peter would assure everyone.

Janet Leigh, Elizabeth Taylor and Margaret O'Brien on the set of *Little Women* (1949, MGM).

LeRoy would start at the very beginning and Peter would come through the door and say, "What have you done? You look like a "porky-pine!" Of course, everyone doubled over with laughter again, except Mary. She had been standing there for some time and was beginning to feel ill from the hot lights and the heavy clothes.

"I couldn't say that I was ill," she said. "I didn't want the kind of attention that would have brought on." As LeRoy began the scene once more, Mary had the first line and realized she could not remember what it was and stood there speechless.

"Cut," LeRoy yelled. "Where's your line, Mary?"

"I don't know Merv," was all she could say, which caused everyone to go to pieces again.[7]

Janet Leigh, who played Meg, remembered that at first Margaret was hesitant to join in on the revelry. "Young Margaret O'Brien took a while before she participated wholeheartedly," Leigh recalled. "She continually looked in her mother's direction for approval. But gradually she loosened up and we won her over to our foolish ways."[8]

Except for the wartime short, *You, John Jones*, *Little Women* was the only film in which one of Margaret's characters dies. That scene took a lot out of both Margaret and June Allyson. Even Mary Astor was impressed with Margaret's ability and proclaimed, "And was that ever a death scene!"[9]

"It was hard for me because June got to cry in that scene and I had to be the strong one," Margaret said. "It was difficult *not* to cry."

June had the same problem—except she couldn't stop crying. In the scene, Beth, who is dying from scarlet fever, comforts Jo and tells her not to be sad because she doesn't mind dying. After the scene was finished, June continued crying and had to be sent home. "I got in my car still blubbering and continued to cry for hours," June said.[10]

After the completion of filming, Margaret was filling out a health questionnaire when her mother noticed that she had checked scarlet fever as one of the diseases she had had. "Why Maggie," her mother exclaimed, "you know very well that you never had scarlet fever."

"Oh yes I did," she replied. "I had scarlet fever and I died from it."[11]

MGM made *Little Women* its opening film for their 25th Anniversary program and it became a big moneymaker for the studio that year. In their publicity, they mentioned that the film reunited four stars from *Meet Me in St. Louis*: Margaret O'Brien, Mary Astor, Leon Ames and Harry Davenport.

Sadly, *Little Women* was the last film for veteran character actor C. Aubrey Smith, who died shortly after filming was completed. This would also be Elizabeth Taylor's last adolescent part. Her next film, *Conspirator* (1950) with Robert Taylor, saw her in a more mature role.

Lee Mortimer of the *Daily Mirror* wrote, "On this photoplay MGM bestowed painstaking and loving care, adhering as much to the warm spirit and restrained actions of the book as it is physically possible in translating words into pictures."[12]

Opposite: **Margaret O'Brien, Janet Leigh, June Allyson and Elizabeth Taylor surround Mary Astor in *Little Women* (1949, MGM).**

Margaret O'Brien as Beth lets June Allyson know she is dying in *Little Women* (1949, MGM; author's collection).

Reviews

"*Little Women* is an American classic, sufficient unto itself. Margaret O'Brien, readily discoverable as herself, portrays sensitive, shy Beth. Miss O'Brien is allotted what are perhaps the film's most touching moments: Beth's joy in the gift of a baby piano and the quiet courage of her farewell speech to Jo." — *Los Angeles Times*, April 10, 1949.

"Margaret O'Brien is nicely restrained as the soulful doomed Beth." — *Newsweek*, March 28, 1949.

"Margaret O'Brien's Beth sends one searching for his handkerchief." — *Hollywood Reporter*, February 23, 1949.

"[*Little Women*] turns in perhaps the best group performances witnessed since *I Remember Mama*." — *Motion Picture Daily*, February 23, 1949.

Additional Reviews: *Commonweal*, 04/01/49; *Cue*, 03/19/40; *Daily News*, 04/18/49; *Film Daily*, 02/25/49, p. 7; *Hollywood Citizen-News*, 04/18/49; *Hollywood Reporter*, 02/23/49, p. 3; *Motion Picture Herald Product Digest*, 02/26/49; *New York Times*, 03/11/49, p. 33; *The New Yorker*, 03/19/49, p. 82; *Rotarian*,

07/49, p. 50; *Time*, 03/14/49, p. 102; *Variety*, 02/23/49.

Academy Award Nominations

Robert Planck and Charles Schoenbaum—Best Cinematography; Cedric Gibbons, Paul Groesse, Jack D. Moore and Edwin B. Willis—Best Art Direction-Set Decoration, Color.

Costar Comments

"Margaret O'Brien and I were known around MGM as 'The Town Criers.' Any role that called for a lot of tears was automatically earmarked for either Maggie or me. Since this put us in a class by ourselves, we formed our own mutual admiration society."—*June Allyson*[13]

"Ever since I have been in pictures I wanted to direct *Little Women*. I always liked the story as long as I can remember. It was a big cast and many of them had reputations for temperament, but everybody got along swimingly."—*Mervyn LeRoy*[14]

"Margaret O'Brien was so talented. My God to be so young and so talented. I saw all of her films. She really brought the people into the theaters; such a gifted child. And I loved *Little Women*, it was a lovely film and such a brilliant cast. Margaret was wonderful in her role."—*Janet Leigh*[15]

Comments by Margaret O'Brien

"*Little Women* was my favorite book, so when I was told I was going to do the movie I was thrilled. I loved Beth and loved the story of *Little Women*. Doing the film made me more interested in the story of Louisa May Alcott and to this day I'm a Civil War buff."

THE SECRET GARDEN

A Metro-Goldwyn-Mayer Picture

1949

"We can come here everyday. We can dig around them and get rid of those weeds. We can make it just the way it used to be. And no one would know—just us. Oh what a secret!"
—Margaret O'Brien to Brian
Roper in *The Secret Garden*.

Opened April 1949 in wide release.
Ad line: "It Was a House of Mystery Until They Found 'The Secret Garden.'"

Statistics

MGM production number 2.
Running time, 92 minutes; black & white with Technicolor sequences; Drama.

Ratings

The Motion Picture Guide, ☆☆☆
Leonard Maltin's Movie and Video Guide, ☆☆☆
Halliwell's Film Guide, ☆

Credits

Produced by Clarence Brown; directed by Fred M. Wilcox; screenplay by Robert Ardrey, based on the novel *The Secret Garden* by Frances Hodgson Burnett (New York: Grosset and Dunlap, 1915); musical score by Bronislau Kaper; music conducted by Andre Previn; art direction by Cedric Gibbons and Urie McCleary; set decoration by Edwin B. Willis and Richard Pefferle; special effects by A. Arnold Gillespie and Warren Newcombe; make-up by Jack Dawn; hairstyles by Sydney Guilaroff; costume design by Walter Plunkett; sound by Douglas Shearer; cinematography by Ray June; film editing by Robert J. Kern.

Song: "Hindu Song of Love" by Lal Chand Mehra.

Cast

Margaret O'Brien (Mary Lennox), Herbert Marshall (Archibald Craven), Dean Stockwell (Colin Craven), Gladys Cooper (Mrs. Medlock), Elsa Lanchester (Martha), Brian Roper (Dickon), Reginald Owen (Ben Weatherstaff), Aubrey Mather (Dr. Griddlestone), George Zucco (Dr. Fortescue), Lowell Gilmore (British Officer), Billy Bevan (Barney), Dennis Hoey (Mr. Pitcher), Mathew Boulton (Mr. Bromley), Isobel Elsom (Governess), Norma Varden (Nurse), Leonard Carey (Charles, Footman), Paul Collins (Peter), Phillis Morris (Grandmother), Kathryn Beaumont (Muriel), Susan Fletcher (Jane, Scullery Maid), Harry Allen (Coachman), John Powers (Friend), Elspeth Dudgeon (Mrs. Sowerby), Vanessa Field, Sherlee Collier, Mora McGivney, Michael McGivney (Four Refugee Children), Jack Deery (Upstairs Servant), William Eddritt (Kitchen Servant), Dick Baron (Kitchen Boy), Barbara Morrison (Cook).

Synopsis

When Mary Lennox is orphaned by a cholera epidemic while living in India, she is brought to live in a gloomy house in England by her uncle Archibald Craven. Mary is a spoiled and ill-tempered child, mostly due to her mother, who resented that her daughter was not pretty. On her arrival in England, Mary discovers a mysterious air about the old English estate and hears weird cries in the night. While investigating, she discovers Colin, her uncle's crippled son. Eventually, the two begin a friendship along with Dickon, a country boy who loves birds and animal life. The children learn of the secret garden, where Craven's wife was accidentally killed, which caused him to keep it forever sealed. Mary and Dickon are determined to rebuild the garden which eventually puts Colin on the road to health and restores his relationship with his father.

Behind the Scenes

The Secret Garden would prove to be one of Margaret O'Brien's favorite films. The screenplay was based on the popular children's novel by Frances Hodgson Burnett who also wrote *Little Lord*

Margaret O'Brien plays with her dolls in *The Secret Garden* (1949, MGM).

Fauntleroy. The story is told through the eyes of three children, played by Margaret, Dean Stockwell and Brian Roper. It begins in India where Margaret's character is orphaned by a cholera epidemic. "I enjoyed doing the part in India," Margaret recalled. "I loved the dolls that were in my bedroom and even got to keep one of them after filming was completed. I still have it today."

Working with her two young costars was also a treat for her. She developed quite a crush on Dean Stockwell, another wonderful child actor, most remembered for his role in *The Boy with*

the Green Hair (1948). "I knew Dean from the MGM school and always had a big crush on him," Margaret said. "I was really excited to work with him. I just thought he was so good looking."

One day Mrs. O'Brien and Mrs. Stockwell were comparing notes about their children and discovered that both began combing their hair without being told shortly after they started work on the picture. Could it be love? they mused. On Margaret's birthday, Dean gave her a strand of simulated pearls that he clasped around her neck with all the flourish of any romantic lead. "Mrs.

Brian Roper, Dean Stockwell and Margaret O'Brien in *The Secret Garden* (1949, MGM).

O'Brien," he said, "you have a very talented child!"[1]

Brian Roper was chosen after a casting call went out for a teenage boy with a Yorkshire accent. He auditioned at MGM's English studios and won the part over dozens of other young hopefuls. Forty-eight hours after leaving his home in Doncaster, Yorkshire, England, he was standing before the cameras opposite Margaret O'Brien. *The Secret Garden* would be his first American film.

When Brian's plane landed at the Burbank airport, he was met by director Fred Wilcox and producer Clarence Brown. His first words to them were, "Who won the World's Series?"[2]

"Brian Roper came from Yorkshire just to do the film," Margaret said. "I really liked him a lot." The adult cast included some of Hollywood's best English actors. Herbert Marshall played Archibald Craven, the brooding master of the English estate. Gladys Cooper, Reginald Owen and Elsa Lanchester rounded out the cast.

Margaret, Dean and Brian spent most of their spare time playing with the animals that Brian Roper's character collected. But the most enjoyment Margaret

Margaret O'Brien as Mary Lennox in *The Secret Garden* (1949, MGM).

had was during the scenes in which she and Dean Stockwell have their screaming tantrums. "We got to yell at one another and it was great fun," she recalled. "And in the beginning of the film I got to play a real mean, haughty type of girl which was also kind of fun."

When the film wrapped, everyone gave each other little gifts to remember their time together. Dean bought Margaret several little trinkets such as a gold rabbit's foot pin for good luck, even though he remarked that she did not need it. Mrs. O'Brien gave Brian Roper a beautiful gold wristwatch which he still had forty years later when Margaret met him again at a showing of *The Secret Garden* in San Francisco. "And it still worked," Margaret marveled.

The Secret Garden was Margaret O'Brien's last film for Metro-Goldwyn-Mayer. Margaret was outgrowing her "cute" roles that the studio usually put her in and they parted amicably. "Performances are competent and production values are high," wrote the *Motion Picture Herald* upon the film's release.[3] *The Secret Garden* has been remade several times since then, but none compare to MGM's classic version.

Reviews

"The role of the girl is well suited to the talents of the little Miss O'Brien who takes its comedy and dramatic moments casually in her stride."—*Hollywood Reporter*, April 22, 1949.

"Miss O'Brien and young Roper, a recent British import, are kept well under reign and are pleasing."—*Variety*, April 27, 1949.

"Stockwell, Roper and O'Brien, due much praise, and the direction is up to par."—*The Exhibitor*, September 14, 1949.

"These three youngsters are the chief figures in a fantasy which despite an occasional false step, maintains its ingratiating air of unreality to create a queer, indefinable appeal that disarms criticisms."—*News Review* (United Kingdom), September 29, 1949.

"It has many dramatic merits, due largely to its fine cast, headed by Margaret O'Brien."—*Motion Picture Daily*, April 22, 1949.

Additional Reviews: *Harrison's Reports*, 04/23/49; *Motion Picture Herald*, 04/23/49.

Costar Comments

"Charles (Laughton) loved some of the people he worked with—Margaret O'Brien for instance. He swore that she must have been a changeling, somehow descended from royalty; perhaps, kidnapped from a Persian King."—*Elsa Lanchester*[4]

Comments by Margaret O'Brien

"*The Secret Garden* was another film based on a wonderful book that I was so lucky to make. I became very good in history because I would do these great historical parts. It was the same with *The Secret Garden* which made me very interested in English history. The film was one of my favorites."

HER FIRST ROMANCE

A Columbia Production
1951

"This isn't junk. It's a real momentum."
—Margaret O'Brien to Jimmy Hunt after picking up a candy wrapper discarded by a boy she likes in *Her First Romance*.

Opened April 1951 in wide release.
Ad line: "The Boys Have Margaret O'Brien Sighing in *Her First Romance*."

Margaret O'Brien dances the Charleston in *Her First Romance* (1951, Columbia).

Jimmy Hunt, Margaret O'Brien, Allen Martin, Jr., and Elinor Donahue in *Her First Romance* (1951, Columbia).

Statistics

Columbia production number 358. Working title: "The Romantic Age." Running time, 73 minutes; black & white; Drama.

Ratings

The Motion Picture Guide, ☆½
Leonard Maltin's Movie and Video Guide, ☆½
Halliwell's Film Guide, 0

Credits

Produced by Seymour Friedman; directed by Seymour Friedman; screenplay by Albert Manheimer, based on the story "City Boy" by Herman Wouk; musical direction by Morris Stoloff; art direction by Ross Bellah; set decoration by Fay Babcock; sound by Jack Goodrich; cinematography by Charles Lawton, Jr.; edited by Jerome Thoms.

Cast

Margaret O'Brien (Betty Foster), Allen Martin, Jr. (Bobby Evans), Jimmy Hunt (Herbie), Sharyn Moffett (Leona Dean), Ann Doran (Mrs. Foster), Lloyd Corrigan (Mr. Gauss), Elinor Donahue (Lucille Stewart), Susan Stevens (Clara), Marissa O'Brien (Tillie), Arthur Space (Mr. Foster), Otto Hulett

Margaret O'Brien and Sharyn Moffett in *Her First Romance* (1951, Columbia).

(Mr. Evans), Lois Pace (Violet), Harlan Warde (Paul Powers), Maudie Prickett (Miss Pond), Norman Ollestad (Cliff), Joseph Sargent (Counselor), Ruth Warren (Mrs. Marsh), Dick Wessell (Night Watchman), Billy Lechner (Counselor), Daria Massey (Clara), Patti Bell (Ad Lib Girl), Bunnie Seidler (Ad Lib Girl), Jeannie Vann (Ad Lib), Brooke Chapin (Ad Lib), Arthur Stone (Boy), Tommy Mann (Boy), Ivor James, Whitney Haupt, Ronnie Gervon, Warren James Farlow, Tony Taylor, Tim Hawkins, Bill McKenzie (Bit Boys), Patty King, Mary Dunn (Bit Girls), Dick Rich (Night Watchman), Paul Dubov (First Counselor), Jerry Paris (Second Counselor), Billy Gray (First Boy), Larry Sims (Military Boy).

Synopsis

Betty Foster and Lucille Stewart, both students, vie for the attention of Bobby Evans, the reigning hunk who is more interested in sports than either of them. Betty and her brother Herbie follow Bobby and Lucille to summer camp where her efforts to have Bobby named king of the camp almost ruin her father financially, but succeed in winning over the young lad.

Behind the Scenes

When Margaret left MGM, she did not stay idle. She went to work in television and on the stage where she worked with a young Steve McQueen in *Peg-O-My-Heart*, which was his first big role. Other roles followed with *Under the Yum-Yum Tree* with James MacArthur and a national tour of *I Remember Mama*.

On television she worked on *Robert Montgomery Presents* where she reprised her role of Lady Jessica in *The Canterville Ghost* and also appeared on *Video Theater* and *Studio One*. Then Columbia called and offered her the starring role in a picture they were preparing to produce called *Her First Romance*. By now Margaret was no longer the little child that everyone remembered. Instead she was beginning to blossom into a very attractive young lady.

She was not that impressed with the script when she read it, but Harry Cohn wanted her and was willing to pay her price. Her meeting with the Columbia mogul was very fleeting and not at all memorable for the young girl. "I met Mr. Cohn very quickly and really didn't get to know him like I did Mr. Mayer at Metro," she recalled.

Filming took place at the studio on Sunset and Gower, on the Columbia back lot in Burbank and at a camp in Northern California. She was reunited with Elinor Donahue, her costar from *The Unfinished Dance*. "They bleached my hair for that one," Elinor recalled. "They said Margaret and I sort of looked alike with our dark hair. The producers thought the villain should have blonde hair."[1]

Margaret also developed a crush on her leading man, Allen Martin, Jr. "We all had a crush on Allen Martin," she

remembered. "And it was fun to be back with Elinor, because we had stayed friends over the years."

Margaret's aunt Marissa was given a small part in the film as a camp counselor and character actress Ann Doran played Margaret's mother—a role she often played in films. "I guess she was everyone's mother at one time or another," Margaret said. "I would always see her when I was friends with Natalie [Wood]. She played James Dean's mother in *Rebel Without a Cause* (1955), the picture he did with Natalie."

Although she enjoyed working with the cast, Margaret was not that fond of *Her First Romance*. "It wasn't my favorite," she said, "I wasn't crazy about the script. I didn't think it was all that good. But they paid me well and I did it."

Although it fared well at the box office, most critics shared Margaret's opinion of *Her First Romance*. The *Hollywood Reporter* told its readers that the "implausible script generates too few interesting sequences."[2]

Reviews

"Margaret O'Brien returns to the screen after going through the 'growing up' stage, and in this first of her semi-grown up roles she emerges quite pleasing in a production that will pass as good clean family fun, a frothy little comedy about adolescent love."—*Motion Picture Daily*, May 3, 1951.

"Margaret O'Brien is completely believable..."—*Box Office*, May 5, 1951.

"Although she is now in what is generally described as the 'awkward age,' Margaret O'Brien has grown into a comely young miss and she makes the most of a part that is not too demanding."—*Harrison's Reports*, May 5, 1955.

"O'Brien fans may be surprised at her lively performance, including a snappy Charleston."—*The Exhibitor*, May 9, 1951.

Additional Reviews: *Hollywood Reporter*, 05/02/51; *Motion Picture Herald*, 05/05/51; *Variety*, 05/02/51.

Costar Comments

"I remember the studio still photographer had to take some shots of Margaret and I. He wanted us to be glaring at each other. Well, we both got into a fit of giggles and we couldn't stop. Remember, Margaret and I were friends; we liked each other. We thought it was fun doing this movie where we are not getting along. The poor photographer finally gave up and never got his shot."—*Elinor Donahue*[3]

Comments by Margaret O'Brien

"*Her First Romance* was my first film since leaving Metro. I had been doing a lot of stage and television work back East when Columbia offered me the role and brought me back to Hollywood. It was my first teenage part."

GIRLS HAND IN HAND

Daiei Motion Picture Company
1953

"When I knew I was coming to Japan, I was so happy. But after I got here and saw those unfortunate children, I knew I could never be happy unless I did something to help them."

—Margaret O'Brien to her Japanese host in *Girls Hand in Hand*.

Statistics

Japanese title, *Futari no Hitomi* (trans. *Two Persons' Eyes*).
Running time, 90 minutes.

Credits

Directed by S. Nakaki; screenplay by N. Ocuni; art direction by K. Takansa; set design by K. Isnida; sound by K. Asnimoto; costumes by I. Onara; cinematography by M. Takanas.

Cast

Margaret O'Brien (Katie McDermott), Hibari Misora (Maria), John Norton (McDermott), Mitsuko Miura (Masako), Tetsunaka Mura (Clergyman), T. Watanabi (Tadao), A. Saito (Senkichi), K. Akano (Moboru), Y. Icarasn (Natsuico), Saito (Welfare Minister), N. Noshi (Carpenter), Okamura (Fumiko), Y. Tashiro (Maid), M. Takata, R. Sugimori, Seiji Izumi,

二人の瞳 23

Margaret O'Brien and Hibari Misora in *Girls Hand in Hand* (1953, Daiei).

M. Sasaki, Gladys O'Brien (Pass-ersby).

Synopsis

The story of an American girl who goes to Japan to visit her father, who is a colonel in the army. There she befriends a Japanese girl who is the leader of an all-child orchestra that plays to collect money to build an orphanage.

Behind the Scenes

In July 1952, Margaret signed with the Japanese motion picture company Daiei to star in the film *Girls Hand in Hand*. Daiei Productions was headed by producer-director Akira Kurosawa, who had just scored a hit with *Rashomon* (1951), which won the Academy Award as the Best Foreign Language Film.

Margaret, who was now fifteen and turning into a very attractive young lady, left for Japan on September 5, along with her mother and tutor. When she arrived in Tokyo, they were greeted by a large crowd of American GIs and

Opposite: Margaret O'Brien dressed in Japanese garb in *Girls Hand in Hand* (1953, Daiei).

Japanese movie fans. Also there to welcome her was her costar, Hibari Misora, a child star who was the equivalent of Margaret in Japan. "They kind of put the Margaret O'Brien of Japan and the real Margaret O'Brien together," Margaret said.

Hibari Misora was the idol of Japanese teenage girls. Making her first film in 1949, she was now doing at least fifteen pictures a year. Also a singer, she was sometimes called the "Judy Garland of Japan."

This was Margaret's first visit to Japan and she fell in love with the country and the people. "It's beautiful in Japan," she said. "I'd love to go there again. I love the rickshaws. I met the Crown Prince and all of the Princesses in Tokyo"

Meanwhile, back in Beverly Hills at the O'Brien home, Margaret's dog was lost while staying with her aunt Marissa. The dog, a miniature fox terrier with black spots that Margaret named Spotty, was a gift from MGM mogul Louis B. Mayer. "Margaret will be heartsick when she finds out," Marissa said, also offering a reward for the pet.[1] Unfortunately, unlike *Lassie Come Home*, Spotty was never found.

Girls Hand in Hand was the story of a young American girl and her father living in Japan who becomes interested in war orphans and befriends a young girl played by Misora. The film had some English dialogue but most of it was shot in Japanese, so the studio hired a tutor to teach Margaret the basics of the language. Margaret was always very proficient in learning languages and picked it up well enough to phonetically learn her lines. "I had a wonderful Japanese tutor," Margaret recalled, "who taught me my lines as we went along. And I also picked some up on my own."

Margaret became very good friends with her tutor, who was about her mother's age. After filming was completed, she kept in touch with her but over the years she lost track of her. Fifteen years later, members of her family wrote Margaret that she was in the United States visiting and wanted to see her. Unfortunately the meeting could not be arranged and they never got together.

In the late 1980s, Margaret was doing a lecture on a Holland-America cruise ship when she discovered that her Japanese tutor and her husband were guests on board. "Finally, after thirty years we were reunited again," Margaret said, "and have kept in touch ever since." Margaret also kept in contact with Hibari Misora, through cards and letters. They met one more time when Misora was in America doing a personal appearance tour.

Over the years, Hibari Misora became a legend to the Japanese populace. She was one of the most adored actresses that country has ever seen. Once in Osaka, a group of fans were waiting for her arrival at the airport when a panic ensued and one young girl was crushed to death. Another time, a deranged fan threw acid in her face. In 1989 she became ill and the American-Japanese press interviewed Margaret to take comforting words back to Hibari in the hospital.

"Why she was such a legend," Margaret explained, "was that she brought Japan and America together after the war, as a goodwill gesture. She is their treasure. So anyone who has made a movie with Hibari Misora is held in great esteem in Japan."

When Hibari Misora died in 1989 at the age of 52, the entire country mourned. Television stations aired documentaries on her life and career and a radio station in Osaka converted to an all–Misora play list. Sales of her records skyrocketed and four of the film companies she worked for, including Daiei, released fifteen of her films on videocassette. The combined sales of her records and videos reached over $4.2 million.

During her time in Japan, Margaret carefully followed the Japanese customs and absorbed the nature of their living. When the film was completed her host gave her the utmost compliment: "You are gentle and tender—more Japanese almost than Japanese girls."[2]

When the film was released, the English title was changed to *Girls Hand in Hand*. "This was a very important picture," Margaret said. "To this day I still get a lot of fan mail from Japan. Working with Hibari kind of made me a legend there also."

Reviews

No data available.

Comments by Margaret O'Brien

"That film was with Hibari Misora, who was a child actress and singer. Some called her the Judy Garland of Japan. She was a legend there because she brought back the goodwill to Japan after the war. I still get requests to do interviews about it."

GLORY

An RKO Release
1956

"Guess you can't go on loving a loser."
—Margaret O'Brien to Charlotte Greenwood in *Glory*.

Opened January 1956 in wide release.
Ad line: "Margaret O'Brien Is Back in a Heartwarming Drama."

Statistics
Running time, 100 minutes; Technicolor (Superscope); Drama/Musical.

Ratings
The Motion Picture Guide, ☆☆½

Leonard Maltin's Movie and Video Guide, ☆☆
Halliwell's Film Guide, 0

Credits
Produced by David Butler; directed

Margaret O'Brien as Clarabel Tilbee in *Glory* (1956, RKO).

by David Butler; assistant directors, Phil Quinn and Grayson Rogers; screenplay by Peter Milne from a story by Gene Markey; musical direction by Frank Perkins; art direction by Albert D'Agostino and John B. Mansbridge; set decoration by Darrell Silvers; make-up by Jack Byron; costume design by Michael Woulfe; sound by Earl Wolcott and Terry Kellum; cinematography by Wilfred M. Cline; film editing by Irene Moura.

Songs: "Glory," "Gettin' Nowhere Road," "Calypso," "Happy Time Again" and "Kentucky (Means Paradise)" by M. K. Jerome and Ted Koehler.

Cast

Margaret O'Brien (Clarabel Tilbee), Walter Brennan (Ned Otis), Charlotte Greenwood (Miz Tilbee), John Lupton (Chad Chadburn), Byron Palmer (Hoppy Hollis), Lisa Davis (Candy Trent), Gus Schilling (Joe Page), Hugh Sanders (Sobbing Sam Cooney), Walter Baldwin (Doc Brock), Harry Tyler (Beed Wickwire), Leonid Kinskey (Vasily), Paul E. Burns (Squeaky Bob), Theron Jackson (Alexander), Madge Blake (Aunt Martha).

Synopsis

When a filly is foaled at Miz Tilbee's stable, her granddaughter Clarabel falls in love with it and names it "Glory." Trouble falls on the Tilbee stable and Glory loses consistently, but Clarabel never loses faith. She falls in love with Chad Chadburn, a millionaire stable owner, but when Glory is sold to him in a claiming race, she vows never to see him again. When Chadburn discovers his stable manager is behind buying Glory, he arranges for Miz Tilbee to win the filly back in a poker game. Because of Clarabel's faith in Glory, Ned Otis, a trainer, prepares the horse for the Kentucky Derby to compete against one of Chadburn's best horses.

Behind the Scenes

The year was 1955 and it had been more than two years since Margaret O'Brien appeared before a motion picture camera. Not one to sit idle, Margaret chose to work in summer stock and the fairly new medium of television, appearing in such early shows as *Lux Video Theatre* and *Studio One*.

Director David Butler, who was responsible for several of Shirley Temple's films, was at the time trying to produce a film about horse racing. He had a screenplay that was based on a story by his friend Gene Markey, who had been the husband of three of Hollywood's most glamorous stars: Joan Bennett, Hedy Lamarr and Myrna Loy.

Markey's story was about a young girl and her grandmother who ran a racing stable and raised a filly called "Glory." Butler's first choice for the young girl was Debbie Reynolds. He had directed Reynolds in her second film, *The Daughter of Rosie O'Grady* (1950) and considered her a good friend. Butler met with Debbie at Goldwyn Studios on Santa Monica Boulevard and brought a piano player with him to play the songs written for the film. "Well, here's how Eddie would sing them," she said after hearing the songs.

Butler knew she was referring to Eddie Fisher, whom she had married earlier that year. He told her to sing them any way she wanted. However, she later turned down the film, which disappointed the director. Next, he went to Columbia Studios and tested Kathryn Grant, who would later become Mrs. Bing Crosby. "I didn't care for the test," he later said. "She was fine, but I thought she was too big and so forth."[1]

Then one night he happened to see Margaret O'Brien on a television show and contacted her about doing the part. After reading the script, Margaret agreed to do it, always having wanted to do a film about horses. "Of course I had to refurbish some of my riding skills for the film," she said. "I really had not done much horseback riding since Wallace Beery's horse ran away with me in *Bad Bascomb*."

Butler was thrilled now that he had found his leading lady. "Finally, I got Margaret O'Brien to play this part," Butler said. "She was a nice girl, and I thought maybe her name would mean something."[2]

When it was certain that Margaret was going to do the part, Mrs. O'Brien called up screenwriter Dalton Trumbo and asked him to rewrite the script for *Glory*. Trumbo was surprised at her request and told Gladys that he did not think that would happen. Trumbo was still blacklisted in Hollywood but sometimes wrote under pseudonyms or the names of people who sympathized with his situation.

One such time was in 1953 when Trumbo conceived the idea for *Roman Holiday*, the film that made Audrey Hepburn a star. The screen credit actually went to Ian McLennan Hunter, but Gladys O'Brien knew that it was really Trumbo who wrote the Academy Award–winning screenplay. So one day she called and asked him to write "another *Roman Holiday*" for Margaret. "That might be difficult," he told Mrs. O'Brien.

"It shouldn't be," she replied. "After all you wrote *Roman Holiday*—didn't you? That's the kind of script Margaret needs."

"Why don't you go to the guy whose name is on it?" he told her, meaning Hunter.

Gus Schilling, Walter Brennan, Margaret O'Brien and Charlotte Greenwood in *Glory* (1956, RKO).

"No, no," she said. "I want you!" Trumbo could not be moved and refused Gladys O'Brien's request.[3]

Because Margaret did not sing, Butler hired Norma Zimmer to dub her musical numbers. The other leads in the film were filled by Charlotte Greenwood as her grandmother, John Lupton as her love interest and Arthur Hunnicutt as the horse trainer. Unfortunately, Hunnicutt had to be replaced after three days of filming because of excessive drinking. Butler then turned to his old friend, Walter Brennan, and paid him $18,000 out of his own pocket to replace

Hunnicutt. Butler had directed Brennan in the 1938 film *Kentucky*, which was also about horse racing.

By this time Butler had already filmed atmospheric shots at the Kentucky Derby and at Calumet Farms, which was a well known racing stable in Kentucky. The rest of *Glory* would be filmed at RKO Studios in Hollywood.

Margaret enjoyed working with her costars Charlotte Greenwood and Walter Brennan. "Through all my years in the movies I had always wanted to work with Walter Brennan," Margaret recalled. "He was everything I always thought he would be—just like the characters he played. The only thing was that he kept taking out his teeth between scenes, which kind of shocked me because I wasn't expecting to see him without his teeth."

And of course Charlotte Greenwood entertained the cast and crew with her trademark high kicks for which she was famous. John Lupton was very nice to her and would make film history as the man to give Margaret O'Brien her first screen kiss. During the filming of that scene, Butler instructed Margaret how to hold her head and Lupton later said he gave her a "real kiss." Afterward Margaret giggled and told everyone it was "wonderful."[4]

Shortly before *Glory* was finished filming, Howard Hughes, who owned RKO, sold the studio to General Tire and Rubber Company for $25 million. And of course the exchange was also sold so when *Glory* was released, it was sent to Universal for distribution. "They never bothered with it at all," Butler later recalled. "Why should Universal exploit a picture for RKO?"

Margaret traveled to Kentucky for the premiere of *Glory*, afterward going to Calumet Farms and visiting with Swaps, the Triple Crown Winner. The critics enjoyed *Glory*, but because of the poor handling between RKO and Universal, the film did not do well at the box office.

"Anyway, I wound up very badly on the picture," Butler said. "It was very good, and Margaret and Charlotte Greenwood were great. But nobody did anything with it. They just left it. I lost quite a little money myself on that picture."[5]

Regardless, Butler signed Margaret to a two-picture contract, but unfortunately it fell through and the films were never made. Gossip columnist Hedda Hopper interviewed Margaret shortly before the film's premiere and declared, "Few moppet stars regain the brilliance of their childhood careers in adult years; but Margaret O'Brien proves the exception to this rule."[6] In their review of the film, *Variety* said that David Butler "produced and directed with skill, realizing the most from the material."[7]

Reviews

"…the sheer pleasure of looking at Margaret O'Brien who has grown from a precocious, talented moppet into a lovely, talented young actress."—*Hollywood Reporter*, January 11, 1956.

"Miss O'Brien registers very nicely in her transition to older roles, and in time should develop into a capable adult actress."—*Hollywood Citizen-News*, March 8, 1956.

"The film will be helped by the O'Brien name and it will be best appreciated by small towns and family audiences."—*The Exhibitor*, January 25, 1956.

"The pleasant news about *Glory* is that Margaret O'Brien, at eighteen, is as much a charmer as she was at four when she tore the heart out of you in *Journey for Margaret*."—*Los Angeles Examiner*, March 8, 1956.

Additional Reviews: *Los Angeles Times*, 03/08/56; *Variety*, 01/11/56.

Costar Comments

"The script for *Glory* called for a girl who was natural and fresh but who was also an experienced actress. When I saw Margaret O'Brien practically all grown-up, I knew she was the one."—*David Butler*[8]

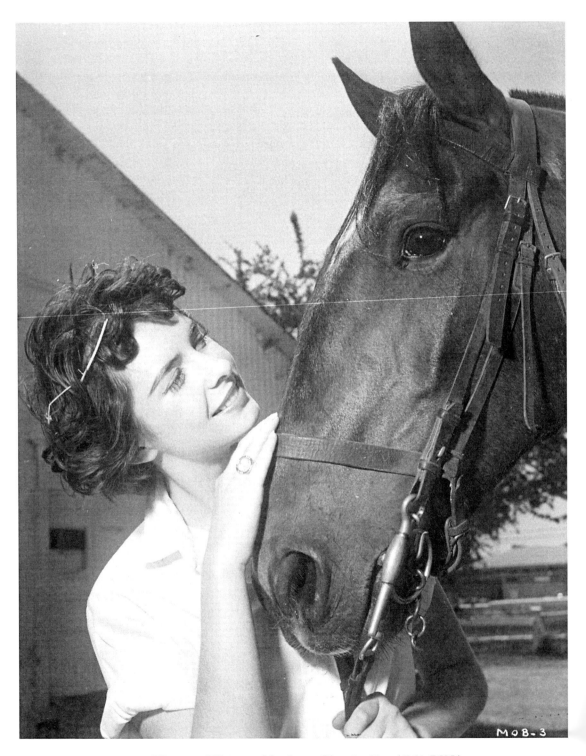

Margaret O'Brien and her horse Glory in *Glory* (1956, RKO).

"I've been in movies since '38; I've never seen a cast so concerned with each other. Nobody steps on anybody else's lines or upstages. I think Margaret's quiet dedication has a lot to do with the whole atmosphere."—*Gus Schilling*[9]

Comments by Margaret O'Brien

"While I was making *Glory* we were out at Hollywood Park, and they let me ride Swaps. He was very gentle—not too high strung like so many race horses. You could get hold of him and he wouldn't go too fast if you didn't want him to."

HELLER IN PINK TIGHTS

A Paramount Picture
1960

"I'm not as young as Mama says I am. Or as you think I am, Tom. I'm twenty years old."
—Margaret O'Brien flirting
with Anthony Quinn in
Heller in Pink Tights.

Opened March 16, 1960, in wide release.
Ad line: "She Had a Way with the Men of the Wild Wild West."

Statistics
Paramount production number 5915.
Running time, 100 minutes; Technicolor (Vistavision); Western.

Ratings
The Motion Picture Guide, ☆☆
Leonard Maltin's Movie and Video Guide, ☆☆½
Halliwell's Film Guide, ☆

Credits
Produced by Carlo Ponti, Marcello Girosi and Lewis E. Ciannelli; directed by George Cukor; assistant director, C. C. Coleman, Jr.; second unit director, Arthur Rosson; screenplay by Dudley Nichols and Walter Bernstein, based on the novel *Heller Without a Gun* by Louis L'Amour; music directed and conducted by Daniele Amfitheatrof; art direction by Hal Pereira and Eugene Allen; set decoration by Sam Comer and Grace Gregory; make-up by Wally Westmore; hairstyles by Nellie Manley; costume design by Edith Head; choreography by Val Raset; technical advisor on theatre scenes, Warren Wade; sound by John Wilkinson and Winston Leverett; color technical

advisor, Hoyningen Huene; color consultant, Richard Mueller; cinematography by Harold Lipstein; second unit cinematography by Irmin Roberts; film editing by Howard Smith.

Songs: "Angela" by Daniele Amfitheatrof; "Beware" by Jack Brooks and Jacques Offenbach; "Love, Lovely Love" by Adolph Deutsch.

Cast

Sophia Loren (Angela Rossini), Anthony Quinn (Tom Healy), Margaret O'Brien (Della Southby), Steve Forrest (Clint Mabry), Eileen Heckart (Lorna Hathaway), Ramon Novarro (De Leon), Edmund Lowe (Manfred "Doc" Montague), George Mathews (Sam Pierce), Frank Cordell (Theodore), Taylor "Cactus" McPeters (William), Edward Binns (Sheriff McClain), Warren Wade (Hodges), Frank Silvera (Santis), Cal Bolder (Goober), Robert Palmer (McAllister), Howard McNear (Photographer), Taggart Casey (First Gunslinger), Leo V. Matranga (Second Gunslinger), Geraldine Wall (Madam), Amanda Randolph (Maid), David Armstrong (Achilles), Alfred Tonkel (Calchas), Bryn Davis (Venus), Cathy Cox (Juno), Robert Darin, Paul T. Salata, John Rockwell (Servants), Sal Lamont, Riza Royce, Ruth Barnell, Allan Paige (Peasants), William Troy, William Vaughn (Noblemen), Richard Shannon (Man at Desk), Harry Cheshire, Brad Johnson, John Benson. Bob Burrows, Jeffrey Sayre (Poker Players), Charles Boaz, Paul J. McGuire, Ralph Neff, Harry J. Fleer, Bill Boyce, Neil K. Hooker (Gamblers), Iron Eyes Cody, Eddie Little Sky, Rodd Redwing, Chief Yow Lachie (Indians), Kenneth D. Clark (Western Union Clerk), Joe Forte (Indian Agent), Dean Williams

(Kansas Sheriff), Gary Armstrong (Office Boy), Bob Adler (Stage Coach Driver), Lorraine Crawford (Madam).

Synopsis

Story of a theatrical troupe headed by Tom Healy, who tries to stay one step ahead of the bill collector. The Healy Dramatic Co., with its cast of vagabond thespians from the beautiful and seductive Angela to the cute little "Baby" (Della) who is no baby at all, travel from one mining town to the next. Eventually they get themselves into more trouble than they can handle and it is up to the beautiful leading lady to save the day.

Behind the Scenes

Heller in Pink Tights was based on a Louis L'Amour western and was directed by the legendary George Cukor. Originally called *Heller Without a Gun*, it told the story of a traveling theatrical troupe—a story which always intrigued Cukor. This would be the director's first and only western.

The script was actually a mix of the L'Amour story and an idea Cukor received from several meetings with the silent screen director D. W. Griffith in 1945. Griffith's outline was based on his own days in a road troupe, and the autobiography of a nineteenth century actor named Joseph Jefferson.

Heller in Pink Tights boasted an all-star cast including Sophia Loren (who was married to *Heller* producer Carlo Ponti), Anthony Quinn, Eileen Heckart, Ramon Novarro and Edmund Lowe, and of course Margaret O'Brien, who received third billing. After four years of appearing on stage and television, Margaret was once again before the movie cameras.

Margaret got along famously with the

Margaret O'Brien as Della Southby in *Heller in Pink Tights* (1960, Paramount).

director, as did every woman who ever worked with Cukor. "George Cukor became one of my favorite directors to work with," Margaret recalled. "He and I got along very well and became very close. He was always very complimentary to me as an actress." Cukor shared that opinion of Margaret and once told a coworker, "She's a real movie actress."[1]

After years of playing moppet roles, it was evident to everyone that little Margaret O'Brien had finally grown up. *Heller in Pink Tights* proved she had outgrown her adolescent cuteness and evolved into a creature of beauty. Paramount publicity played on that evolution when they wrote, "In the beginning of the film she is fighting off pigtails and at the end she's an adult."[2]

Even compared to her costar, the alluring Sophia Loren, Margaret mesmerized audiences with her emerging sexiness. However, Margaret saw one feature about Loren which she coveted—her doe-like eyes. One day she had the make-up man pull her eyes up with her hair and secure it underneath the wig. When Sophia saw Margaret's new look, she was not pleased. "Your eyes are up," Sophia remarked. "The eyes come down." Eileen Heckart, who was standing nearby, became very impatient. "Eyes up—eyes down," Heckart responded. "Let's get this picture finished so I can get home."

"Sophia's reaction made me unhappy for awhile," Margaret remembered.

On the set, Margaret became Cukor's technical expert on certain aspects of the filming. In one scene, she was having an argument with her mother, played by Eileen Heckart, and she told Cukor, "When I'm having a row with my mother, I break off to smile very sweetly at anyone who passes, then go back to the row."[3]

This impressed the director, who knew that of his principal stars, Margaret had the most years as a star before the camera—even at such a young age. The only actors in the film who had more experience were former silent film stars Edmund Lowe and Ramon Novarro. Novarro was best known as the original *Ben-Hur* (1926) and thrilled moviegoers at the time with his Latin charisma. Now, thirty-five years later, he was doing television and an occasional supporting role. "Ramon Novarro was very sweet and very shy and quiet," Margaret said. "He kind of kept to himself, but was not haughty even though he was once a very big star."

Much of the film was shot on location including some scenes in the mountains where it was quite cold, which is what the script called for. However, Margaret was the only one of the cast that was not affected by the biting wind. "But I like the cold weather," Margaret explained. "Perhaps if I had lighter clothing." Finally, Cukor stopped filming and called for make-up. "Grey her face; muss up her hair," the director ordered. "She must look cold no matter how she feels." Cukor found it hard to believe that any girl with Spanish blood really enjoyed the snow. "I think," Margaret said, "I was born with a busted thermostat."[4]

Because *Heller in Pink Tights* was not the typical western, Paramount did not know what to do with it once filming was completed. Instead, they edited the film to fit their mold instead of Cukor's vision. Cukor called the cuts idiotic but knew he did not have control and accepted it.

Heller in Pink Tights was met with mixed reviews, but overall was an enjoyable experience. Many complained that there was no recognizable plot—mostly because of the studio's edits—but everyone raved about the beautiful cinematography and the gorgeous costumes by Edith Head. One critic said that *Heller in Pink Tights* had "a welcome individuality which is never quite smothered by its lapses into convention."[5]

Reviews

"Margaret O'Brien's new sexiness will probably astound onlookers."—*Beverly Hills Citizen*, March 9, 1960.

"Miss O'Brien shows indications of becoming as successful in grown-up roles as she has been as a child star."—*Motion Picture Herald*, March 12, 1960.

"The ingenue is played by Margaret O'Brien, the child-star of *Journey for Margaret*. Now 21, she seems to be serious about learning the acting art."—*Films in Review*, April 1960.

"One-time child actress O'Brien, here 21, is surprisingly good as the ingenue."—*The Motion Picture Guide*, *H–K*, p. 1194.

Additional Reviews: *America*, 03/26/60; *BFI/Monthly Film Bulletin*, 05/60, p. 64; *Commonweal*, 03/04/60; *Cue*, 03/19/60; *Film Daily*, 03/08/60; *Film Quarterly*, Spr/60, p. 60; *Films and Filming*, 05/60, p. 26; *Hollywood Citizen-News*, 03/10/60; *Hollywood Reporter*, 03/07/60, p. 3; *Los Angeles Examiner*, 03/10/60; *Los Angeles Mirror-News*, 03/10/60; *Los Angeles Times*, 03/10/60; *The New Yorker*, 03/26/60; *New York Times*, 03/17/60, p. 28; *New York Times*, 03/20/60, sec. 2, p. 1; *Newsweek*, 03/14/60, p. 100; *Saturday Review*, 03/05/60, p. 35; *Sight and Sound*, Sum/60, p. 147; *Time*, 04/04/60, p. 81; *Variety*, 03/09/60, p. 6.

Costar Comments

"(Margaret) was our technical expert on certain things, because she was a famous child actress. She's a real movie actress, she looks at the dead bodies and you know they're dead, she feels cold and makes you feel cold."—*George Cukor*[6]

Comments by Margaret O'Brien

"My role in *Heller in Pink Tights* was a fun part because I was kind of a vixen in a way. It was my first western since doing *Bad Bascomb* with Wallace Beery. The entire cast of *Heller*, from Sophia Loren to Ramon Novarro, were a class act. I also loved Edith Head's costumes and George Cukor's penchant for authenticity."

DIABOLIC WEDDING

Panamericana Produccions
Ellman Enterprises
1972

Released July 17, 1972, in the U.S.
Note: Film unavailable for viewing.

Statistics

Running time 84 minutes; color; Horror; Rated R.

Credits

Produced by Enrique Torres Tudela; directed by Gene Nash (no other credit information available).

Cast

Margaret O'Brien, Dom Furneau, Mary Anne Sarmiento, Fernando Larranaga, Patricia Aspillaga, Elvira Travesl (no other cast information available).

Synopsis

Things go haywire during a wedding celebration.

Behind the Scenes

It had been nearly ten years since Margaret O'Brien appeared in a motion picture when Mexican producer Enrique Torres Tudela approached her about making a series of horror films in Peru. She signed for two pictures that were to be filmed simultaneously in Spanish and English. The first was *Diabolic Wedding* and the other was *Annabelle Lee*, which was based on the lyric poem by Edgar Allan Poe.

Margaret was very well versed in the Spanish language, being half Spanish herself on her mother's side; however she was not prepared for the work schedule. After shooting a scene in Spanish, they would go back and shoot the exact same scene in English, which became rather monotonous. It was like shooting two pictures, and became exhausting after a while.

Another difference from her American-made movies was the discipline of the cast. At night everyone would attend parties and then be expected on the set for make-up at nine o'clock the next morning. Because Margaret was trained at MGM, she would be on the set on time but her South American counterparts would not show up until eleven or twelve. "So we would be sitting there waiting for several hours before any arrived," Margaret recalled. "But we caught on to that after awhile so the American group started doing the same thing."

Reviews

"Margaret O'Brien conveys the proper admixture of winsomeness-and-fright in the course of this drama of a nightmarish wedding. It should play well in those situations with a track record of profitable horror entertainment."—*Horror Film Review*, July 17, 1972.

Comments by Margaret O'Brien

"Ricky Torres Tudela was looking for an American actress to play in a film to be shown in Mexico and South American countries. He knew I was part Spanish so he called me to do it and the roles sounded real interesting, so we all went on location to Peru. I enjoyed the experience very much."

ANNABELLE LEE

Panamericana Produccions
Ellman Enterprises
1972

Released date unknown.
Note: Film unavailable for viewing.

Statistics

Running time, 91 minutes; Horror; Rated R.

Credits

Produced by Enrique Torres Tudela; directed by Gene Nash (no other credit information available).

Cast

Margaret O'Brien, Dom Furneau, Mary Anne Sarmiento, Fernando Larranaga, Patricia Aspillaga, Elvira Travesl (no other cast information available).

Synopsis

Story based on Edgar Allan Poe's classic poem.

Behind the Scenes

As soon as *Diabolic Wedding* was completed, the same cast and crew went into production for *Annabelle Lee*. Margaret worked for more than five months in Peru making both films. Afterward, she was signed by the Panamericana Television Network as the host for a soap opera based on *Diabolic Wedding*. Several of the film's costars also worked on the television show. Later, tapes of the series were offered to Puerto Rico, Ecuador, other key spots in Latin America and the Spanish-language television stations in the United States. Margaret enjoyed working on an old-fashioned horror movie, which was a change of pace to what she was usually accustomed.

Reviews

"Margaret O'Brien has come a long way career wise, from the wistful little girl roles at MGM a generation ago. The film should play well in those situations with a track record of profitable horror entertainment."—*Horror Film Review*, undated.

Comments by Margaret O'Brien

"I love doing horror movies. I love things like that. *Annabelle Lee* was shot in some beautiful old buildings in Peru and had some of the most gorgeous costumes I've ever worked with."

AMY

A Walt Disney Production
1981

Opened April 1981 in wide release.

Statistics

Working Title: "Amy on the Lips."
Running time, 100 minutes; Technicolor; Children's Drama.

Ratings

The Motion Picture Guide, ☆☆½
Leonard Maltin's Movie and Video Guide, ☆☆☆
Halliwell's Film Guide, 0

Credits

Produced by Jerome Courtland and William Robert Yates; directed by Vincent McEveety; screenplay by Noreen Stone; music composed and conducted by Robert F. Brunner; art direction by John B. Mansbridge and Mark W. Mansbridge; set decoration by Roger M. Shook; costume supervision by Jack Sandeen; sound by Henry A. Maffett; cinematography by Leonard J. South, A.S.C.; film editing by Gregg McLaughlin, A.C.E.

Song: "So Many Ways" by Bruce Belland and Robert F. Brunner, sung by Julie Budd.

Cast

Jenny Agutter (Amy Medford), Barry Newman (Dr. Ben Corcoran), Kathleen Nolan (Helen Gibbs), Chris Robinson (Elliott Medford), Lou Fant (Lyle Ferguson), Margaret O'Brien (Hazel Johnson), Nanette Fabray (Malvina), Otto Rechenberg (Henry Watkins), David Hollander (Just George), Bumper (Wesley Moods), Alban Branton (Eugene), Ronnie Scribner (Walter Ray), Lance Le Gault (Edgar), Lucille Benson (Rose), Jonathan Daly (Clyde), Lonny Chapman (Virgil), Brian Freshman (Melvin), Jane Daly (Molly Tribble), Dawn Jeffory (Carolyn Chapman), Frances Bay (Mrs. Lindey), Peggy McCay (Mrs. Grimes), Len Wayland (Mr. Grimes), Virginia Vincent (Edna), Norman Burton (Caruthers); Kevin Van Wieringen (Owen Corner), Seamon Glass (Mr. Watkins), Nancy Jeris (Mrs. Watkins), Randy Morton (Teenage Boy), Lance R. Gordon (Referee), John Arndt (Mr. Pool), Michelle Downey (Essie), Carson Sipes (Dwayne), Diana Boyd (Loretta), Flavia Fleischer (Iris), David Jacob Weiss (Glenn), Oscar Arturo Aguillar (Chester).

Synopsis

The story about a young woman who leaves her wealthy and domineering husband to take a job as a teacher at a school for the deaf and blind. In this new world without sight and sound, she teaches the deaf children to read lips and speak. They in return, teach her to love again.

Behind the Scenes

Margaret's appearance in *Amy* was the first time that the actress ever worked on the Disney lot. That was part of the reason she agreed to work in what amounted to a cameo appearance. In it she played Hazel Johnson, the nurse at a deaf and blind school sometime during the early part of this century.

The stars were Jenny Agutter, herself an English child actress and the winner of the British Academy Award for Best Supporting Actress for her role in *Equus* (1977). Others in the cast included Barry Newman, best known to American television audiences as *Petrocelli*, Kathleen Nolan and Nanette Fabray, who herself was hearing impaired.

Many of the children in the film were played by deaf and blind actors, which gave it a sense of realism. The entire cast learned sign language so they could communicate with the children, including Margaret, who never got a chance to use it in the film.

Amy was originally slated as a television movie of the week, but was so highly thought of by the people at Disney that they decided to release it theatrically in the States and in Europe. The reviews for *Amy* were mixed, but it treated the problems of deaf children with compassion and warmth. The *Los Angeles Times* called *Amy* a "rare gem … A glowing and lovely film."[1]

Reviews

"Funny as well as heartwarming, it's the sort of well-told tale for which Disney Studios became famous. Film has enough humor and human interest to appeal to both kids and adults."—*Variety*, March 27, 1981.

"Margaret O'Brien and Kathleen Nolan impart great compassion to their roles."—*Los Angeles Times*, April 10, 1981.

"Though the script doesn't realistically deal with the male mentality of the early 1900s, which would have made Agutter's achievements more difficult, the film is admirable and a good bet for children."—*The Motion Picture Guide, A-B*, p. 62.

Additional Reviews: *Box Office*, 05/81; *Hollywood Reporter*, 03/27/81; *Los Angeles Herald-Examiner*, 04/14/81.

Awards

Southern Motion Picture Council Golden Halo Award: Outstanding All-Family Viewing.

Lutheran Deaf Association Award of Merit.

Comments by Margaret O'Brien

"*Amy* was really an amazing, and what is now, a somewhat overlooked picture. It was shot for Disney and was about a school for the deaf and blind. I played a nurse and was taught some sign language, even though I did not use it in the film. I wouldn't say the cast was close, but it was a nice shoot."

SUNSET AFTER DARK

Wildcat Entertainment
1996

"I think that's absolutely horrid of you to tear apart my good name on the tragedy of my poor husband's death. Especially when everybody knows you were the biggest slut in Hollywood."

—Margaret O'Brien to Anita
Page in *Sunset After Dark*.

Opened in wide release in 1996.

Statistics

Running time, 90 minutes; color; Drama; MPAA: Rated R for nudity and strong sexuality, and for some violence and language.

Credits

Executive produced by Albert J. Gordon; produced by Mark J. Gordon; associate producers, Steve Harpst and Margaret O'Brien; directed by Mark J. Gordon; first assistant director, Robert Sidis; second assistant director, Mimi Douglas; screenplay by Frank Spotnitz; music by Fernando Cavazos; art direction by Robert Joseph; assistant art director, Scott Duthie; set decoration by Darla Hitchcock; costume design by Katzoff; make-up and hair by James Robert Mackinnon; sound by Marty Kasparian; cinematography by David Hallinger; first assistant camera, Kurt Fry; film editing by Craig Kitson.

Cast

Tony Maggio (John Harbert), Monique Parent (Gina Darnell), Anita Page (Anita Bronson), Margaret O'Brien (Betty Corman), Randal Malone (Gaylord Van Slyke), Corbin Timbrook (Peter D'Angelo), George Kuchar (George Kilman), April Breneman (Michelle Martin), J. Lyle Randolph (Case), Miranda Gibson (Arletta), Jeffrey Markle (Detective Flynn), Paul Brewster (Haskell), Steve Harpst (Bennett), Scott Forrest (Todd), Andrea Riave (Stripper), Rick Bennett (Second Detective), Mio Miyake (Geisha Girl), Misako (Geisha Girl), Paolo Nona (Poolman), Dale Vandegriff (Cameraman).

Synopsis

To find inspiration, a struggling screenwriter rents a room in an eerie old mansion on Sunset Boulevard. He soon becomes involved with the wife of a missing man and the plot of an unsolved murder. Mix in the disappointments of a fading silent screen star and the bitterness of a former child actress and you have a plot of intrigue and suspense.

Behind the Scenes

When Margaret O'Brien agreed to take the part of Betty Corman in *Sunset After Dark*, it had been more than twenty years since she stood before a motion picture camera. During that time she had worked on television and in theater, but she was basically retired. She had been offered many parts and still continues to receive them, but because she had been working since she was four years old, she felt she deserved a rest.

The idea for *Sunset After Dark* came one evening while the director, Mark Gordon, was interviewing silent film star Anita Page. The interview was arranged by Anita's manager, actor Randal Malone, who is also good friends with Margaret. During the interview, he had the idea of writing a script involving a great silent movie star, which he hoped would be played by Anita Page.

Several months later, with a completed script in hand, Mark Gordon presented it to Anita and Randal. The script was written by Frank Spotnitz, who would later gain fame for his work on the highly successful television show *The X-Files*. In the script was a part for a former child star and Randal immediately thought of Margaret. "You know, Mark," Randal told him, "I know Margaret O'Brien and she'd be wonderful for this part."

"That would be great. Do you think she'd do it?" he asked.[1] After much consideration, Margaret agreed to come out of retirement and do it as a favor to her friend Randal, who considered it a dream come true to not only work with Anita Page but also Margaret O'Brien.

The film was shot in the old "Sugar Hill" district of Los Angeles in a mansion once owned by banker Harry Crocker. The neighborhood, where actress Hattie McDaniel also owned a house, was once a grand showplace for the rich and elite, but was now somewhat run down.

One evening they were filming a dinner scene in which Randal, Anita and Margaret all appeared together. When Randal asked Margaret if she had gone over the script, she replied that she had, however Randal had some doubts about certain lines with Anita. "I'm not worried," Margaret assured him. "It will go all right."

"Can we run the lines anyway?" Randal asked.

"I don't do that," she told him. "I've already looked over it and it will be all right."

"I wish I had your confidence," he remarked. When the time came to film the dinner scene and the cameras began to roll, Margaret breezed through it without ever missing a line or a cue. "She has the gift of having a great ability for acting and for drama with very little preparation," Randal said. "That's an actor's gift. She truly is unique."[2]

Margaret returned the admiration and felt that Malone gave an outstanding performance as the mysterious Gaylord Van Slyke. "His bigger-than-life style really proved him to be a great showman," Margaret said. "The way he burlesqued himself across the screen with that cigarette holder was so funny."[3]

During the dinner scene, Margaret has a line where she calls Anita Page's

Randal Malone and Margaret O'Brien in *Sunset After Dark* (1996, Wildcat Entertainment; courtesy of Michael Schwibs).

Anita Page, Randal Malone and Margaret O'Brien in *Sunset After Dark* (1996, Wildcat Entertainment; courtesy of Michael Schwibs).

character a tramp. "It's one of my favorite scenes in the film," recalled Mark Gordon. "We wanted to show the jealousy and rivalry that exist between fallen stars and they played along with that beautifully."[4] For some reason Anita was opposed to using the word "tramp" so Gordon and writer Frank Spotnitz explained that they had tried many variations and the word "tramp" seemed to work the best. "I don't like tramp. I think tramp is terrible and I don't want you to use it," Anita insisted.

"Well Anita," Randal asked, "What about slut? Do you think that sounds better?"

"Yes, slut is fine," Anita replied. "I can live with that."[5] And with that the entire set broke into laughter. In Anita's day, to be called a tramp was a scandalous thing, but the word slut was hardly used, so it did not mean as much to her. To

Margaret, working with Anita Page was an interesting experience in itself. In the film, Anita plays a character much like herself. "Anita really was a silent film star," Margaret said. "She had a very fascinating look about her and a real flair for the dramatic which she still has."

On one occasion, Anita Page gave Margaret the chance to show how much of a professional she really was. While filming a scene with Tony Maggio, Margaret asked if it would be all right to change a few of the lines. The writer, Frank Spotnitz, was brought in and he agreed to the changes. Off to the side, Anita was sitting with Randal Malone, and overheard Margaret's suggestions.

Anita was a star during the silent and early talkies when the studio ran everything and the actor had very little say unless they were a big star like Garbo. You were expected to arrive at the studio, say your lines and that was it, so to hear Margaret ask for changes in the script was something she associated with great stardom. In a voice that could be heard on the entire set, Anita asked, "Don't you think that's bold changing the lines like that?"

"Apparently it's for the better or they wouldn't let her do it," Randal told her.

"I think she's doing that because she thinks she's the star of this picture," Anita replied.[6]

Suddenly everything got very quiet on the set. Margaret glanced at Randal and smiled and continued with her scene; she completely let it go. Even though Anita acknowledged that Margaret was a remarkable child actress, she felt that she was trying to manipulate all of Malone's time on the set. "I was a big star too," Anita said, "and I was not about to play second fiddle to anyone."[7]

Many actresses would have become upset, but Margaret knew Anita's background and understood her reaction. "Anita has the temperament of the twenties," Margaret said. "From when the stars were very grand and they would sweep in and sweep out. We actually were in awe of her."

Sunset After Dark was put in limited release in the United States, but in Europe and South America it had a popular and very successful run. The film proved once again that Margaret O'Brien is still remembered today and her many fans hope to see her again soon on the silver screen.

Reviews

"Great acting on the part of Margaret O'Brien, Anita Page and Randal Malone."—*California Motion Picture Council*, undated.

Comments

"Of course I was aware of Miss O'Brien's great talent, although I'd never worked with her until this film. I have always admired her work and she still has a very natural appeal. It was a thrill to actually work with her."—*Anita Page*[8]

"Working with Margaret was one of the greatest acting experiences of my life. It was a dream come true. She was marvelous; a constant professional. She's not a method actress, but she has the ability to step into the character which she conceives and then step right out of it."—*Randal Malone*[9]

"As you know, Margaret was one of the biggest child stars at MGM. Casting her as Betty Corman, the embittered ex–child star, seemed perfect. She really has a great sense of humor and was able to have a lot of fun with the role without any second thoughts. There are a lot of great inside jokes in her scenes. I think she gave a delightful performance."—*Mark Gordon*[10]

Comments by Margaret O'Brien

"That part in *Sunset After Dark* was a lot of fun for me because it was a different kind of role than what I'm normally offered. In it I played a bitchy actress—a sort of Joan Collins type of role; a very temperamental former child actress."

HOLLYWOOD MORTUARY

Brimstone Productions
1999

"I remember listening outside the door one day, when Arlene Borakoff—she was such a dear sweet woman—poured out her very heart and soul to my mother. She said that Pratt actually sat up and spoke with her in the funeral home. I mean really."

—Margaret O'Brien telling of her experiences in *Hollywood Mortuary*.

Opened June 16, 1999, at "Monster Bash," Pittsburgh, Pennsylvania.

Statistics
Running time, 90 minutes; color; Horror/Spoof.

Credits
Line produced by David Benjamin; associate producers, Michael W. Schwibs and Randal Malone; produced by Ron Ford and Paula Pointer-Ford; directed by Ron Ford; assistant director, Larry Richards; second assistant, Greg Cannone; production assistant, Robert Orentlicher; screenplay by Ron Ford; music by Robert Van and Kevin Parcher; art direction by Billie Hagle; special make-up effects by Kelly Beatty, Melanie Robinette, Susan Romero, Anna R. Futrell, Tyson Fontaine, Faith Griffin and Jennifer Donish; jewelry by Nate Waxman; Mr. Malone's hairstyles by Michelle of Beverly Hills; cinematography by Jeff Leroy and Clark Jordan; film editing by Jeff Leroy.

Cast
Randal Malone (Pierce Jackson Dawn), Tim Sullivan (Prat Borakoff), Ron Ford (Janos Balasco), Joseph Haggerty (Corey Mackerman), Wesley Deitrich (Mr. Shine), Denice Stradling (Mrs. Borakoff), Tim Murphy (Himself), Greg Cannone (Mr. Blevins), Athena Worthy (Fortune Teller), Margaret O'Brien (Herself), Anita Page (Herself), Conrad Brooks (Himself), Wesley Keitrick (Himself), David DeCoteau (Himself), Oriana Nicole Tavoularis (Secretary), Adriane Belle (Fan), John Ellis (Dancer), Michael Schwibs (Boyfriend), Judy Weaver (Girlfriend), Tyler Feneck (Comedian), Jon Trapnell (Customer), Holly Regan (Dancer), Cooper Johnson (Jitterbug

Margaret O'Brien, Randal Malone and Anita Page in *Hollywood Mortuary* (1999, Brimstone Productions; courtesy of Michael Schwibs).

Dancer), Becka Robbins (Jitterbug Dancer), Josh Young (Jitterbug Dancer), Danielle O'Neill (Jitterbug Dancer), Michael Pozo (Jitterbug Dancer), Cloud Michaels (Jitterbug Dancer), Paula Pointer-Ford (Murder Victim), Precious Baby Malone (Fifi).

Synopsis

A tongue-in-cheek story of an insolent horror make-up king named Pierce Jackson Dawn, who is ousted from his studio when they decide to stop making horror films. Dawn then decides that the only way to salvage his career is by making horror stories a front page reality, in turn, convincing the studios to once again make them. After learning about an ancient form of voodoo, Dawn murders one of Hollywood's former horror stars and brings him and his former film rival back from the dead. The zombies

Anita Page, Margaret O'Brien and Randal Malone in *Hollywood Mortuary* (1999, Brimstone Productions; courtesy of Michael Schwibs).

he creates go on a killing spree, but the entire scheme meets with a tragic ending before Dawn achieves his dream.

Behind the Scenes

Hollywood Mortuary was originally a project for Margaret's good friend, MTV Film Star Randal Malone. They had recently worked together in *Sunset After Dark*, along with silent film star Anita Page, who also had a role in this film. Malone had created quite a successful career as a B-actor in such films as *Alien Force* and *George's Garage* and had recently completed a stint on the popular MTV show *Singled Out*. Margaret had been friends with him for almost fifteen years and the two had always hoped to work together. After their success in *Sunset After Dark*, they wanted to do it again sometime.

After Malone worked in several films for director Ron Ford, it was decided to find a starring vehicle for him. "As it turned out," Ford recalled, "Randal himself had an idea for a project which he had been mulling around for some time. An idea which played right into my love of old horror films and my sense of camp."[1] What resulted was a kind of spoof of the legendary rivalry between Bela Lugosi and Boris Karloff, two of the biggest names in horror films.

Ford thought that Malone would be perfect to play the lead, Pierce Jackson Dawn, an arrogant monster make-up king. Margaret agreed with Ford's choice. "I must say, Randy was at his flamboyant best in this one. He brilliantly portrayed this fictitious makeup artist who loses his mind and commits murders and mayhem in Hollywood."[2]

Costar Anita Page, who had worked with such Hollywood greats as Ramon Novarro, Lon Chaney and Clark Gable, agreed, saying, "If all my leading men would have been like Randy, I could have just relaxed."[3]

When Margaret read the script, she agreed to play herself in a documentary-style portion of the film. "I liked the script and thought it would be an interesting project," she said. This was an unusual kind of role for Margaret since she had never before played herself in a film. "Getting into a different role and a different person is what I'm used to doing," Margaret said. "It's much harder to play yourself, I think."

The lead character's name, Pierce Jackson Dawn, was a take-off on several real make-up artists including Jack Pierce, and Jack Dawn (whom Margaret knew as a child at MGM). "I knew him very well," Margaret recalled, "so it was really almost like talking about a person I knew."[4]

Besides legendary silent film actress Anita Page, the film also costarred actor and author Tim Sullivan, horror film director David DeCoteau and cult movie star Conrad Brooks. Brooks, who appeared in several Ed Wood classics, including *Plan 9 from Outer Space*, had a huge infatuation with Margaret O'Brien and always made it a point to kiss her when they met.

Perhaps *Hollywood Mortuary* will not be Margaret O'Brien's last film. At this point in her life, it is her luxury to be able to pick and choose her roles. Margaret says she will never retire, and for her fans' sake, this author wholeheartedly approves.

Reviews

"The best independent effort of the year, no contest."—*Video Graveyard*, June 1999.

Comments

"And of course working with the wonderful Margaret O'Brien was almost more than I could stand. She overwhelms me."—*Randal Malone*[5]

"Margaret O'Brien has always been one of my favorite actresses."—*Conrad Brooks*[6]

Comments by Margaret O'Brien

"[*Hollywood Mortuary*] was a cute story. Sort of a spoof on the horror films, which was kind of fun. I always enjoyed the Bela Lugosi and the Boris Karloff movies. I grew up with them. It was fun to do this, and I think it will become sort of a cult spoof on Hollywood horror films."[7]

Radio

"The greatest Christmas present I've ever received was having Margaret O'Brien guest star on my radio show."
—Frank Sinatra, *Command Performance*, December 25, 1945

Shortly after the success of *Lost Angel*, Cecil B. DeMille decided to dramatize it for his *Lux Radio Theatre*. Since Margaret could not read, she would have to memorize the entire script—her part as well as the other actors'. Everyone thought it was too much of a risk, but DeMille chose to do it anyway.

They did three rehearsals and Margaret was perfect each time. However, the executives were afraid that she would get stage fright and forget her lines on live radio and ruin the entire show. Everyone was nervous, except for Margaret, who was the only calm one in the studio. True to her ability, she didn't miss a word or a cue; she was letter perfect. Reportedly after the performance, two nerve-wracked radio executives ran across the street to the Brown Derby bar and stayed there until sunrise.

Margaret O'Brien made numerous appearances on radio during her career at MGM, usually recreating roles that she had made famous on the screen. A listing of many of those appearances follows.

Radio Appearances

Screen Guild Players (CBS); April 5, 1943; episode "Journey for Margaret"; produced and directed by William (Bill) Lawrence; written by Harry Kronman; host/announcer, Truman Bradley; orchestra, Wilbur Hatch; cast: Robert Young, Margaret O'Brien, Anita Louise, William Severn.

Lux Radio Theatre of the Air (CBS); June 19, 1944; episode "Lost Angel"; host, Cecil B. DeMille; cast: Margaret O'Brien (Alpha), James Craig, Marsha Hunt, Keenan Wynn.

Lux Radio Theatre of the Air (CBS);

November 6, 1944; episode "The Pied Piper"; host, Cecil B. DeMille; cast: Frank Morgan, Margaret O'Brien, Signe Hasso, Cathy Lewis, Noreen Gammell.

Suspense (CBS); March 15, 1945; episode "Cricket"; cast: Margaret O'Brien, Dame Mae Whitty.

Lux Radio Theatre of the Air (CBS); June 18, 1945; episode "The Canterville Ghost"; guest host, Hal B. Wallis; cast: Margaret O'Brien, Charles Laughton, Tom Drake.

Lux Radio Theatre of the Air (CBS); October 22, 1945; episode "Lost Angel"; guest host, Mitchell Leisen; intermission guest, Marissa O'Brien, MGM starlet; cast: Margaret O'Brien, George Murphy, Donna Reed.

The Edgar Bergen/Charlie McCarthy Show (NBC); November 18, 1945; episode "Miles Standish"; guest: Margaret O'Brien.

Command Performance (Syn); December 24, 1945 episode #16; cast: The Crosby Kids, Peggy Ann Garner, Frances Langford, Roddy McDowall, Margaret O'Brien, Frank Sinatra, Elizabeth Taylor.

Lux Radio Theatre of the Air (CBS); February 18, 1946; episode "Captain January"; cast: Margaret O'Brien, Lionel Barrymore, Cliff Clark.

Lux Radio Theatre of the Air (CBS); May 27, 1946; episode "Music for Millions"; host, William Keighley; cast: Margaret O'Brien, Jimmy Durante, Jose Iturbi, Frances Gifford, Marissa O'Brien.

Lux Radio Theatre of the Air (CBS); September 2, 1946; episode "Our Vines Have Tender Grapes"; host, William Keighley; cast: Margaret O'Brien, Frances Gifford, James Craig, Joseph Kearns.

Lux Radio Theatre of the Air (CBS); December 2, 1946; episode "Meet Me in St. Louis"; produced by William Keighley; written by Sally Benson; musical direction by Louis Silvers; hosted by William Keighley; announcer, John Milton Kennedy; cast: Judy Garland, Margaret O'Brien, Tom Drake, Gale Gordon.

Academy Award Theatre; December 8, 1946; episode "Lost Angel"; cast: Margaret O'Brien, Jeff Chandler (last show).

Lux Radio Theatre of the Air (CBS); September 1, 1947; episode "Three Wise Fools"; host, William Keighley; cast: Margaret O'Brien, Lionel Barrymore, Edward Arnold, Lewis Stone.

Philco Radio Time (CBS); May 28, 1947; host: Bing Crosby; guest: Margaret O'Brien.

The Jimmy Durante Show (CBS); December 24, 1947; episode "Christmas Show"; guest: Margaret O'Brien.

Lux Radio Theatre of the Air (CBS); March 1, 1948; episode "Bad Bascomb"; cast: Margaret O'Brien, Wallace Beery.

Philco Radio Time (CBS); March 17, 1948; host: Bing Crosby; guest: Margaret O'Brien.

Screen Guild Players (CBS); June 7, 1948; episode "Snow White"; produced and directed by William (Bill) Lawrence; written by Harry Kronman; announcer, Michael Ray; orchestra, Wilbur Hatch; cast: Margaret O'Brien, Jimmy Durante, Mary Jane Smith.

Suspense (CBS); November 25, 1948; episode "The Screaming Woman"; cast: Margaret O'Brien.

Lux Radio Theatre of the Air (CBS); March 13, 1950; episode "Little Women"; host, William Keighley; cast: June Allyson, Margaret O'Brien, Janet Leigh.

Tom Drake, Margaret O'Brien and Judy Garland prepare for the radio presentation of *Meet Me in St. Louis* for the *Lux Radio Theatre*.

The Big Show (NBC); December 24, 1950; emcee and host: Tallulah Bankhead; guests: Jimmy Durante, Bert Lahr, Ed Wynn, Fran Warren, Margaret O'Brien.

The Big Show (NBC); December 31, 1950; emcee and host: Tallulah Bankhead; guests: Margaret O'Brien, Ken Murray, Vivian Blaine, Sam Levine, Jose Ferrer, Gloria Swanson; excerpt "The Twentieth Century," Jose Ferrer, Gloria Swanson; excerpt "Romeo and Juliet," Jose Ferrer, Margaret O'Brien.

The U.S. Treasury Department; August 7, 1955; episode #437, "The Red Evening Gown"; guest: Margaret O'Brien.

The U.S. Treasury Department; August 14, 1955; episode #438; guests: Margaret O'Brien, Margaret Whiting.

Theater

Margaret O'Brien made her stage debut in the Clare Boothe Luce drama *Child of Morning*. The play opened at the Broadway Theater in Springfield, Massachusetts, where the critics praised Margaret's ability, comparing her to a young Helen Hayes. The show, however, was not taken to New York, and closed two weeks later in Boston. "They seemed to think the Luce play, which was about a saint, was too religious," Margaret recalled. "*Joan of Arc* seems to be the only one about a saint they ever produce."[1]

O'Brien also appeared with actor Steve McQueen in his stage debut in the play *Peg o' My Heart*. Of the experience, McQueen later recalled, "I was real nervous, and forgot some of my lines. I remember one of the other actors comin' to me after the curtain went down and saying, very slowly and seriously, 'I want you to know that your performance was just embarrassing.' That kinda took the wind out of my sails."[2]

When *Romeo and Juliet* was being staged at the prestigious Pasadena Playhouse, Margaret was cast in one of the title roles opposite John Barrymore, Jr.

Later, when Margaret won a nomination for her performance in *Jennie Kissed Me* from Chicago's Sarah Siddons Society, she was ecstatic, not so much at winning the award, but rather that she was competing with Lillian Gish and Deborah Kerr. Her performance in Chicago broke all records for four years. "I love the stage," Margaret once said. "Especially since I've known the different forms and expressions which it can take."[3]

THEATER CREDITS

Child of the Morning. A drama in three acts by Clare Boothe Luce; produced by Eddie Dowling and John MacArthur; directed by Eddie Dowling; sets, costumes and lighting by John Blankenchip. Opened at the Broadway Theater, Springfield, Massachusetts, November 16, 1951, and closed at the Shubert in Boston, Massachusetts, on December 1, 1951.

Cast: Margaret O'Brien (Cathy), Sylvia Field (Anna), Una O'Connor (Aunt Nell), Donald McClelland (Fred

Margaret O'Brien as Juliet for the stage production of *Romeo and Juliet*.

Worth), Arthur O'Connell (Father John), Joseph Roman (Spade), P. J. Kelly (Father Pasco), Betty Lou Keim (Jane Moser), Leigh Whipper, Jr. (Joe Washington), Joseph Sullivan (Tom Meehan), Peg Hillias (Zoe), Richard Gaines (Mr. Ordway), John Hamilton* (Gramps).

Synopsis: A Brooklyn Catholic family is thrown into turmoil when their daughter decides not to enter a convent as had been planned since her birth. Source: *Theatre World, Season 1951-1952*. Review: "As the child, the movie actress Margaret O'Brien demonstrated great power, suggesting with complete conviction the perfect sanctity and serenity of the mystic."—*The Best Plays of 1951-1952*, p. 16.

The Intruder. By Edwin Bronner; presented by John D. MacArthur; directed by Eddie Dowling; sets and costumes by Edward Gilbert. Opened December 4, 1952, at the Locust Theater, Philadelphia, Pennsylvania, and closed January 12, 1953, in Northampton, Massachusetts.

Cast: Ann Shoemaker (Serena), Eddie Dowling (Robert), Julie Hayden (Catherine), Margaret O'Brien (Alison), Lionel Wilson (Tommy). General manager: Byron Bentley; press: Dick Williams; stage manager: Freeman Hammond. Source: *Theatre World, Season 1952-1953*.

A Thousand Clowns. By Herb Gardner; directed by Fred Coe; scenery designed and lighted by George Jenkins; costumes, Ruth Morley; production supervisor, Porter Van Zandt; presented by Fred Coe and Arthur Cantor. Opened Wednesday, September 11, 1963, at the Playhouse, Wilmington, Delaware, and closed April 18, 1964, at the American, St. Louis, Missouri.

Cast: Dane Clark (Murray Burns), Barry Gordon (Nick Burns), Conrad Fowkes (Albert Amundson), Margaret O'Brien (Sandra Markowitz), Marc London (Arnold Burns), Paul E. Richards (Leo Herman). Standbys: Ardyth Kaiser (Sandra), Barry Pearl (Nick), Harry Basch (Albert, Arnold, Leo).

Synopsis: A comedy in three acts and five scenes. The action takes place in Murray Burns' Manhattan apartment at the present time. General managers: Joseph Harris, Ira Bernstein; company manager: Emmett Callahan; press: George Deber; stage managers: Tom Porter, Harry Basch. Source: *Theatre World, Season 1963-1964*.

Since 1951, Margaret O'Brien has appeared in hundreds of stage productions. Among them are: *Barefoot in the Park, Secret Service, Romeo and Juliet, The Moon Is Blue, Star Spangled Girl, Young and Beautiful, I Remember Mama, Sabrina Fair, Sunday in New York, Jenny Kissed Me, Love from a Stranger, Kiss and Tell, Peg o' My Heart, Smiling Through, Gigi, Under the Yum-Yum Tree* and *Meet Me in St. Louis*.

*replaced by Eddie Dowling

Television

"When she was doing live television shows in New York, fellow actors said her complete calmness made everyone else more nervous than usual."[1]

—Sidney Skolsky, Hollywood columnist.

Not many people are aware that Margaret O'Brien has appeared in scores of television programs since 1949. She was present during the "Golden Age" of television and during that time appeared in many landmark programs. In the early 1960s Margaret returned to MGM studios for the first time in more than twelve years to appear in an episode of the popular medical drama *Dr. Kildare*. Coincidentally, her third picture at the studio was in *Dr. Gillespie's Criminal Case*, which featured Dr. Kildare's boss, then played by Lionel Barrymore.

"I remember it all quite well," she told a reporter. "Donna Reed and Marilyn Maxwell were nurses and Van Johnson played an intern. Mr. Barrymore used to make rag dolls for me when we weren't shooting."

While back on the MGM lot, Margaret took some time to reminisce about the place that was her home for more than nine years. She remarked that working at MGM now seemed like working at an aircraft plant, because everyone had to punch in and punch out. And the commissary, where everyone ate Mayer's special chicken soup, had a much different ambiance about it.

"I can still see Louis B. Mayer as he used to walk into the commissary then," Margaret recalled. "When he arrived, everybody stopped talking. The waitresses even stopped serving. He was like a king. There's no caste system in the commissary now, but there was then, and where you ate depended upon who you were and how much money you made."[2]

The schoolhouse where Margaret spent three hours of every day was gone now. So were many of the people she worked with, though some still remained after all those years. "I saw a lot of people who are still there," she recalled, "like the wardrobe mistress, and on this *Dr. Kildare* I had the same soundman and cameraman who were on my pictures then."

She even ran into a couple of her old costars including Jimmy Durante, who was back again at MGM filming *Jumbo*. There was also Leon Ames, her father from *Meet Me in St. Louis* and *Little Women*. He was appearing in MGM's *Father of the Bride* television series.

Another significant television appearance occurred ten years later when she had a role in an episode of *Marcus Welby, M.D.* with her friend, Robert Young. Margaret is always open to a good role and still receives many offers every year to appear on television. Don't be surprised if you turn on your television one day soon and see Margaret O'Brien doing what she loves to do best—acting.

TELEVISION APPEARANCES

Inside USA with Chevrolet (CBS)—variety, 30 min.; October 5, 1949; produced by Arthur Schwartz; directed by Sherman Marks; written by Sam Taylor; lyrics by Ira Gershwin, Oscar Hammerstein II, Albert Stillman, Howard Dietz; music by Arthur Schwartz; choreographed by Paul Godkin; with Peter Lind Hayes, Mary Healy, Sheila Bond, Marion Colby, Jay Blackton Orchestra; guest, Margaret O'Brien.

Review: "Skit 'The Head of the Family' with Margaret O'Brien, Hayes and Miss Healy, was very good, not so much for the comedy but in the proper utilization of guest talent and the camera's

enhancement of the personality."—*Variety*, October 5, 1949.

Toast of the Town (CBS)—variety, 60 min.; March 8, 1950; hosted by Ed Sullivan; guests: Margaret O'Brien, Vic Damone, Monica Lewis, Anton Karas, Trini Rayes, Jimmy Valentine, Micki Deems.

Review: "With filmster Margaret O'Brien as guest, Sullivan reprised those old silent clips' routine he did in vaude to demonstrate a possible yesteryear TV 'Toast of the Town.' Sullivan did an okay narration and the spot emerged pleasantly nostalgic."—*Variety*, March 8, 1950.

Robert Montgomery Presents (NBC)—anthology; November 20, 1950; episode #17, "The Canterville Ghost"; adapted from the Oscar Wilde play; cast: Margaret O'Brien, Cecil Parker.

Review: "The excellent performances of the stars did not extend to the supporting company."—*Variety*, November 22, 1950.

Lux Video Theatre (CBS)—anthology, 60 min.; February 19, 1951; episode #21, "To The Lovely Margaret"; directed by Fielder Cook; sets by William Gray Smith; cast: Margaret O'Brien (Margaret), Skip Homeier (Kirk), Anna Lee (Julia), Ivan Simpson (Professor Adams), Pat Gage (Jackie).

Four Star Review (NBC); March 7, 1951; host, Danny Thomas; guests: Margaret O'Brien, Peggy Ryan, Ray McDonald.

Review: "Miss O'Brien finally gives some good material, demonstrated nice comedic talents."—*Variety*, March 7, 1951.

Margaret O'Brien guest stars with Raymond Burr on the television series *Perry Mason*.

Garry Moore Evening Show (CBS)—variety, 30 min.; October 24, 1951; produced by Herb Sanford; directed by Clarence Schimmel; hosted by Garry Moore; cast: Durwood Kirby, Ken Carson, Ilene Woods; guests: James Dunn, Margaret O'Brien, Phil Foster.

Review: "Dramatic spot starred Margaret O'Brien and James Dunn in the daughter-coming-of-age scene from *Tree Grows in Brooklyn*. Pair did a nice thesping job in a moving segment. However, its brevity reduced its impact and didn't utilize the O'Brien-Dunn talents fully."—*Variety*, October 24, 1951.

Lux Video Theatre (CBS)—anthology, 60 min.; February 2, 1953; episode #114, "The White Gown"; directed by Fielder Cook; teleplay by Cyrus Cunion; cast: Margaret O'Brien (Laura), Walter Abel (Father), John Kerr (Tony), Valerie Cossart (Mother), Georgianne Johnson (Maggie), Marcel Hillaire (Headwaiter), William Penn (Bob), Geoffrey Lamb (Professor), Ethel Remey (Chaperone), Dorothy Elder (Professor's Wife), John Weaver, Garry Walluz, Germaine Raphael, May Johnson, Sherman Brown, Hal Hamilton, Nancy Livingston (Extras).

Studio One (CBS); March 16, 1953; episode #193, "A Breath of Air"; cast: Margaret O'Brien, Everett Sloane.

Lux Video Theatre (NBC)—anthology, 60 min.; April 1, 1954; episode "The Way I Feel"; directed by Richard Goode; teleplay by William Kendall Clark; story by Jeff Brown; intermission guest, Sheila Graham; cast: Margaret O'Brien (Elaine), Michael Chapin (George), Duane Hickman (Charlie), Michael

Morrow (Pete), Mae Clarke (Mother), Sidney Mason (Father), Joseph Crehan (Doctor).

Review: "Miss O'Brien, although rating star billing, has very little to do but die, but even the death scene is omitted."—*Daily Variety*, April 5, 1954.

Ford Television Theatre (NBC)—anthology, 30 min.; October 7, 1954; episode #79, "Daughter of Mine"; produced by Irving Starr; directed by Arnold Laven; teleplay by Lillian Hayward, based on a story by Dale Eunson and Katherine Albers; cameraman, Gert Anderson; film editor, Richard Fantl; cast: Margaret O'Brien, Maureen O'Sullivan, Pat O'Brien, Richard Jaeckel.

Review: "The two O'Brien's—Margaret and Pat—play their roles with deep feeling and give the piece its poignant movement."—*Daily Variety*, October 12, 1954.

Climax! (CBS)—anthology, 60 min.; March 3, 1955; episode #23, "South of the Sun"; hosts: William Lundigan, Mary Costa; cast: Jeffrey Hunter, Margaret O'Brien, Thomas Gomez, Edward Arnold.

Review: "Jeffrey Hunter failed to measure up to the demands either dramatically or romantically and on the distaff side Margaret O'Brien was only occasionally impressive in her grown-up role."—*Daily Variety*, March 9, 1955.

Matinee Theatre (NBC); November 21, 1955; episode #16, "Midsummer"; teleplay by Robert Nathan; host: John Conte; cast: Margaret O'Brien.

Lux Video Theatre (NBC)—anthology; December 8, 1955; episode "Suspicion"; directed by Richard Goode, adapted by

R. Goode; guests: David Butler, Margaret O'Brien; cast: Dan O'Herlihy (Jeremy), Kim Hunter (Lina), Melville Cooper (Flaky), Beryl Machin (Isobel), Tito Furden (Ethel), Jack Raine (Captain Melbeck), Richard Peel (Benson), Terrence DeMarney (Dr. Medrusk).

Review: "RKO's payoff was a ploy for *Glory* with producer David Butler and Margaret O'Brien on hand to tubthumb the pic. Clip shown was not the type which would make the watcher wanta go buy a ticket."—*Daily Variety*, December 12, 1955.

Lux Video Theatre (NBC)—anthology; December 22, 1955; episode "Holiday Affair"; directed by Earl Ebi; adaptation by Harry Kronmar; guests: Margaret O'Brien, Walter Brennan; cast: Scott Brady (Steve), Phyllis Thaxter (Connie), Elliott Reid (Carl), Chris Olsen (Timmy), Herb Butterfield (Grandpa), May Adams (Grandma), George Baxter (Mr. Goro), Charles R. Cane (Cop), Paul Bryan (Desk Sergeant).

Front Row Center (CBS)—anthology, 60 min.; March 4, 1956; episode #20, "Innocent Witness"; directed by Ralph Nelson; teleplay by Marc Brandell; cast: Margaret O'Brien, Dean Stockwell, John McIntire, Don Beddoe, Edward Binns, Virginia Christine, Kem Dibbs, Tommy Ivo, Kay Kuter, Jeanette Nolan, James O'Rear, Betsy Paul, Ralph Reed.

Review: "Play moved with measured stride through the hour (no commercial interruptions) with a brace of youngsters, Dean Stockwell and Margaret O'Brien, who has acquired considerable dramatic poise since she traded pigtail for ponytail, the chief motivators."—*Daily Variety*, March 6, 1956.

Climax! (CBS); March 7, 1957; episode #127, "Night of the Rebel" (aka "Nine-Day Wonder"); directed by Buzz Kulick; hosts: William Lundigan, Mary Costa; cast: John Kerr, Margaret O'Brien, Edward Ciannelli, Harry Townes.

The Steve Allen Show (NBC); 1957.

Matinee Theatre (NBC); April 22, 1957; episode #105, "Winter in April"; teleplay by Robert Nathan; host: John Conte; cast: Margaret O'Brien.

Climax! (CBS)—anthology, 60 min.; September 19, 1957; episode #155, "The Necessary Evil"; directed by Buzz Kulik; teleplay by Harold Jack Bloom; hosts: William Lundigan, Mary Costa; cast: Dewey Martin, Victor Jory, Margaret O'Brien, Lon Chaney, Jr., Karl Lucas, Rusty Lane, Sarah Selby, Don Gordon.

Review: "All the performances are skillfully handled, and Jory receives fine support."—*Daily Variety*, September 24, 1957.

Playhouse 90 (CBS); October 24, 1957; episode #46, "The Mystery of Thirteen"; produced by Martin Manulus; directed by Robert Mulligan; teleplay by David Shaw from the Robert Graves novel *They Hanged My Saintly Billy*; cast: Margaret O'Brien, Jack Lemmon, Gladys Cooper, Herbert Marshall, Henry Jones, Romney Brent, John Baragrey.

Review: "Miss O'Brien was very good as the wife who eventually dies—with the help of her husband."—*Daily Variety*, October 28, 1957.

Suspicion (NBC)—anthology, 60 min.; October 28, 1957; episode #5, "The Story of Margery Reardon"; directed by

John Brahm; teleplay adapted by John Kneubuhl from the story by Susan Seavy; host: Dennis O'Keefe; cast: Margaret O'Brien (Margery), Rod Taylor (Jim), Henry Silva (Dick), Sara Haden.

Jane Wyman Presents the Fireside Theatre (NBC)—anthology, 30 min.; November 7, 1957; episode #342, "Roadblock Number Seven"; directed by George Waggner; teleplay by George Waggner from a story by Bruno Fischer; cameraman, John L. Russell, editor, Marston Fay, art director, George Patrick; cast: Margaret O'Brien, Mark Richman, Robert Armstrong, Gordon Jones, Dabbs Greer, Richard Shannon, Frank Gerstle.

Review: "Margaret O'Brien capably projected all the dimension her role provided."—*Daily Variety*, November 11, 1957.

Kraft Television Theatre (NBC); December 4, 1957; episode #539, "Come to Me"; teleplay by Peter Lind Hayes and Robert J. Crean; Hayes, with Robert Allen, also authored the title song and "Lilac Chiffon"; cast: Margaret O'Brien, Farley Granger, Julie Wilson, J. Pat O'Malley, Steve Dunne.

General Electric Theatre (CBS); December 22, 1957; episode #83, "The Young Years"; directed by Herschel Daugherty; host: Ronald Reagan; cast: Margaret O'Brien, Rod Taylor, Dorothy Stickney.

Matinee Theatre (NBC); December 26, 1957; episode #541, "The Little Minister"; teleplay adapted by Helene Hanff from the James M. Barrie Story; cast: Margaret O'Brien, Ben Cooper, Henry Daniell.

Studio One in Hollywood (CBS)—

anthology, 60 min.; January 20, 1958; episode #435, "Trial by Slander"; produced by Gordon Duff; directed by Tom Donovan; teleplay by Roger O. Hirson; cast: Franchot Tone, Jackie Coogan, Margaret O'Brien, Dennis Hopper, Whit Bissell, Rosemary DeCamp.

Review: "Margaret O'Brien was good as the protegee."—*Daily Variety*, January 22, 1958.

Studio One in Hollywood (CBS)—anthology, 60 min.; March 17, 1958; episode #443, "Tongues of Angels"; directed by Herbert Hirschman; teleplay by John Vlahos; cast: Margaret O'Brien (Jenny Walker), James MacArthur (Ben Adams), Leon Ames (Cyrus Walker), Frances Farmer (Mrs. Walker).

Review: "Giving the show its acting excellence were Margaret O'Brien, grown to full ladyhood and with commensurate thespic stature, and James MacArthur, son of the Charles MacArthurs (Helen Hayes). Their touching, tender scenes had an infectious warmth."—*Daily Variety*, March 19, 1958.

Person to Person (CBS)—interview; June 6, 1958; hosted by Edward R. Murrow; guest: Margaret O'Brien.

Steve Allen Presents the Steve Lawrence–Eydie Gorme Show (NBC)—variety, 60 mins.; July 13, 1958, debut episode; produced by Nick Vanoff; directed by Dwight Hemion; written by Johnny Bradford, Fill Dana, Frank Peppiat, Jud Holstein; musical direction by Jack Kane; hosted by Steve Lawrence and Eydie Gorme; guest: Baccaloni, Jackie Cooper, Margaret O'Brien, Shari Lewis.

Review: "Jackie Cooper also registered neatly in a vocal duet with Lawrence and in some hoofing turns, a tympany exhibition and a cute sketch with Margaret O'Brien in which they played a couple of old codgers in 1988 looking back to 1958. Miss O'Brien's bit with Miss Gorme, in which a split-screen illusion had her standing in Miss Gorme's palm during inside show biz monolog, was shaky."—*Variety*, July 16, 1958.

Wagon Train (NBC); September 24, 1958; episode #39, "The Sacramento Story"; cast: Ward Bond (Major Seth Adams), Robert Horton (Flint McCullough), Terry Wilson (Bill Hawks) Frank McGrath (Charlie Wooster); guests: Dan Duryea, Margaret O'Brien, Linda Darnell, Marjorie Main.

Little Women (CBS)—musical special, 60 min.; October 16, 1958; produced by David Susskind; directed by William Corrigan; teleplay by Wilson Lehr; music and lyrics by Richard Adler; orchestration by Don Walker; cast: Florence Henderson (Meg March), Jeanie Carson (Jo March), Margaret O'Brien (Beth March), Zina Bethune (Amy March), Rise Stevens (Margaret March), Joel Grey (Theodore Lawrence), Bill Hayes (John Brooks), Roland Winters (Mr. Lawrence).
    Review: "Television in one hour Thursday did the impossible. In that brief time it destroyed and mutilated Louisa M. Alcott's classic, *Little Women*, with an emasculated, musicalized version which made a farce of the original, beautiful story."—*Daily Variety*, October 20, 1958.

Pursuit (CBS)—anthology, 60 min.; November 19, 1958; episode #5, "Kiss

Me Again, Stranger"; directed by David Greene; teleplay adapted by Leonard Kantor from a story by Daphne du Maurier; cast: Jeffrey Hunter (Lt. Aaron Gibbs), Margaret O'Brien (Mara), Myron McCormick (Colonel), Mort Saul (Skip), Mary Beth Hughes (Evelyn), Yvette Dugay.
    Review: "For Margaret O'Brien it was a good display of emotional acting."—*Daily Variety*, November 21, 1958.

Rawhide (CBS); March 6, 1959; episode #9, "Incident of the Town in Terror"; guest stars: Russ Conway, Kem Dibbs, James Gavin, Don C. Harvey, Margaret O'Brien, Patrick O'Moore, Harry Townes, Garry Walberg, Dan White.

Arthur Murray Party (NBC)—variety; 1959 (exact air date not known).

Playhouse 90 (CBS)—anthology, 90 min.; June 25, 1959; episode #117, "Second Happiest Day"; produced by Peter Kortner; directed by Ralph Nelson; teleplay by Steven Gethers from the novel by John Phillips; cast: Tony Randall, Judith Anderson, Margaret O'Brien, Fay Wray, Ron Ely, Jack Mullaney.
    Review: "This was a hapless task for the director and cast. The best Randall could do was to posture his caricature of a role. Miss O'Brien managed to appear properly sexy, also properly moronic."—*Daily Variety*, June 29, 1959.

The United States Steel Hour (CBS)—anthology, 60 min.; November 4, 1959; episode #265, "Big Doc's Girl"; teleplay adapted by Leonard Moran from the story by Mary Medearis; cast: Robert Lansing, Margaret O'Brien, Gene Hackman.

Review: "Miss O'Brien lost her usual quaver for this one, which was a sort of blessing."—*Variety*, November 11, 1959.

June Allyson Show (CBS); February 22, 1960; episode #22, "Escape"; hosted by June Allyson; cast: Sylvia Sidney, Brian Donlevy, Frank Lovejoy, Margaret O'Brien.

New Comedy Showcase: Maggie (CBS)— unsold pilot, 30 min.; August 29, 1960; executive producer, George Burns; produced by Bill Manhoff; directed by Rod Amateau; teleplay by Bill Manoff; cameraman, James Van Trees; editor, Rex Lipton; cast: Margaret O'Brien (Maggie Bradley), Leon Ames (Mark Bradley), Fay Baker (Annie Bradley), Jesslyn Fax (Miss Caldwell), also, Jeanne Tatum, Charles Cantor, Edwin Bruce, Michael Emmet and Mona Knox.

Review: "This combo deserved a better fate but they paid the penalty of swinging too wildly at zany situations with a brash youngster, Margaret O'Brien, not quite past apprenticeship for such a heavy load. Femmes with a comedy flair haven't done too well in television and Miss O'Brien wasn't about to change things."—*Daily Variety*, August 31, 1960.

Checkmate (CBS); November 12, 1960; episode #8, "Deadly Shadow"; cast: Don Corey, Anthony George, Ted Sills, Doug McClure, Dr. Carl Hyatt, Sebastian Cabot; guests: Margaret O'Brien, Ken Lynch.

The Aquanauts (CBS); January 4, 1961; episode #13, "River Gold"; cast: Drake Andrews, Keith Larson, Larry Lehr, Jeremy Slate, Mike Madison, Ron Ely,

Charles Thompson; guests: James Coburn, Margaret O'Brien.

Here's Hollywood (NBC)—interview; 1961 (exact air date not known).

Adventures in Paradise (ABC); December 17, 1961; episode #76, "The Trial of Adam Troy"; guests: Margaret O'Brien, Ben Cooper.

Dr. Kildare (NBC); February 15, 1962; episode #20, "The Dragon"; guests: Margaret O'Brien, Ben Cooper.

Dupont Show of the Week (NBC); October 21, 1962; episode #33, "The Betrayal"; teleplay adapted by Ernest Pendrell from Joseph Conrad's *Under Western Eyes*; cast: Franchot Tone, Burt Brinckerhoff, Margaret O'Brien, Blanche Yurkon.

Perry Mason (CBS)—drama; January 3, 1963; episode #166, "The Case of the Shoplifter's Shoe"; directed by Arthur Marks; teleplay by Jackson Gillis based on Erle Stanley Gardner's 1938 novel; cast: Raymond Burr (Perry Mason); guests: Lurene Tuttle, Blair Davies, Margaret O'Brien, Leonard Nimoy, Melora Conway, Richard Coogan, Arthur Batanides, Shirley Mitchell, James Millhollin, Charles Irving, Kenneth Patterson, Walter Kelly, Bernard Fein, Vincent Troy, Lee Miller.

Legacy of Light (NBC); July 20, 1963.

The Mike Douglas Show (Syn)—talk show, 90 min.; 1964 (exact air date not known).

Bob Hope Chrysler Theatre (NBC); October 23, 1964; episode #31, "The

Turncoat"; cast: George Hamilton, Rodolfo Acosta, Margaret O'Brien, Jack Weston, Carroll O'Connor.

Combat! (ABC)—drama, 60 min.; January 3, 1967; episode #143 "Entombed"; produced by Richard Caffey; directed by Bernard McEveety; story by William Bast; teleplay by Paul Playdon and Bob Frederick; cast: Rick Jason (Lt. Hanley), Vic Morrow (Sgt. Saunders); guests: Margaret O'Brien (Marianne Fraisnet), Skip Homeier (Lt. Karl Mauer), Michael Constantine (Jacques Patron), Tom Fielding (Pfc. Tommy Bishop), King Moody (Toulon), Mark de Vries (Pvt. Wexler), Michael Hausserman (Johann Schiller), Barry Ford (German Captain), Beau Vann den Ecker (Emile).

Ironside (NBC)—drama; September 26, 1968; episode "Split Second to an Epitaph"; executive producer Frank Pierce; produced by Paul Mason; directed by Leonard Horn; teleplay by Don Mankiewicz, Sy Salkowitz and Collier Young; original music by Quincy Jones; cinematography by Bud Thackery; film editing by Edward W. Williams; cast: Raymond Burr (Chief Robert Ironside), Barbara Anderson (Eve Whitfield), Don Mitchell (Mark Sanger); guests: Joseph Cotten (Dr. Ben Stern), Margaret O'Brien (Louise Prescott), Troy Donahue (Father Dugan), Andrew Princ (Ernie Clark), Mel Scott (Ralph Fellows), Lilia Skala (Sister Agatha), Don Stroud (Albee).

Love, American Style (ABC)—anthology, 60 min.; October 6, 1969; episode "Love and the Letter."

The Movie Game (Syn); 1970 (exact air date not known).

Adam-12 (NBC)—police drama, 30 min.; August 19, 1971; episode "Sign of the Times."

Marcus Welby, M.D. (ABC)—drama, 60 min.; December 19, 1972; episode #88, "Dinner of Herbs"; guests: Margaret O'Brien, Anthony Eisley, Vincent Van Lynn, Marjorie Arnold, Richard Derr.

Wide World of Mystery (ABC); June 17, 1974; episode "Death in Space."

Testimony of Two Men (Syn)—miniseries, 120 min.; May 2, May 9 and May 16, 1977; cast: David Birney, Steve Forrest, William Shatner, Margaret O'Brien, Ray Milland, Linda Purl.

Quincy (NBC)—medical drama, 60 minutes; 1982; episode "Across the Line."

Hotel (ABC)—drama, 60 min.; December 7, 1983; episode #11, "The Offer"; directed by Don Chaffey; teleplay by Ross Teal and Geoffrey Fischer; guests: Lorenzo Lamas, Arte Johnson, Margaret O'Brien, Donald O'Connor, Craig Stevens, Eleanor Parker, Albert Hague, Dianne Kaye.

Tales from the Darkside (HBO)—mystery; May 23, 1987; episode "Black Widows"; cast: Margaret O'Brien, Theresa Saldano.

America's All-Star Tribute to Elizabeth Taylor (ABC)—variety special, 60 min.; March 9, 1989; produced and directed by Marty Pasetta; written by Stephen Pouliot, Ken Welch and Mitzie Welch; music by Lenny Stack; host: Charles Bronson; guest of honor: Elizabeth Taylor; guests: June Allyson, Beau Bridges,

Carol Burnett, Bob Hope, Roddy McDowall, Vera Miles, Margaret O'Brien, Mickey Rooney, Robert Stack, Stevie Wonder.

When We Were Young: Growing Up on the Silver Screen (PBS)—documentary, 95 minutes; December 7, 1989; produced by Glen DuBose, James Arntz and Shelly Spencer; directed by Dick Carter; written by James Arntz and Katherine McMillan; hosted by Maureen Stapleton; guests: Angela Cartwright, Jackie Cooper, Daryl Hickman, Roddy McDowall, Spanky McFarland, Haley Mills, Dick Moore, Margaret O'Brien, Tommy Rettig, Mickey Rooney, Dean Stockwell, Jane Withers.

Murder, She Wrote (CBS)—drama/mystery, 60 minutes; February 10, 1991; episode #7.14, "Who Killed J. B. Fletcher?"; cast: Angela Lansbury (Jessica Fletcher); guests: Betty Garrett (Kit Parkins), Jamie Rose (Lisa McCauley), Max Baer, Jr. (State Trooper Boone Willoughby), Earl Holliman (Sheriff Tanner), Tom Shanley (Rick, the Kennel Groomer), Margaret O'Brien (Jane), Lyman Ward (Mitchell Lawrence), Marie Windsor (Caroline), Terry Moore (Florence), Jane Withers (Marge Allen), Janet Blair (Bertie), David Cowgill (Deputy), Rod Britt (Hotel Clerk), Curt Booker (Security Guard), Marilyn Byrkett (Technician), Michael Leopard (Cabbie), Mario Machado (Anchor), Marc Marcosi (Waiter), Tom Menuh (Kennel Clerk).

Lassie (Syn)—drama, 30 min.; episode #25; cast: Christopher Stone (Chris McCullough), Dee Wallace Stone (Dee McCullough), Jon Provost (Uncle Steve), Wendy Cox (Megan McCullough), Will Nipper (Will McCullough); guests: Margaret O'Brien, Gale Gordon.

Magazine References

Collier's, November 28, 1942.

Motion Picture Herald, November 6, 1943.

Showmen's Trade Review, undated.

"At Age of Seven, This Personable Child Is One of Hollywood's Most Gifted Actresses," *Life*, April 3, 1944.

Photoplay, May 1944.

"Little Miss Magic," *Movie Stars*, June 1944.

"Little Miss Margaret: America's Newest Sweetheart," *Movieland* (cover), September 1944.

"She Might Be Your Child," *New York Times Magazine*, October 1, 1944.

"Child Actress," *Nation*, November 25, 1944.

"Close-up of Margaret O'Brien, Our Cover Girl," *Motion Picture* (cover), February 1945.

"Margaret O'Brien Is My Darling," *Sunday Dispatch* (London), February 25, 1945.

"A Journey for Margaret," *Movieland*, April 1945.

"Margaret O'Brien," *Movie Show*, April 1945.

"Margaret O'Brien at Eight," *Look* (cover), April 17, 1945.

"Little Miss Remarkable," *Modern Screen*, May 1945.

"Junior Pin-up," *Photoplay*, May 1945.

"There's Magic in Margaret," *Screenland*, May 1945.

Le Petite Revue (cover), June 1945 (Canada).

"Education for Margaret," *Woman's Home*, August 1945.

"Our Vines Have Tender Grapes," *Movie Story* (cover), September, 1945.

"My Favorite Movie Scene," *Saturday Evening Post*, October 27, 1945.

"Maggie Settles Down," *This Week Magazine*, December 9, 1945.

"Margaret O'Brien," *Life*, December 10, 1945.

"Maggie's Scrapbook," *Photoplay* (cover), January 1946.

"Margaret O'Brien," *Reader's Digest*," February 1946.

"Margaret O'Brien," *Family Circle*, February 8, 1946.

"Maggie Was a Cover Girl," *American Magazine*, March 1946.

"Shirley Temple's Advice to Margaret O'Brien," *Movieland*, May 1946.

Cover portrait, *Movies*, July 1946.

"Happiest Day of My Life," *Woman's Home*, August 1946.

Cover portrait, *Screenland*, December 1946.

Cover portrait, *Silver Screen*, January 1947.

"Maggie's Dreamy," *Photoplay*, February 1947.

Cover portrait, *Polly Pigtails*, February 1947.

"Speaking of Pictures," *Life*, April 7, 1947.

Cover portrait, *Movies*, July 1947.

"My Little Girl's Name Is Margaret O'Brien," *McCall's*, August 1947.

"This Is Myself ... Margaret O'Brien," *Movieland*, August 1947.

"I Sightsee in New York," *Family Circle*, September 1947.

Cover portrait, *Parents*, October 1947.

"Did I Say Candy?" *Photoplay*, November 1947.

Cinema (cover), December 1, 1947 (Spain).

"My Trip to Honolulu," *Family Circle*, January 1948.

Cover portrait, *Movie Teen*, July 1948.

"The Role I Liked Best," *Saturday Evening Post*, July 24, 1948.

"Princess Margaret of Hollywood," *Collier's*, January 29, 1949.

"My Mother Understands," *Photoplay*, June 1949.

"Maggie Shows Her Age," *Photoplay*, August 1952.

"The Case of Margaret O'Brien," *Good Housekeeping*, April 1953.

"Margaret O'Brien Grows Up," *Collier's*, September 4, 1953.

Portrait, *Saturday Evening Post*, January 2, 1954.

Portrait, *Time*, May 24, 1954.

Portrait, *Look*, August 10, 1954.

"Grown-up Graduation," *Newsweek*, June 27, 1955.

Portrait, *Time*, June 27, 1955.

"All Teenagers Aren't Delinquent," *Photoplay*, December 1955.

"Adult Margaret O'Brien," *Cosmopolitan*, January 1956.

"Margaret O'Brien, the Girl Who Refused to Grow Up," *Redbook*, January 1956.

"Child Stars Who Came Back," *Coronet*, March 1958.

"How the Girls Grown," *Life* (cover), May 19, 1958.

"Who Can I Turn to Now That I'm All Alone," *Photoplay*, December 1958.

"Princess of Pretend," *Holiday*, March 1959.

"Actress O'Brien: 'Why It Was Hard for Me to Grow Up,'" *Parade* (cover), April 19, 1959.

"I Miss My Mother Most of All Now," *Photoplay*, September 1959.

"A Journey for Margaret into Mother-Daughter Fashions," *Photoplay*, December 1977.

"Margaret O'Brien," *Cine Review* (Paris), August 21, 1980.

"Margaret O'Brien: A Star Waiting to Shine Again," *Hollywood Studio Magazine*, December 1983.

"Margaret O'Brien," *Film Dope* (England), July 1992.

"The Journeys of Margaret," *Classic Images #218*, August 1993.

"Journey for Margaret's Oscar," *Classic Images #237*, March 1995.

"Tea with Vivien Leigh," *Films of the Golden Age*, Summer 1995.

"An Interview with Margaret O'Brien: The MGM Years," *Classic Images*, December 1998.

Newspaper References

"Seeing Styles," *Los Angeles Times,* December 6, 1942.

Virginia Wright column, *Los Angeles Daily News,* February 17, 1943.

"New Film Star Sheds Tears in Every Picture," *New York Herald-Tribune,* March 21, 1943.

"Young Actor Has First Villain Role," *MGM News,* September 3, 1943.

"Laughton Learns Prestidigator's [*sic*] Art," *MGM News,* October 5, 1943.

"Margaret O'Brien Is 'Teardrop' to Stars," unidentified and undated newspaper.

"Child Actress Gains Screen Fame Quickly," Hedda Hopper column, November 21, 1943.

"A Glamor Nightie for Miss O'Brien, Please," *Hollywood Citizen-News,* November 22, 1943.

"Ghosts Lack Terrors for Moppet Star," *MGM News,* December 16, 1943.

"Mrs. Long-Run Is Back at Music Hall," *New York Herald-Tribune,* January 23, 1944.

Trade Views column, *Hollywood Reporter,* February 21, 1944.

"Movie Queen at Age of 7—Margaret O'Brien," *Hollywood Citizen-News,* March 1, 1944.

"Lost Angel," *New York Herald-Tribune,* April 9, 1944.

"Tiny Film Star Not a Prodigy, Avers Mother," *MGM News,* June 13, 1944.

"Pink Horse Wins," *Los Angeles Times,* January 2, 1945.

"A Special Screen Award," *New York Times,* March 16, 1945.

"Hollywood's Veterans," *New York Times,* September 16, 1945.

"Maggie Settles Down," *Los Angeles Times,* December 9, 1945.

"Child Star Gets $2500 Weekly Pay," *Los Angeles Times,* October 12, 1946.

"Hollywood Agenda," *New York Times,* February 9, 1947.

"Margaret O'Brien's Record Contract Approved by Court," *Los Angeles Examiner,* June 27, 1947.

"Touring the Hollywood Studios," *New York Times,* July 13, 1947.

"Dazzling Ballet Effects Glorify O'Brien Feature," *Los Angeles Times,* undated article.

"Tiny Star Off to N.Y. to Study Role," unidentified and undated newspaper.

"Radio Station KMGM Opened," *Los Angeles Times,* March 28, 1948.

"Europe Trip 'Wonderful,' Says Margaret

O'Brien," *Los Angeles Times*, May 24, 1948.

"Margaret O'Brien's Mama Tells Trials of Her Job," unidentified and undated article, circa 1948.

"Margaret O'Brien Honored," *New York Times*, undated article, circa 1948.

"Opening Crusade for Children," *New York Times*, undated article, circa 1948.

"Miss O'Brien Gets Housed for $25,000," unidentified newspaper, July 24, 1948.

"Margaret O'Brien Investment Ok'd," *Hollywood Citizen-News*, July 24, 1948.

"Child Actress Gets Permission for Investment," *Los Angeles Times*, July 24, 1948.

"Margaret O'Brien Becomes Landlady," *MGM News*, August 9, 1948.

"Margaret O'Brien Income Set at $193,848 in 1947," *Los Angeles Examiner*, October 25, 1948.

"Margaret O'Brien Nets $18,530 Out of $193,848," *Los Angeles Times*, October 25, 1948.

"Margaret and Her Little Lamb," *Los Angeles Times*, November 15, 1948.

"Margaret O'Brien Mother Will Wed," *Los Angeles Times*, February 17, 1949.

"Margaret Weeps as Mrs. O'Brien Plans to Wed," *Los Angeles Times*, February 18, 1949.

"Margaret O'Brien Shuns Stepfather," *Los Angeles Examiner*, February 23, 1949.

"Margaret Wet Blanket on Ma's Bridal Altar," *Los Angeles Mirror*, February 23, 1949.

"Tearful O'Brien: Child Film Star Weeps as Mother Weds," *Los Angeles Times*, February 23, 1949.

"Step-Father Very Nice Young Star Decides," *Los Angeles Times*, February 24, 1949.

"Archbishop Scolds Margaret O'Brien for Her Bobby Sox," *Los Angeles Examiner*, February 27, 1949.

"Journey for Margaret Fails to Sweeten Her to Sylvio," *Los Angeles Daily News*, March 16, 1949.

"Film Goal Achieved by LeRoy," *Los Angeles Times*, April 10, 1949.

"'Little Women' Revives Era of Gracious Living," *Los Angeles Times*, April 18, 1949.

"Maggie O'Brien Mother to Ask Annulment," unidentified newspaper, June 1, 1949.

"Margaret O'Brien, MGM Sever Pact," *Hollywood Reporter*, June 1, 1949.

"Margaret O'Brien Gets 'Peter Pan' Stage Offer," unidentified newspaper, June 2, 1949.

"Battle Looms; Sylvio to Fight Annulment," *Hollywood Citizen-News*, June 2, 1949.

"Don Sylvio to Fight Annulment," *Los Angeles Daily News*, June 2, 1949.

"Mate Opposing Annulment by Margaret O'Brien Mother," *Los Angeles Examiner*, June 2, 1949.

"Margaret O'Brien to Be Voice of Disney's 'Alice,'" unidentified newspaper, June 3, 1949.

"Margaret O'Brien, 'Upset' Over Mother, to Take Rest," unidentified newspaper, June 6, 1949.

"Margaret O'Brien's Plans Won't Halt Film," *Los Angeles Times*, June 6, 1949.

"Varied Hollywood Matters," *New York Times*, June 12, 1947.

"Touring the Hollywood Studios," *New York Times*, July 13, 1949.

"Margaret O'Brien's Mother Files New Charge in Sylvio's Divorce Suit," *Los Angeles Times*, September 9, 1949.

"Don Sylvio Contests O'Brien Divorce; Puts Blame on Margaret," *Hollywood Citizen-News*, October 21, 1949.

"Actress O'Brien's Mother Reveals Sylvio Demands," *Los Angeles Times*, December 16, 1949.

Earl Wilson column, *Los Angeles Daily News*, March 13, 1950.

"Court Gets Plan to Save Margaret

O'Brien's Cash," *Los Angeles Times*, August 31, 1950.

"Margaret O'Brien's Piggy Bank Bulges with $176,577," *Los Angeles Daily News*, September 1, 1950.

"Margaret O'Brien's Mother Tells Threats, Gets Divorce," *Los Angeles Herald-Express*, September 5, 1950.

"Margaret O'Brien to Be Confirmed," *Los Angeles Times*, April 24, 1951.

"Daughter of Danny Thomas, Margaret O'Brien Confirmed," *Los Angeles Herald-Examiner*, April 25, 1951.

"Margaret O'Brien Gets Confirmation Sacrament," *Los Angeles Times*, April 25, 1951.

"Mrs. O'Brien Seeks OK to Sell Margaret's Half of Family Home," *Hollywood Citizen-News*, June 15, 1951.

"Margaret, Mama in Court on House-Sale Deal," *Los Angeles Daily News*, June 15, 1951.

"Margaret O'Brien in 'Affairs of Maggie,'" *Variety*, July 16, 1951.

"Wherefore Art Thou Romeo?" *New York Picture Newspaper*, October 21, 1951.

"Margaret O'Brien Set to Star in Japanese Picture," *Hollywood Citizen-News*, July 17, 1952.

"Margaret O'Brien Arrives in Japan to Costar in Film," *Los Angeles Times*, September 5, 1952.

"Help Asked to Find Margaret O'Brien's Dog," *Hollywood Citizen-News*, September 20, 1952.

"Ex-Child Star's Funds Questioned," *Los Angeles Examiner*, October 21, 1953.

"Margaret O'Brien's Finances Reported," *Los Angeles Times*, October 21, 1953.

"Margaret O'Brien in Court," *Los Angeles Daily News*, October 21, 1953.

"Court, Star's Mother at Odds Over Finances," *Los Angeles Examiner*, May 24, 1954.

"Margaret O'Brien Wins Contracts Okay," *Los Angeles Times*, March 15, 1955.

"Margaret O'Brien to Get High School Diploma," *Los Angeles Mirror-News*, June 15, 1955.

"Margaret O'Brien Ready for Work After Graduation," *Daily Newslife*, June 20, 1955.

"Margaret O'Brien Set for Grown-up Career," *Los Angeles Times*, July 17, 1955.

"Margaret O'Brien to Get First Screen Kiss," *Los Angeles Herald-Express*, July 25, 1955.

"Court OK's Film for Miss O'Brien; Warns on Pacts," *Los Angeles Examiner*, October 8, 1955.

"Famous Laps I've Sat In," *Los Angeles Times*, January 15, 1956.

"Margaret O'Brien Breaks Moppets Jinx," *Los Angeles Times*, May 6, 1956.

"Where Are the Tots?" *New York Times*, May 12, 1957.

"Margaret O'Brien Gets Okay on Latest Contract," *Los Angeles Times*, June 8, 1957.

"Star Margaret O'Brien's Mother Dies," *Beverly Hills Citizen*, August 28, 1958.

"Margaret O'Brien's Mother Dies," *Hollywood Citizen-News*, August 28, 1958.

"Rosary Set Tonight for Mrs. O'Brien," *Hollywood Citizen-News*, August 29, 1958.

"Mother of Margaret O'Brien Laid to Rest," *Los Angeles Times*, August 31, 1958.

"Margaret O'Brien Won't Be a Hot Rod Girl," *Los Angeles Mirror-News*, September 10, 1958.

"Margaret O'Brien to Marry," *Los Angeles Mirror-News*, January 23, 1959.

"The New Margaret O'Brien Looks Ahead," *Los Angeles Herald-Examiner*, March 15, 1959.

"Margaret's 21, Rich, Lonely," *Hollywood Citizen-News*, March 25, 1959.

"Margaret O'Brien Gets Permit to Wed," *Los Angeles Examiner*, August 7, 1959.

"Margaret O'Brien, Art Student, Say

'I Do'," *Los Angeles Examiner*, August 9, 1959.

"Margaret O'Brien Hawaii-Bound After Wedding," *Hollywood Citizen-News*, August 10, 1959.

"At Home with Margaret O'Brien," *New York News*, March 26, 1961.

"Little Maggie's Back in the Hospital Again," *Los Angeles Times*, December 25, 1961.

"Margaret O'Brien, One Child Star Able to Qualify as an Adult Professional," *Variety*, January 10, 1962.

"Margaret O'Brien Revisits Kildare," *Los Angeles Times*, February 11, 1962.

"Names at Fairfield College Include Maggie Truman," *Variety*, June 23, 1965.

"Margaret O'Brien's Soap Opera in Peru," *Variety*, October 23, 1965.

"Margaret O'Brien, Sally Rand Co-stars," *Los Angeles Times*, September 20, 1966.

"Television Makes Margaret O'Brien Feel So Young Again," *Los Angeles Times*, January 16, 1967.

"Margaret's Sunny Side Ascending," *Los Angeles Herald-Examiner*, May 7, 1967.

"Margaret O'Brien for Peru's 'Annabelle Lee,'" *Hollywood Reporter*, February 8, 1968.

"Miss O'Brien Seeks Divorce," *Los Angeles Herald-Examiner*, November 26, 1968.

"Actress O'Brien Loses $5400 to Burglar," *Los Angeles Herald-Examiner*, March 11, 1970.

"Robert Young: Welby Has the Right Rx for Life," *Los Angeles Times*, February 21, 1971.

"Mexican Producer Torres Here to Cast Two Films," *Hollywood Reporter*, April 26, 1971.

"Miss O'Brien Slated for Welby Role," *Los Angeles Times*, June 6, 1972.

New York Times, November 19, 1972.

"Little Margaret O'Brien—as a Fattie?" *Los Angeles Times*, December 15, 1972.

"New Career for Margaret O'Brien," *Beverly Hills Independent*, October 21, 1973.

"New Career for O'Brien," *Los Angeles Times*, May 22, 1977.

"The Death of a Monument to Innocence," *Los Angeles Times*, April 29, 1979.

"Margaret O'Brien Backs Rejection of Jane Fonda," *Los Angeles Times*, August 12, 1979.

"New Career for Margaret O'Brien," *Beverly Hills Independent*, October 21, 1979.

"Academy Salutes Child Stars of 30s and 40s," *Los Angeles Times*, July 16, 1980.

Rambling Reporter column, *Variety*, December 5, 1990.

"Margaret O'Brien to Read from 'The Secret Garden,'" *Los Angeles Times*, July 31, 1993.

"Child Star Wins Back Oscar After 40 Years," *London Times*, February 9, 1995.

"Back Where He Belongs," *Minneapolis Star Tribune*, February 9, 1995.

"Academy Award to Be Returned to Actress Forty Years After Theft," *West Hollywood Weekly*, February 10, 1995.

"Oscar Tale with a Happy Ending," *Los Angeles Times*, March 7, 1995.

"Lights, Camera, Narration," *Los Angeles Times*, August 3, 1995.

"Vintage Hollywood: The Stars from Yesteryear Came Out Saturday Night," *Newsday*, October 29, 1996.

"Whatever Happened to Child Star Margaret O'Brien," *The Christian Science Monitor*, July 30, 1998.

"No Business Like Snow Business," *Independent on Sunday*, December 13, 1998.

Endnotes

Unless otherwise noted, all quotes by Margaret O'Brien are taken from a series of interviews at the Roosevelt Hotel, Hollywood, California, on May 28, 1995, July 2, 1995, and September 10, 1995.

INTRODUCTION

1. Ephraim Katz, *The Film Encyclopedia* (New York: HarperPerennial), p. 451.

2. "Margaret O'Brien," *Life*, December 10, 1945.

3. Trade Views column, *Hollywood Reporter*, February 21, 1944.

4. "Adult Margaret O'Brien," *Cosmopolitan*, January 1956.

5. "Tiny Film Star Not a Prodigy, Avers Mother," *MGM Publicity*, June 13, 1944, AMPAS.

6. Theresa Saldana at the Pacific Pioneer Broadcasters banquet for the presentation of the Lifetime Achievement Award to Margaret O'Brien, Sportsmen Lodge, Studio City, California, May 1994.

7. Patti Andrews interview, Los Angeles, California, March 1996.

8. David Shipman, *The Great Movie Stars: The Golden Years* (New York: Bonanza Books), p. 419.

9. Ann Miller interview, Beverly Hills, California, April 1996.

10. Del Reisman, letter to author, Los Angeles, California, August 17, 1999.

11. Jimmy Bangley to author, West Hollywood, California, August 27, 1999.

12. Roddy McDowall at the Pacific Pioneer Broadcasters banquet for the presentation of the Lifetime Achievement Award to Margaret O'Brien, Sportsmen Lodge, Studio City, California, May 1994.

MARGARET O'BRIEN— HER JOURNEY

1. Virginia Wright column, *Los Angeles Daily News*, February 17, 1943.

2. "Maggie Was a Cover Girl," *American Magazine*, March 1946.

3. Margaret O'Brien's MGM Biography, Margaret Herrick Library, AMPAS.

4. "Margaret O'Brien," *Life*, December 10, 1945.

5. Vincente Minnelli, *I Remember It Well* (New York: Doubleday & Company), p. 118.

6. "Margaret O'Brien," *Life*, December 10, 1945.

7. "Margaret O'Brien, The Girl Who

Refused to Grow Up," *Redbook*, January 1956.

8. "She Might Be Your Child," *New York Times Magazine*, October 1, 1944.

9. *Collier's*, November 28, 1942.

10. "Margaret O'Brien," *Life*, December 10, 1945.

11. *Motion Picture Herald*, November 6, 1943.

12. *Showmen's Trade Review*, undated.

13. "Margaret O'Brien," *Life*, December 10, 1945.

14. Dick Moore, *Twinkle, Twinkle, Little Star, but Don't Have Sex or Take the Car* (New York: Harper & Row Publishers), p. 136.

15. "Junior Pin-up," *Photoplay*, May 1945.

16. Lionel Barrymore, *We Barrymores* (New York: Appleton-Century-Crofts), p. 248.

17. "Junior Pin-up," *Photoplay*, May 1945.

18. "Maggie Was a Cover Girl," *American Magazine*, March 1946.

19. "Robert Young: Welby Has the Right Rx for Life," *Los Angeles Times*, February 21, 1971.

20. Elsa Lanchester, *Elsa Lanchester, Herself* (New York: St. Martin's Press), p. 178.

21. "Margaret O'Brien's Mama Tells Trials of Her Job," undated.

22. Elinor Donahue interview, Studio City, California, August 14, 1999.

23. "Princess Margaret of Hollywood," *Collier's*, January 29, 1949.

24. Margaret O'Brien interview, Turner Classic Movies archives, Los Angeles, California, 1999.

25. "Pink Horse Wins," *Los Angeles Times*, January 2, 1945.

26. "She Might Be Your Child," *New York Times Magazine*, October 1, 1944.

27. "Margaret O'Brien," *Family Circle*, February 8, 1946.

28. "Princess Margaret of Hollywood," *Collier's*, January 29, 1949.

29. "Child Actress," *The Nation*, November 25, 1944.

30. Margaret O'Brien interview, Hollywood, California, July 2, 1995.

31. Dick Moore, *Twinkle, Twinkle, Little Star, but Don't Have Sex or Take the Car*, p. 93.

32. Hearst Newsreel, March 16, 1945.

33. Margaret O'Brien interview, Turner Classic Movies archives, Los Angeles, California, 1999.

34. Margaret O'Brien, *My Diary* (Philadelphia: J. B. Lippincott Co.), p. 18.

35. "Margaret O'Brien's Mama Tells Trials of Her Job," undated.

36. Hedda Hopper Collection, Margaret Herrick Library, AMPAS.

37. "Europe Trip 'Wonderful,' Says Margaret O'Brien," *Los Angeles Times*, May 24, 1948.

38. *Movie Teen*, January 1948.

39. "The Case of Margaret O'Brien," *Good Housekeeping*, April 1953.

40. Elinor Donahue interview, Studio City, California, August 14, 1999.

41. "Margaret O'Brien," *Life*, December 10, 1945.

42. "Margaret O'Brien, the Girl Who Refused to Grow Up," *Redbook*, January 1956.

43. "My Mother Understands," *Photoplay*, June 1949.

44. "Margaret O'Brien Shuns Stepfather," *Los Angeles Examiner*, February 23, 1949.

45. "My Mother Understands," *Photoplay*, June 1949.

46. "Journey for Margaret Fails to Sweeten Her to Sylvio," *Los Angeles Daily News*, March 16, 1949.

47. "Battle Looms; Sylvio to Fight Annulment," *Hollywood Citizen-News*, June 2, 1949.

48. "Mate Opposing Annulment by

Margaret O'Brien Mother," *Los Angeles Examiner*, June 2, 1949.

49. "Margaret O'Brien's Plans Won't Halt Film," *Los Angeles Times*, June 6, 1949.

50. "Margaret O'Brien Gets 'Peter Pan' Stage Offer," *Los Angeles Daily News*, June 2, 1949.

51. "Margaret O'Brien, 'Upset' Over Mother, to Take Rest," unidentified publication, June 6, 1949.

52. "Margaret O'Brien, the Girl Who Refused to Grow Up," *Redbook*, January 1956.

53. Earl Wilson column, *Los Angeles Daily News*, March 13, 1950.

54. "Margaret O'Brien, the Girl Who Refused to Grow Up," *Redbook*, January 1956.

55. Roddy McDowall to Jimmy Bangley, September 1996.

56. "Margaret Grows Up!" unidentified and undated publication.

57. *New York Times*, November 19, 1972.

58. "Little Margaret O'Brien—as a Fattie?" *Los Angeles Times*, December 15, 1972.

59. Unidentified and undated publication, Margaret Herrick Library, AMPAS.

60. "Wherefore Art Thou Romeo?" *New York Picture Newspaper*, October 21, 1951.

61. Dick Moore, *Twinkle, Twinkle, Little Star, but Don't Have Sex or Take the Car*, p. 61.

62. "Margaret O'Brien, the Girl Who Refused to Grow Up," *Redbook*, January 1956.

63. Ibid.

64. "The Case of Margaret O'Brien," *Good Housekeeping*, April 1953.

65. Ibid.

66. "Margaret O'Brien Set for Grown-up Career," *Los Angeles Times*, July 17, 1955.

67. Ibid.

68. "Margaret O'Brien to Get First Screen Kiss," *Los Angeles Herald-Express*, July 25, 1955.

69. "Adult Margaret O'Brien," *Cosmopolitan*, January 1956.

70. "Who Can I Turn to Now That I'm All Alone," *Photoplay*, December 1958.

71. "Rosary Set Tonight for Mrs. O'Brien," *Hollywood Citizen-News*, August 29, 1958.

72. "Margaret's 21, Rich, Lonely," *Hollywood Citizen-News*, March 25, 1959.

73. Ibid.

74. *Beverly Hills Citizen*, March 9, 1960.

75. "Margaret Grows Up!" unidentified and undated publication.

76. "Margaret's 21, Rich, Lonely," *Hollywood Citizen-News*, March 25, 1959.

77. "Margaret O'Brien Revisits Kildare," *Los Angeles Times*, February 11, 1962.

78. "Margaret O'Brien, Sally Rand Co-Stars," *Los Angeles Times*, September 20, 1966.

79. Ibid.

80. "Margaret O'Brien Set for Grown-up Career," *Los Angeles Times*, July 17, 1955.

81. "Little Maggie's Back in the Hospital Again," *Los Angeles Times*, December 25, 1961.

82. "Child Stars: Where Are They Now?" *Buffalo Sun*, undated.

83. "Little Margaret O'Brien—as a Fattie?" *Los Angeles Times*, December 15, 1972.

84. Unidentified and undated publication, Margaret Herrick Library, AMPAS.

85. "Margaret's 21, Rich, Lonely," *Hollywood Citizen-News*, March 25, 1959.

86. "Child Stars: Where Are They Now?" *Buffalo Sun*, undated.

87. Ibid.

88. David Ragan, *Who's Who in Hollywood, 1900–1976* (New Rochelle: Arlington House), p. 333.

THE FILMS

Babes on Broadway (1941)

1. Margaret O'Brien interview, Los Angeles, California, Turner Classic Movies Archive, 1999.
2. *Halliwell's Film Guide*, p. 68.
3. Mickey Rooney interview, Hollywood, California, July 21, 1999.
4. "Lost Angel," *New York Herald-Tribune*, April 9, 1944.

Journey for Margaret (1942)

1. "Margaret O'Brien," *Life*, December 10, 1945.
2. MGM Publicity Service, Margaret Herrick Library, AMPAS.
3. Virginia Wright column, *Los Angeles Daily News*, February 17, 1943.
4. Diana Serra Cary, *Hollywood's Children* (Boston: Houghton Mifflin Company), p. 252.
5. *The Exhibitor*, November 4, 1942.
6. Joan Rivers, *Enter Talking* (New York: Delacorte Press), p. 29.
7. *Harrison's Reports*, October 31, 1942.
8. "Margaret O'Brien, the Girl Who Refused to Grow Up," *Redbook*, January 1956.
9. Lorraine Day, Academy Oral History Program, Margaret Herrick Library, AMPAS, p. 114.

Dr. Gillespie's Criminal Case (1943)

1. Lionel Barrymore, *We Barrymores* (New York: Appleton-Century-Crofts), p. 249.
2. Unidentified and undated publication, Margaret Herrick Library, AMPAS.
3. *Film Fan Monthly*, May 1973.
4. "Margaret O'Brien Is 'Teardrop' to Stars," unidentified and undated publication, AMPAS.
5. "Margaret O'Brien," *Life*, December 10, 1945.

6. *Motion Picture Daily*, May 4, 1943.
7. Lionel Barrymore, *We Barrymores*, p. 248.

Thousands Cheer (1943)

1. John Wakeman, *World Film Directors, Volume 1, 1890–1945* (New York: The H. P. Wilson Co.), p. 993.
2. *New York Times*, September 14, 1943.
3. Joe Pasternak, *Easy the Hard Way* (New York: Putnam), pp. 241–242.
4. Red Skelton to Randal Malone, Long Beach, California, 1992.

Madame Curie (1943)

1. "Mrs. Long-Run Is Back at Music Hall," *New York Herald-Tribune*, January 23, 1944.

Lost Angel (1944)

1. "Lost Angel," *New York Herald Tribune*, April 9, 1944.
2. Marsha Hunt interview, Sherman Oaks, California, July 17, 1997.
3. Ned Wynn, *We Will Always Live in Beverly Hills* (New York: W. Morrow), p. 32.
4. "Maggie, I Am Far Away," *This Week Magazine*, undated.
5. "She Might Be Your Child," *New York Times*, October 1, 1944.
6. *New York News*, April 9, 1944.
7. *Los Angeles Examiner*, March 3, 1944.
8. *Showmen's Trade Review*, November 6, 1943.
9. Marsha Hunt interview, Sherman Oaks, California, July 17, 1997.
10. *New York Herald-Tribune*, April 19, 1944.
11. Robert Blake interview, Los Angeles, California, July 21, 1999.

Jane Eyre (1944)

1. Virginia Wright column, *Los Angeles Daily News*, February 17, 1943.

2. Ibid.

3. Barbara Leaming, *Orson Welles, a Biography* (New York: Viking), p. 259.

4. *New York Times*, February 4, 1944.

5. *Hollywood Reporter*, February 2, 1944.

6. "At Age of Seven, This Personable Child Is One of Hollywood's Most Gifted Actresses," *Life*, April 3, 1944.

7. Joan Fontaine, letter to author, February 15, 1996.

The Canterville Ghost (1944)

1. *MGM News*, December 16, 1943, Margaret Herrick Library, AMPAS.

2. "Robert Young: Welby Has the Right Rx for Life," *Los Angeles Times*, February 21, 1971.

3. *New York Sun*, July 29, 1944.

4. Gladys Hall Collection, Margaret Herrick Library, AMPAS.

5. Ibid.

Music for Millions (1944)

1. June Allyson, *June Allyson* (Thorndike, Maine: Thorndike Press), p. 42.

2. "Child Actress," *Nation*, November 25, 1944.

3. "She Might Be Your Child," *New York Times Magazine*, October 1, 1944.

4. Ibid.

5. John Wakeman, *World Film Directors, Volume 1, 1890–1945* (New York: The H. P. Wilson Co.), p. 569.

6. Henry Koster, *Henry Koster: A Director's Guild of America Oral History* (Metuchen, New Jersey, and London: The Director's Guild of America and Scarecrow Press, Inc.), pp. 79–80.

7. *Hollywood Reporter*, December 13, 1944.

8. Unidentified and undated publication, Margaret Herrick Library, AMPAS.

9. June Allyson, *June Allyson*, p. 51.

Meet Me in St. Louis (1944)

1. Hugh Fordin, *The World of Entertainment: Hollywood's Greatest Musicals* (Garden City, New York: Doubleday & Company, Inc.), p. 91–93.

2. Ibid.

3. Ibid.

4. From the documentary, *Meet Me in St. Louis: The Making of An American Classic*, Turner Home Entertainment, 1994.

5. Ibid.

6. Margaret O'Brien interview, Hollywood, California, July 2, 1995.

7. Mary Astor, *A Life on Film* (New York: Delacorte Press), p. 177.

8. Hugh Fordin, *The World of Entertainment: Hollywood's Greatest Musicals*, p. 91–93.

9. Del Reisman, letter to author, Los Angeles, California, August 17, 1999.

10. *Harrison's Reports*, November 4, 1944.

11. John Fricke, *Judy Garland: World's Greatest Entertainer* (New York: Henry Holt & Co.), p. 89.

12. Vincente Minnelli, *I Remember It Well* (Garden City, New York: Doubleday & Company, Inc.), pp. 132–133.

13. Mary Astor, *A Life on Film*, p. 177.

Our Vines Have Tender Grapes (1945)

1. Gladys Hall Collection, Margaret Herrick Library, AMPAS.

2. "A Glamor Nightie for Miss O'Brien, Please," *Hollywood Citizen-News*, November 22, 1944.

3. Ibid.

4. Alan L. Gansberg, *Little Caesar: A Biography of Edward G. Robinson* (Sevenoaks, Kent: New English Library), p. 102.

5. *Variety*, July 18, 1945.

6. *PM Reviews*, undated review.

7. "Big Jim," *Photoplay*, July 1944.

8. Bruce Cook, *Dalton Trumbo* (New York: Charles Scribner's Sons), p. 159.

Bad Bascomb (1946)

1. *New York Times*, May 23, 1946.

2. "Maggie Was a Cover Girl," *American Magazine*, March 1946.

Three Wise Fools (1946)

1. "Veteran Actors Say Tiny Star Wonder of Age," unidentified and undated publication.
2. "Movie Midgets Are Real Live Pixies to Star," unidentified and undated publication.
3. Ibid.
4. "Real Eclipse Pictured in New Film," unidentified and undated publication.
5. Lionel Barrymore, *We Barrymores* (New York: Appleton-Century-Crofts), p. 250.
6. *Film Daily*, June 14, 1946.
7. Lionel Barrymore, *We Barrymores*, p. 249.
8. "Veteran Actors Say Tiny Star Wonder of Age," unidentified and undated publication.
9. Ibid.

The Unfinished Dance (1947)

1. John Wakeman, *World Film Directors, Volume 1, 1890–1945*, (New York: The H. P. Wilson Co.), p. 569.
2. "Maggie's Dreamy," *Photoplay*, February 1947.
3. Elinor Donahue interview, Studio City, California, August 14, 1999.
4. Danny Thomas, *Make Room for Danny* (Boston: G. K. Hall), p. 153.
5. "The Role I Liked Best," *Saturday Evening Post*, July 24, 1948.
6. *Los Angeles Times*, September 20, 1947.
7. Elinor Donahue interview, Studio City, California, August 14, 1999.
8. Henry Koster, *Henry Koster: A Director's Guild of America Oral History* (Metuchen, New Jersey, and London: The Director's Guild of America and Scarecrow Press, Inc.), p. 79.

Tenth Avenue Angel (1948)

1. "Tiny Star Off to N.Y. to Study Role," unidentified and undated publication.
2. Margaret O'Brien interview, Hollywood, California, July 2, 1995.
3. *Variety*, January 21, 1948.
4. Elinor Donahue interview, Studio City, California, August 14, 1999.
5. Unidentified and undated review, Margaret Herrick Library, AMPAS.
6. Robert Edelman and Audrey E. Kupferberg, *Angela Lansbury: A Life on Stage and Screen* (New York: A Birch Lane Press Book, published by Carol Publishing Group), p. 63.
7. George Murphy to Randal Malone, Los Angeles, California, 1990.

Big City (1948)

1. Betty Garrett, *Betty Garrett and Other Songs* (New York: Madison Books), p. 96.
2. Jay Robert Nash and Stanley Ralph Ross, *The Motion Picture Guide, 1927–1983* (Chicago: Cinebooks, Inc.), p. 192.
3. Betty Garrett to Randal Malone, Los Angeles, California, July 1999.
4. Joe Pasternak, *Easy the Hard Way* (New York: Putnam), p. 242.

Little Women (1949)

1. Mervyn LeRoy, *Mervyn LeRoy: Take One* (New York: Hawthorn Books), p. 165.
2. Ibid, p. 165.
3. "Film Goal Achieved by LeRoy," *Los Angeles Times*, April 10, 1949.
4. Mervyn LeRoy, *Mervyn LeRoy: Take One*, p. 166.
5. Margaret O'Brien interview, Hollywood, California, July 2, 1995.
6. Mary Astor, *A Life on Film* (New York: Delacorte Press), p. 198.
7. Ibid.
8. Janet Leigh, *There Really Was a Hollywood* (Garden City, New York: Doubleday), p. 81.
9. Mary Astor, *A Life on Film*, p. 197.

10. June Allyson, *June Allyson* (Thorndike, Maine: Thorndike Press), p. 124.

11. "Princess Margaret of Hollywood," *Collier's*, January 29, 1949.

12. *Daily Mirror*, February 23, 1949.

13. June Allyson, *June Allyson*, p. 51.

14. Mervyn LeRoy, *Mervyn LeRoy: Take One*, p. 166.

15. Janet Leigh to Jimmy Bangley, Beverly Hills, California, August 13, 1999.

The Secret Garden (1949)

1. "Princess Margaret of Hollywood," *Collier's*, January 29, 1949.

2. Brian Roper Studio Biography, Margaret Herrick Library, AMPAS.

3. *Motion Picture Herald*, April 23, 1949.

4. Elsa Lanchester, *Elsa Lanchester, Herself* (New York: St. Martin's Press), p. 178.

Her First Romance (1951)

1. Elinor Donahue interview, Studio City, California, August 14, 1999.

2. *Hollywood Reporter*, May 2, 1951.

3. Elinor Donahue interview, Studio City, California, August 14, 1999.

Girls Hand in Hand (1953)

1. "Help Asked to Find Margaret O'Brien's Dog," *Hollywood Citizen-News*, September 20, 1952.

2. "All Teenagers Aren't Delinquent," *Photoplay*, December 1955.

Glory (1956)

1. David Butler, *David Butler: A Director's Guild of America Oral History* (Metuchen, New Jersey, and London: The Director's Guild of America and Scarecrow Press, Inc.), p. 260.

2. Ibid.

3. Bruce Cook, *Dalton Trumbo* (New York: Charles Scribner's Sons), pp. 243–244.

4. "Margaret O'Brien to Get First Screen Kiss," *Los Angeles Herald-Express*, July 25, 1955.

5. David Butler, *David Butler: A Director's Guild of America Oral History*, p. 261.

6. "Margaret Grows Up!" *Collier's*, September 4, 1953.

7. *Variety*, January 11, 1956.

8. David Butler, *David Butler: A Director's Guild of America Oral History*, p. 260.

9. "All Teenagers Aren't Delinquent," *Photoplay*, December 1955.

Heller in Pink Tights (1960)

1. David Ragan, *Who's Who in Hollywood, Vol. 2, M–Z* (New York: Facts on File), p. 1254.

2. George Cukor Collection, Margaret Herrick Library, AMPAS.

3. David Ragan, *Who's Who in Hollywood*, p. 332.

4. Paramount Production Files, Margaret Herrick Library, AMPAS.

5. Unidentified and undated review, Margaret Herrick Library, AMPAS.

6. David Ragan, *Who's Who in Hollywood*, p. 332.

Amy (1981)

1. *Los Angeles Times*, April 10, 1981.

Sunset After Dark (1996)

1. Randal Malone interview, South Pasadena, California, September 17, 1995.

2. Ibid.

3. Margaret O'Brien interview, Sherman Oaks, California, July 22, 1999.

4. *The Making of Sunset After Dark: An Interview with Film Director Mark J. Gordon*, Internet interview, 1996.

5. Randal Malone interview, South Pasadena, California, September 17, 1995.

6. Ibid.

7. Anita Page interview, South Pasadena, California, July 20, 1999.

8. Anita Page interview, South Pasadena, California, August 20, 1995.

9. Randal Malone interview, South Pasadena, California, September 17, 1995.

10. *The Making of Sunset After Dark: An Interview with Film Director Mark J. Gordon*, Internet interview, 1996.

Hollywood Mortuary (1999)

1. "*Hollywood Mortuary: Behind the Scenes*," Internet interview, 1999.

2. Margaret O'Brien interview, Sherman Oaks, California, July 22, 1999.

3. Anita Page interview, South Pasadena, California, July 20, 1999.

4. Margaret O'Brien interview, Sherman Oaks, California, July 22, 1999.

5. "*Hollywood Mortuary: Behind the Scenes*," Internet interview, 1999.

6. Conrad Brooks to Randal Malone, Los Angeles, California, 1999.

7. Margaret O'Brien interview, Sherman Oaks, California, July 22, 1999.

THEATER

1. Hedda Hopper interview, February 21, 1956, Margaret Herrick Library, AMPAS.

2. William F. Nolan, *McQueen* (New York: Congdon & Weed, Inc.), p. 21.

3. Hedda Hopper interview, February 21, 1956, Margaret Herrick Library, AMPAS.

TELEVISION

1. Sidney Skolsky Collection, Margaret Herrick Library, AMPAS.

2. "Margaret O'Brien Revisits Kildare," *Los Angeles Times*, February 11, 1962.

Bibliography

Agee, James. *Agee on Film*. New York: McDowell, Obolensky, 1958–1960.

Alcott, Louisa May. *Little Women*. Boston: Little, Brown, 1912.

Allyson, June, with Frances Spatz Leighton. *June Allyson*. Thorndike, Maine: Thorndike Press, 1982.

"An Oral History with Laraine Day." Interviewed by Barbara Hall. Academy of Motion Picture Arts and Sciences, 1998.

Astor, Mary. *My Story: An Autobiography*. Garden City, New York: Doubleday, 1959.

_____. *A Life on Film*. New York: Delacorte Press, 1971.

Barrymore, Lionel, with Cameron Shipp. *We Barrymores*. New York: Appleton-Century-Crofts, 1951.

Benson, Sally. *Meet Me in St. Louis*. New York: Random House, 1942.

Best, Marc. *Those Endearing Young Charms: Child Performers of the Screen*. New York: A. S. Barnes and Company, 1971.

Billips, Connie, and Arthur Pierce. *Lux Presents Hollywood: A Show by Show History of the Lux Radio Theatre and the Lux Video Theatre, 1934–1957*. Jefferson, North Carolina, and London: McFarland & Company, Inc., Publishers, 1995.

Bloom, Ken. *Hollywood Song: The Complete Film & Musical Companion, Volume 1, Films A–L*. New York: Facts on File, 1995.

_____. *Hollywood Song: The Complete Film & Musical Companion, Volume 2, Films M–Z*. New York: Facts on File, 1995.

_____. *Hollywood Song: The Complete Film & Musical Companion, Volume 3, Chronology, Personnel Index, Song Index*. New York: Facts on File, 1995.

Blum, Daniel. *TheatreWorld, Season 1951-1952*. New York: Greenberg Publishers, 1952.

_____. *TheatreWorld, Season 1952-1953*. New York: Greenberg Publishers, 1953.

_____. *TheatreWorld, Season 1963-1964*. Philadelphia-New York: Chilton Books, 1964.

Brontë, Charlotte. *Jane Eyre*. New York: Harper, 1848.

Brown, Les. *Encyclopedia of Television, 3rd Edition*. Detroit, London: Gale Research, 1992.

Burnett, Frances Hodgson. *The Secret Garden*. New York: Grosset and Dunlap, 1915.

Butler, David, interviewed by Irene Kahn Atkins. *David Butler: A Director's Guild of America Oral History.* Metuchen, New Jersey, and London: The Director's Guild of America and Scarecrow Press, Inc., 1993.

Cary, Diana Serra. *Hollywood's Children: An Inside Account of the Child Star Era.* Boston: Houghton Mifflin Company, 1978.

Chapman, John. *The Best Plays of 1951-1952: And the Year Book of the Drama in America.* New York, Toronto: Dodd, Mead and Company, 1952.

Cook, Bruce. *Dalton Trumbo.* New York: Charles Scribner's Sons, 1977.

Crowther, Bosley. *The Lion's Share: The Story of an Entertainment Empire.* New York: Dutton, 1957.

_____. *Hollywood Rajah: The Life and Times of Louis B. Mayer.* New York: Henry Holt, 1960.

Curie, Eve. *Madame Curie.* New York: Doubleday, Doran, 1939.

Dimmitt, Richard Bertrand. *A Title Guide to the Talkies.* New York & London: The Scarecrow Press, 1965.

Dunning, John. *Tune In Yesterday: The Ultimate Encyclopedia of Old-Time Radio, 1925-1976.* Englewood Cliffs, New Jersey: Prentice Hall, Inc., 1976.

Dye, David. *Child and Youth Actors: Filmographies of Their Entire Career, 1914-1985.* Jefferson, North Carolina, and London: McFarland & Company, Inc., Publishers, 1988.

Edelman, Robert, and Audrey E. Kupferberg. *Angela Lansbury: A Life on Stage and Screen.* New York: A Birch Lane Press Book, published by Carol Publishing Group, 1996.

Ellenberger, Allan R. *Ramon Novarro: A Biography of the Silent Film Idol, 1899-1968.* Jefferson, North Carolina, and London: McFarland & Company, Inc., Publishers, 1999.

Endres, Stacey, and Robert Cushman. *Hollywood at Your Feet: The Story of the World-Famous Chinese Theater from the Silents to "Star Trek."* Los Angeles: Pomegranate Press, 1992.

Fontaine, Joan. *No Bed of Roses.* New York: Morrow, 1978.

Fordin, Hugh. *The World of Entertainment: Hollywood's Greatest Musicals.* Garden City, New York: Doubleday & Company, Inc., 1975.

Fricke, John. *Judy Garland: World's Greatest Entertainer.* New York: Henry Holt & Co., 1992.

Gansberg, Alan L. *Little Caesar: A Biography of Edward G. Robinson.* Sevenoaks, Kent: New English Library, 1983.

Garrett, Betty, with Ron Rapoport. *Betty Garrett and Other Songs.* New York: Madison Books, 1998.

Gevinson, Alan (ed.). *American Film Institute Catalog, Within Our Gates: Ethnicity in American Feature Films, 1911-1960.* Berkeley, Los Angeles, London: University of California Press, 1997.

Gianakos, Larry James. *Television Drama Series Programing, 1947-1959: A Comprehensive Chronicle.* Metuchen, New Jersey, and London: The Scarecrow Press, 1980.

_____. *Television Drama Series Programing, 1959-1975: A Comprehensive Chronicle.* Metuchen, New Jersey, and London: The Scarecrow Press, 1978.

_____. *Television Drama Series Programing, 1982-1984: A Comprehensive Chronicle.* Metuchen, New Jersey, and London: The Scarecrow Press, 1987.

Hanson, Patricia King, and Stephen L. Hanson. *Film Review Index, Volume 2: 1950-1985.* Phoenix, Arizona: Oryx Press, 1987.

Higham, Charles. *Merchant of Dreams: Louis B. Mayer, M.G.M. and the Secret Hollywood.* New York: Donald I. Fine, Inc., 1993.

Katz, Ephraim. *The Film Encyclopedia.* New York: HarperPerennial, 1994.

Kear, Lynn. *Agnes Moorehead: A Bio-Bibliography.* New York; Westport, Connecticut; London: Greenwood Press, 1992.

Koster, Henry, interviewed by Irene Kahn Atkins. *Henry Koster: A Director's Guild of America Oral History.* Metuchen, New Jersey, and London: The Director's Guild of America and Scarecrow Press, Inc., 1987.

Lackmann, Ron. *Same Time, Same Station: An A–Z Guide to Radio from Jack Benny to Howard Stern.* New York: Facts on File, 1996.

Lanchester, Elsa. *Elsa Lanchester, Herself.* New York: St. Martin's Press, 1983.

Leaming, Barbara. *Orson Welles, a Biography.* New York: Viking, 1985.

Leigh, Janet. *There Really Was a Hollywood.* Garden City, New York: Doubleday, 1984.

LeRoy, Mervyn, as told to Dick Kleiner. *Mervyn LeRoy: Take One.* New York: Hawthorn Books, 1974.

Lyon, Christopher (ed.). *The International Dictionary of Films and Filmmakers: Vol. 1, Films.* Chicago: St. James Press, 1984.

Maltin, Leonard. *TV Movies and Video Guide.* New York: New American Library, 1987.

Martin, George Victor. *For Our Vines Have Tender Grapes.* New York: W. Funk Inc., 1940.

Michael, Paul (editor-in-chief). *The American Movies Reference Book: The Sound Era.* Englewood Cliffs, New Jersey: Prentice Hall, Inc., 1969.

Minnelli, Vincente, with Hector Arce. *I Remember It Well.* Garden City, New York: Doubleday & Company, Inc., 1974.

Monder, Eric. *George Sidney: A Bio-Bibliography.* Westport, Connecticut: Greenwood Press, 1994.

Moore, Dick. *Twinkle, Twinkle, Little Star, but Don't Have Sex or Take the Car.* New York: Harper & Row Publishers, 1984.

Mordden, Ethan. *The Hollywood Musical.* New York: St. Martin's Press, 1981.

Nash, Jay Robert, and Stanley Ralph Ross. *The Motion Picture Guide, 1927–1983.* Chicago: Cinebooks, Inc., 1985.

Nolan, William F. *McQueen.* New York: Congdon & Weed, Inc., 1984.

O'Brien, Margaret. *My Diary.* Philadelphia: J. B. Lippincott Co., 1948.

Osborne, Robert. *70 Years of the Oscar: The Official History of the Academy Awards.* New York, London, Paris: Abbeville Press, 1999.

Parish, James Robert. *The M.G.M. Stock Company.* New York: Bonanza, 1972.

_____. *Great Child Stars.* New York: Ace Books, 1976.

_____. *The Unofficial Murder, She Wrote Casebook.* New York: Kensington Books, 1997.

_____, and Gregory Mank. *The Best of MGM: The Golden Years: 1928–1959.* Westport, Connecticut: Arlington House, 1981.

Pasternak, Joe as told to David Chandler. *Easy the Hard Way.* New York: Putnam, 1956.

Pratt, Carol Issacs. *A Study of the Motion Picture Relief Fund's Screen Guild Radio Program, 1939–1952.* Louisiana State University, 1976.

Ragan, David. *Who's Who in Hollywood, 1900–1976.* New Rochelle: Arlington House, 1976.

_____. *Who's Who in Hollywood: The Largest Cast of International Film Personalities Ever Assembled, Vol. 2, M–Z.* New York: Facts on File, 1992.

Rivers, Joan, with Richard Meryman. *Enter Talking.* New York: Delacorte Press, 1986.

Sackett, Susan. *The Hollywood Reporter*

Book of Box Office Hits. New York: Billboard Books, 1991.

Schuchman, John S. *Hollywood Speaks: Deafness and the Film Entertainment Industry*. Urbana and Chicago: University of Illinois Press, 1988.

Schultz, Margie. *Ann Sothern: A Bio-Bibliography*. New York; Westport, Connecticut; London: Greenwood Press, 1990.

Shipman, David. *The Great Movie Stars: The Golden Years*. New York: Bonanza Books, 1970.

Terrace, Vincent. *Radio's Golden Years: The Encyclopedia of Radio Programs, 1930–1960*. San Diego, New York: A. S. Barnes & Co., Inc., 1998.

_____. *Television Specials: 3,201 Entertainment Spectaculars, 1939–1993*. Jefferson, North Carolina, and London: McFarland & Company, Inc., Publishers, 1995.

Thomas, Danny, with Bill Davidson. *Make Room for Danny*. Boston: G. K. Hall, 1991.

Wakeman, John (ed.). *World Film Directors, Volume 1, 1890–1945*. The H. P. Wilson Co., 1945.

Walker, John (ed.). *Halliwell's Film Guide (Eighth Edition)*. New York: Harper-Collins, 1991.

White, William L. *Journey for Margaret*. New York: Harcourt, Brace, 1941.

Wiley, Mason, and Damien Bona. *Inside Oscar: The Unofficial History of the Academy Awards*. New York: Ballantine Books, 1986.

Wouk, Herman. *City Boy*. New York: Doubleday, 1952.

Wynn, Ned. *We Will Always Live in Beverly Hills: Growing Up Crazy in Hollywood*. New York: W. Morrow, 1990.

Index